Contents

Introduction: Reading Literary Modernities on the Horizon of World Literature	1
1. Literary Modernity and the Emancipation of Voice: Defences of Poetry by Percy Bysshe Shelley and Lu Xun	23
2. Shakespearean Retellings and the Question of the Common Reader: Charles and Mary Lamb's *Tales from Shakespeare* and Lin Shu's *Yinbian Yanyu*	50
3. Estrangements of the World in the Familiar Essay: Charles Lamb and Zhou Zuoren's Approaches to the Ordinary	73
4. Between the Theater and the Novel: Woman, Modernity, and the Restaging of the Ordinary in *Mansfield Park* and *The Rouge of the North*	92
Coda	137
Acknowledgments	141
Notes	145
Index	161

ON THE HORIZON
OF WORLD LITERATURE

Sara Guyer and Brian McGrath, series editors

Lit Z embraces models of criticism uncontained by conventional notions of history, periodicity, and culture, and committed to the work of reading. Books in the series may seem untimely, anachronistic, or out of touch with contemporary trends because they have arrived too early or too late. Lit Z creates a space for books that exceed and challenge the tendencies of our field and in doing so reflect on the concerns of literary studies here and abroad.

At least since Friedrich Schlegel, thinking that affirms literature's own untimeliness has been named romanticism. Recalling this history, Lit Z exemplifies the survival of romanticism as a mode of contemporary criticism, as well as forms of contemporary criticism that demonstrate the unfulfilled possibilities of romanticism. Whether or not they focus on the romantic period, books in this series epitomize romanticism as a way of thinking that compels another relation to the present. Lit Z is the first book series to take seriously this capacious sense of romanticism.

In 1977, Paul de Man and Geoffrey Hartman, two scholars of romanticism, team-taught a course called Literature Z that aimed to make an intervention into the fundamentals of literary study. Hartman and de Man invited students to read a series of increasingly difficult texts and through attention to language and rhetoric compelled them to encounter "the bewildering variety of ways such texts could be read." The series' conceptual resonances with that class register the importance of recollection, reinvention, and reading to contemporary criticism. Its books explore the creative potential of reading's untimeliness and history's enigmatic force.

ON THE HORIZON
OF WORLD LITERATURE

*Forms of Modernity in Romantic England
and Republican China*

Emily Sun

Fordham University Press
New York 2021

Copyright © 2021 Fordham University Press

All rights reserved. No part of this publication may be reproduced, stored in a retrieval system, or transmitted in any form or by any means—electronic, mechanical, photocopy, recording, or any other—except for brief quotations in printed reviews, without the prior permission of the publisher.

Fordham University Press has no responsibility for the persistence or accuracy of URLs for external or third-party Internet websites referred to in this publication and does not guarantee that any content on such websites is, or will remain, accurate or appropriate.

Fordham University Press also publishes its books in a variety of electronic formats. Some content that appears in print may not be available in electronic books.

Visit us online at www.fordhampress.com.

Library of Congress Cataloging-in-Publication Data

Names: Sun, Emily, author.
Title: On the horizon of world literature : forms of modernity in romantic England and republican China / Emily Sun.
Description: New York : Fordham University Press, 2021. | Series: Lit Z | Includes bibliographical references and index.
Identifiers: LCCN 2020051686 | ISBN 9780823294787 (hardback) | ISBN 9780823294787 (paperback) | ISBN 9780823294800 (epub)
Subjects: LCSH: Literature—Philosophy. | Civilization, Modern, in literature. | Comparative literature—English and Chinese. | Comparative literature—Chinese and English.
Classification: LCC PN49 .S846 2021 | DDC 801—dc23
LC record available at https://lccn.loc.gov/2020051686

Printed in the United States of America

23 22 21   5 4 3 2 1

First edition

*To Clay, and to the memory of my grandmother
Alice Tsai Yu, listeners extraordinaire*

ON THE HORIZON
OF WORLD LITERATURE

Introduction

Reading Literary Modernities on the Horizon of World Literature

It was on a winter evening in Weimar in 1827, so the story goes, that Johann Wolfgang von Goethe coined the term *Weltliteratur*. In conversation with his assistant Eckermann, he remarks, "I am more and more convinced that poetry is a common property of humanity, revealing itself everywhere and at all times in hundreds and hundreds of human beings."[1] Following the capacious universalism of this claim, he comments, "National literature does not mean much at present; the epoch of world literature is now at hand, and everyone must strive to hasten its approach."[2] What Goethe calls "national literature"—the classification of texts of imaginative writing according to national categories—may be old and even self-evident for us but was, we need to remind ourselves, a more recent phenomenon for him. As Raymond Williams traces in his influential study *Keywords: A Vocabulary of Culture and Society*, the specific definition of literature as "imaginative writing"—a shift away from an earlier definition as general "polite learning"—had only gained currency in Europe in the second half of the eighteenth century.[3] The study of literature so defined, and its division into "old" and "new" philologies, were correspondingly relatively recent developments in the modern European university.[4] In the context of the radical changes in the organization of knowledge that took place during his lifetime in Europe, Goethe takes an expansive view, supplementing the narrower category of "national literature" with the unbounded notion of "world literature."

Since Eckermann's publication of the *Conversations* in 1835, Goethe's term achieved global circulation and currency over the course of the nineteenth century. By the end of that century, on the other side of the globe in late Qing dynasty China, reformist scholar-statesmen such as Liang Qichao and Chen Jitong were calling for new writing practices and a revolution in poetry (*shijie geming*) that would promote Chinese participation in world literature (*shijie de wenxue*).⁵ Such a move to recontextualize and reorient Chinese writing practices in relation to the concept of world literature would yield in the first decades of the twentieth century in China reconfigurations of old and new, native and foreign, as succinctly expressed in the four-character idiom *gujin zhongwai*, a temporal-spatial quadrant denoting "ancient/modern, Chinese/foreign," with limber relations among its four elements.⁶ Initially coined and conceptualized by Goethe, achieving textual organizational impact and currency first in Europe and then globally, world literature acquired through this process the status of founding concept of comparative literature, prompting scholars in the discipline to revisit it periodically to reestablish its significance.

From the perspective of the twenty-first century, almost two hundred years after Goethe coined the term, this book joins the efforts of other contemporary scholars in revisiting world literature and reaffirming its significance for reading comparatively. It does so by bringing to light the often overlooked disciplinary-historical impact the term has already had in forming and re-forming literary traditions and practices in different sites around the world. It situates itself in relation to comparative literature as an international and polycentric enterprise that depends on the participation of readers and writers in multiple sites. For its focus, it zooms in on literary texts written in two asynchronous periods in disparate parts of the world: the late eighteenth and early nineteenth centuries in England, a period commonly designated as "Romantic" in terms of Western literary historiography, and the early twentieth century in China, a time of cultural and political transition from the imperial dynastic order to modern republicanism. Both of these periods saw the emergence of self-conscious—and, to varying degrees, programmatic—critical efforts to redefine literature and to realize literature as new or modern in linguistically and culturally separate spheres. Each functions as a pivotal moment of incipient literary modernity in lived and ongoing literary and cultural traditions. By examining connected yet asynchronous and heterogeneous moments of literary modernity in, respectively, a Western and non-Western context, this book argues and shows how the notion of world literature has provided and continues to provide the epistemic condition of possibility and discursive framework for articulations of local literary histories and literary modernities in relation to other literary histories and literary modernities. In disciplinary historical terms, "world literature" designates a framework for processes of textual classification, revaluation, and production in a plurality of connected yet differently inherited and inhabited lifeworlds. These diverse traditions present varying local configurations of native and foreign literatures, distributions of major and minor languages, and asynchronous divisions between premodern and modern. Beyond functioning as such as a condition of possibility and framework, world literature, this book proposes, serves also on a more abstract level as an ideal that continues to orient and motivate ongoing exposure to and exchange with the foreign. In this latter sense, the "world" of "world literature" does not already exist as the equivalent of a map or other representation of the inhabited globe, but rather continually comes into being as that which is activated and reactivated in processes of exposure and exchange. World literature thus designates not only what already is or has been ascertained, but future, yet unknown possibilities that unfold in practices of reading.

This book situates itself alongside recent reassessments of the notion of world literature by scholars in the U.S. academy aiming to move the discipline of comparative literature away from its perceived European, even Eurocentric, bias at the end of the twentieth century and toward the expansive promise of Goethe's formulation. Among these reassessments, I highlight a few paradigmatic ones. In his 2000 essay "Conjectures on World Literature," a programmatic document for the digital project of "distant reading," Franco Moretti remarks, "Comparative literature has not lived up to [its] beginnings. It's been a much more modest intellectual enterprise, fundamentally limited to western Europe."[7] In his 2003 book *What Is World Literature?*, David Damrosch aims to make texts from a greater range of places and periods manageable for practical criticism by redefining world literature as a para-canonical "elliptical space" of works that "refract national literatures" and "gain" in translation, rather than as an inexhaustible collection of national canons.[8] In her provocatively titled 2013 book *Against World Literature: On the Politics of Untranslatability*, Emily Apter critiques the rise at the turn of the twenty-first century of programs and curricula of World Literature, primarily in U.S. higher education but also internationally. While such programs and curricula aim to expand the range of comparative reading beyond Western literature, they do so by teaching texts in English translation, very often at the expense of engaging with the foreignness of foreign languages. In so doing, they tend to operate with underexamined assumptions of "cultural equivalence and substitutability" and to celebrate "nationally and ethnically branded 'differences' that have been niche-marketed as commercialized 'identities.'"[9] Against such a well-meaningly multi-culturalist but, ultimately, naïvely monocultural and perhaps even neoliberalist paradigm, Apter proposes instead the study of foreign languages and the specific foregrounding therein of questions of untranslatability as nodes of cultural difference and geopolitical contention.

While this book joins such peers in the common project of expanding the disciplinary scope of comparative literature for educating cosmopolitan global citizens in the twenty-first century, it takes a different starting point by bringing to light the global epistemic significance of the term "world literature" and the impact it has already had on the classification and production of literary traditions around the world. By paying critical attention to links between local, international, and cross-cultural issues of disciplinary historiography, it elucidates how the definition of literature that emerged in eighteenth-century Europe was fundamental to the reclassification and revaluation of textual practices in China at the beginning of the twentieth century. World literature has provided and continues to provide the framework of connection whereby unassimilable differences between diverse textual traditions can appear—and thus enter into conversation—in relation to the shared heuristic of literature as imaginative writing. Europe as a cultural sphere functions, in this light, not as the center of world literature but as one region among others, in relation to which it has always already been provincialized.[10] World literature, in turn, serves as the framework wherein this mutual provincialization and conversation between literatures and cultures can take place and wherein the "world" of world literature can emerge accordingly.

This book adopts a limited and strategic focus on one Western literature and one non-Western literature to offer an adaptable approach to reading between Western and non-Western literatures. It makes no pretense of providing comprehensive or exhaustive coverage of the sum of the world's languages and literatures. Such an ambition of comprehensiveness has often been expressed in tandem with a sense of defeatism before the prospect of quantitatively inclusive representation. So Moretti: "Many people have read more and better than I have, of course, but still, we are talking of hundreds of languages and literatures here. Reading 'more' seems hardly to be the solution."[11] Damrosch channels the comic horror of a predecessor comparatist, Claudio Guillén, exclaiming, "The sum total of all national literatures? A wild idea, unattainable in practice, worthy not of an actual reader but a deluded keeper of archives who is also a multimillionaire."[12] Apter refers in her critique of the enterprise of World-Literature-in-Translation to the "expansionism and gargantuan scale of world-literary endeavors."[13] Such remarks repeat a topos that is well described by Immanuel Kant's notion of the mathematical sublime in the *Critique of Judgment*: the sensation of being overwhelmed by magnitudes that exceed the mind's capacity for comprehension.[14] This study puts into question the very ambition of comprehensiveness and quantitative representation that would lead to the sensation of being overwhelmed in the first place. Such an ambition implicitly positions the inquiring subject in a space suspended outside of languages and cultures, as if there could be a meta- or supra-perspective—an Archimedean point—from which to survey and study the world's languages and cultures.[15] This book proposes, rather, that we approach the fact of linguistic and cultural plurality predicated by the notion of world literature immanently as a lived, historical condition—an exposure to difference already experienced in our various ties and debts, both given and chosen, to actual communities—rather than as an externality that threatens the inquiring subject with dizzying quantitative excess.

By adopting a limited and strategic focus on two moments of incipient literary modernity that continue to be vital for ongoing literary and cultural traditions, this book reaffirms the value and renews the method of close reading for both expanding the scope of comparative literature and deepening its stakes. The task of living up to the capacious promise of world literature, this book aims to show, involves careful, philologically and philosophically informed reading. By philology, I mean here the scrutiny of semantic shifts as well as nuances of meaning produced by manipulations of diction, rhythm, meter, allusion, and devices of repetition.[16] By philosophy, I imply not just Western philosophy or late twentieth-century to contemporary Western theory but also non-Western traditions of thought—for instance, Confucianism, Daoism, and Buddhism—that persist in evolving discursive patterns and enter into conversation with Western conceptual categories. This book aims to offer careful readings between different traditions of poetics and theory in chapter-by-chapter analyses of select literary forms. In its attention to disciplinary historiographical issues, this book compares not just texts but textual and historical processes that condition acts of iteration. It treats texts as fields of interlocking developments wherein processes in one culture and locale connect to processes in another within a common epistemic framework but depend for their meaningfulness on heterogeneous traditions and cultural contexts of address. In so doing, this book models a deprovincialized close reading that loosens the practice of close reading from confinement within monocultural hermeneutic circles while remaining attuned to linguistic and cultural differences. A comparative literature that turns away from the intimate demands of close reading risks missing the surprises within texts in languages one may call one's own.[17] Even more, it risks missing the surprises of texts and cultural patterns in languages and regions beyond one's native or customary habitat. In another vein, a comparative literature that diminishes the importance of local canons and traditions in favor of a utopic, para-canonical "elliptical space" risks missing the very real and weighty consequences that semantic shifts, textual afterlives, and processes of revaluation within traditions have on actual histories and communities.

Finally, in situating this book alongside recent revisitations of the notion of world literature, I make the simple and obvious point that this book performs close readings across languages and cultures. It advocates multilingualism as fundamental to the task of living up to the promise of a genuinely plural and cosmopolitan world literature. As such, it provides an alternative to studies of cross-cultural literary relations that focus on how a non-Western culture is depicted or imagined in the West, in which Western texts are prioritized as the subjects of readings and misreadings that produce discourses about the non-Western culture in question. This book aims to open up, rather, analysis of multilateral interactions in a complex, polycentric world. It issues also an invitation and a provocation to postcolonial approaches to world literature that either privilege or read exclusively texts written in English or other languages of former European colonizers. In his 2016 book *What Is a World? On Postcolonial Literature as World Literature*, Pheng Cheah defines the "world" in temporal, rather than spatial, terms as a futurity that literature may bring into being in resistance to and in excess of the world qua product of the capitalist world-system.[18] The hopefulness of such an orientation can only be enhanced by further engagement among comparatists with the complex multilingualism, Western and non-Western, that informs the experience and inheritance of postcoloniality.

Toward Literary Modernity: Reading between Literary Histories and Literary Modernities

This study examines in juxtaposition literary texts from two periods written in disparate parts of the world. The period in question in England, the late eighteenth to the early nineteenth centuries, was a time of political and social transformation and colonial extension accelerated by industrial and technological change. The period in question in China, the early twentieth century, saw the end of the dynastic, imperial order alongside the end of the traditional Confucian civil service examination system. It was a time in which revolutionary social and political change was accompanied by a radical epistemic shift and transformation of culture. Significantly, these moments of historical crisis and transformation saw the emergence of self-conscious—and, to varying degrees, programmatic—critical efforts to redefine literature and to realize literature as new or modern. They constitute moments of incipience for literary modernity and modern literature in separate but connected linguistic and cultural spheres.

Underlying and connecting the two moments of incipient literary modernity in England and China is a common definition of literature as specifically imaginative writing. While corpuses of imaginative writing preexist such a designation, it is this designation, issuing from a particular epistemic framework, that has allowed for imaginative writing in multiple languages and forms to be variously classified, reevaluated, and produced as such. In *Keywords*, as mentioned previously, Raymond Williams traces a major shift in the definition of the word "literature" itself in eighteenth-century England from its earlier sense as "polite learning through reading" toward the specific sense of "imaginative" or "creative," rather than "general and discursive," writing.[19] This new usage was roughly contemporaneous with similar usages in other European languages, for which Williams chooses a few titles as examples: "*Über die neuere deutsche Litteratur* (Herder, 1767); *Les Siècles de littérature française* (1772); *Storia della letteratura italiana* (1772)."[20] The redefinition of literature in the European eighteenth century tended to be modified by adjectives that connote both national and linguistic categories, whose separateness or conflation with one another remains a question whose decidability is the matter of ideology.

The European eighteenth-century definition of literature as imaginative writing emerged within the context of a secular-historicist reorganization of knowledge that yielded the modern university and the three-part division of the natural sciences, the humanities, and the social sciences that still obtains around the world today and organizes international scholarly collaboration. This definition reached China in the late nineteenth and early twentieth centuries through informal means as well as through scholarship whose impact was exerted in a disciplinary-institutional context. Besides the informal channel of translations of literature for popular reading, a scholarly corpus consisting of literary histories, anthologies, biographies, and other taxonomic enterprises circulated to China as it did to other parts of the world throughout the nineteenth century. Such scholarship occasioned in China redefinitions, reclassifications, and revaluations of existing textual practices and forms of writing and often served as sources for translation, imitation, and adaptation. As an effect of the circulation of such a corpus of knowledge, the first Western-style literary history of China appeared in 1904, written by Lin Chuanjia on commission from the

Imperial University of Peking, established in 1898, for use in its literature program. As David Der-wei Wang writes, looking back at precursors of his own editorial project in *A New Literary History of Modern China* (2017), "Lin's history is an eclectic undertaking that comprises genre classification, philological inquiry and chronological periodization and was modeled after the Japanese scholar Sasagawa Rinpu's . . . *History of Chinese Literature* (1898), which was in turn inspired by European literary histories."[21] Lin's 1904 text was the first among numerous endeavors in late Qing and Republican China to reclassify and reevaluate, with varying degrees of critical sophistication, the tradition of Chinese letters according to criteria attending the definition of literature within the structure of the modern Enlightenment university.[22] Such historiographical efforts were contemporaneous with public calls, often with pronouncedly nationalistic inflections, for the writing of a modern literature imagined as adequate to a new China. Significantly, in both European and Chinese contexts on opposite ends of the long nineteenth century, literary history appears to be cognate with literary modernity: a particular conception of the latter gives rise to the former, which in circular fashion produces lines and logics of division between old and new, ancient and modern. The global transmission of positivistic scholarship about literature in the long nineteenth century serves as condition of possibility for heterogeneous linguistic and cultural traditions—among them English and Chinese—to enter into conversation with one another.

But, as Paul de Man cautions with rigorous clarity in his 1969 essay "Literary History and Literary Modernity," literary modernity is an unstable concept that unsettles the claims of literary history.[23] Literary modernity is unstable for two reasons. First, literature is ontologically a self-contradictory entity. Defined as imaginative writing within a modern epistemic configuration grounded on the authority of reason, literature haunts this very framework as an excess that exposes the limits of reason, manifesting itself negatively in modes of irony and ambiguity and gesturing beyond what can simply be stated as known. Second, modernity is a temporal category of presentness and immediacy and, as such, exists in amnesiac tension with history defined according to a model of patrilineal, genetic extension. Given the conceptual instability of literary modernity, de Man infers that "a positivist history of literature, [as] a collection of empirical data, can only be a history of what literature is not. At best," he adds, "it would be a preliminary classification opening the way for actual literary study, and at worst, an obstacle in the way of literary understanding."[24]

De Man's remarks about the challenge of reading literary modernity with and against literary history are directed intensively to the context of Western Europe. My study is concerned with a comparative reading of greater cross-cultural scope: the languages in question are radically different; the traditions do not share a past in the Latin Middle Ages or a nexus in the Abrahamic religions. As such, it argues that literary history does not just serve as a preliminary classification for literary study but has indispensable heuristic value for opening up hermeneutic circles of monolingualism or monoculturalism, be these Eurocentric, Sinocentric, or a scientistic aculturalist globalism. Approached through the modes of cross-cultural comparative reading performed in this study, literary history and literary modernity become realized in the plural as literary histories and literary modernities. In the plural, moreover, these histories and modernities work in productive tension with one another insofar as the former are not just inventories of facts about languages and literatures but vitally operative as elements of linguistically embedded and culturally differentiated pasts that return in and animate enactments of literary modernity. Literary modernity thus no longer can appear in the singular as an inherent or self-evident attribute of what is called world literature. Instead, it reemerges as the effect of the plurality and complexity of literary modernities.

But this does not mean that the notion of literary modernity, in the singular, has no place. Once we recognize that the singular category of literary modernity is not adequate to the plurality of literary histories and modernities, we can see it instead as itself an effect of their encounter. In other words, literary modernity does not already exist as an attribute of world literature, it does not take place in any language, it has no language of its own. It is activated rather in the movement of reading between languages that constitute the particular and actual mediums of literary modernities and inform the terms and conditions of lived and evolving histories and traditions. The notion of world literature can thus be said to serve as the horizon for literary modernity in two senses and on two levels: on one level, as the framework for encounter and connection between national or regional literary histories and literary modernities, which define and redefine themselves dialectically in relation to one another; and, on another, as that which, in a more abstract sense, orients them, including orienting them mutually toward one another.

These double senses of world literature are active already in Goethe's coining of the term in 1827. To repeat his comment on that winter evening, "I am more and more convinced that poetry is a common property [*Gemeingut*] of humanity, revealing itself everywhere and at all times in hundreds and hundreds of human beings."[25] This idea that poetry belongs to humanity [*Menschheit*] as a universal category, rather than to human beings in their particular divisions into nationalities, serves as the premise for the ensuing pronouncement that "national literature does not mean much at present; the epoch of world literature is now at hand, and everyone must strive to hasten its approach."[26]

Earlier that day, before Eckermann's visit, Goethe had been reading a Chinese novel. A consideration of this occasion of reading illustrates the extent to which world literature already depended in 1827 on a process of encounter and connection between literary histories and literary modernities. Goethe does not name the novel in question but compares it to his own 1796–97 idyll *Hermann und Dorothea* and to the novels of Samuel Richardson. From the details he mentions, scholars have inferred that the novel he was reading may have been *Haoqiu zhuan*, an early Qing dynasty or late seventeenth-century work of anonymous authorship.[27] While this work enjoys only minor prestige within the sphere of Chinese letters, it has the distinction of being the first full-length work of Chinese fiction to be introduced to European readers. The story of its introduction to Europe is worth retelling. It began with a preliminary and partial translation dated 1719 by James Wilkinson, a British East India Company merchant who was learning Chinese while stationed in Canton, nowadays Guangzhou. The translation was then completed by an unknown hand in Portuguese, probably by a Jesuit missionary. This bilingual manuscript then passed through the translation and editorship of none other than Bishop Thomas Percy, who published the work in four volumes in London in 1761 with the title *Hao Kiouu Chouan, or The Pleasing History*, with notes and appendices, including the "Argument or Story of a Chinese Play," "A Collection of Chinese Proverbs," and "Fragments of Chinese Poetry." In his Preface, Percy identified the text as "a novel."[28] And this novel was then retranslated in the next few years from English into French, German, and Dutch. It is quite possible that Goethe was reading the German or French edition that January day in 1827.

While there is much that is remarkable about the history of transmission and reception of this text, I limit myself to two sets of observations. First, the editor who introduced the novel to England was the same who would, four years later, publish in 1765 the *Reliques of Ancient English Poetry*, a collection central to the ballad revival in late eighteenth-century Britain and thus to the establishment of local, non-Greco-Roman origins for English national literature. The *Reliques* also inspired Wordsworth and Coleridge's "modern" experiments with "ancient" ballad form in their breakthrough 1798 volume *Lyrical Ballads*. As Eun Kyung Min has traced in her recent book *China and the Writing of English Literary Modernity, 1690–1770*, comparisons with China, however rudimentary, second- or third-hand, and sometimes defensively chauvinistic, aided Percy and others in Restoration and eighteenth-century England to articulate new logics of division between ancient and modern as well as relations between genres in the historiography of English national literature.[29] This shows that the articulation of ostensibly vertical divisions did not take place within national literatures in isolation from one another but developed, rather, in encounters among civilizations, languages, and cultures within a framework of horizontality.[30]

Second, the epoch of world literature whose time Goethe says has come in 1827 (the phrase he uses is "an der Zeit") seems already to have begun over sixty years earlier in the practices of an English clergyman and, before that, a colonial merchant, his Chinese tutor, and a Portuguese Jesuit, and, before that, a seventeenth-century Chinese author. However, it is crucial to recognize, against the simple logic of linear chronology, that it is only from the deferred vantage point of 1827, with the operativity of concepts and classifications facilitated by the prior operations of translation and collection, that the possibility of a new kind of reading practice and new criticality can take effect with the conceptualization of world literature. In the preliminary comparisons Goethe was making between (presumably) *Haoqiu zhuan*, *Hermann und Dorothea*, and Richardson's novels, he was activating already a new way of reading that would become inaugural of the discipline of comparative literature and that looks forward, strikingly, to present-day comparative work on heterogeneous traditions of prose fiction and the polycentric, rather than Eurocentric, genesis of the novel as a global form.[31] Proceeding from the premise that poetry is the property of humanity as universal category, Goethe activates the promise of literary modernity as attribute of world literature.

In the strictest sense, logically speaking, literary modernity in the singular and world literature in the singular do not exist. They derive from the actuality of literatures phenomenally available in a diversity of languages and forms and that issue from the diversity of forms of human life. They emerge as effects of the reading of actual literary texts in their foreignness, heterogeneity, and diversity. Such reading is aided by the processes of translation, collection, classification, and reclassification that produce and reproduce heuristic guides to reading but, grounded in the claim to knowledge, are not themselves literary texts. Perhaps Borges showed greater understanding than anyone in his encyclopedist fables and allegories of reading how indispensable yet provisional world literature is as a formation for the forking encounters between languages and cultures.[32] In an interview published in 1991, Derrida shows similar insight when he defines succinctly "the space of literature" within the modern framework of knowledge as "that of an instituted *fiction* but also a *fictive institution* which in principle allows one to say everything."[33] The classifications and guides to literatures generated in the horizontal encounters among languages, cultures, and literatures institute the space of literature as one wherein literary authority continually puts into question, by means of fiction, the institutions of fiction itself.

Forms of Modernity

This study approaches the writing of literary modernity in Romantic England and Republican China by focusing on a selection of literary forms that serve as testing grounds for the enactment of new sociopolitical forms of life. These literary forms—the literary manifesto, the tale collection, the familiar essay, and the domestic novel—serve as sites in which questions of simultaneously literary-aesthetic and sociopolitical importance are tested. These questions include: what does it mean to attain a voice? What is a common reader? How does one dwell in the ordinary? What is a woman? In different languages, activating elements of heterogeneous literary and philosophical traditions, these texts explore by literary means the far from self-evident question of how to be modern in different lifeworlds.

I would like to comment here further on the specificity of the term "Romantic," a category that appears somewhat of an oddity in terms of English literary history. Whereas "Elizabethan," "Restoration," and "Victorian" are terms that correspond to categories of sovereign succession, Romanticism, like modernism, does not fit so neatly within the nomenclature or period logic of English national literature. Its origins are more cosmopolitan, developing as a Western European phenomenon with iterations throughout Europe and the Americas, gaining impetus from the philosophical and political claims informing the political revolutions of the late eighteenth century. Its complexity manifests itself in the bardic nationalisms of Percy and Pseudo-Ossian, among others, as well as in decontextualizing assimilations by writers everywhere, including early twentieth-century China, who equate Romanticism simply with the subjectivist expression of untrammeled feeling.[34] What makes Romanticism most significant, however, as both a moment and a corollary of world literature, is its disposition as a textual practice that contains its own critique, that theorizes and reflects on its own conditions of reading and its status as imaginative literature.[35] It is this critical disposition, issuing from the conversation between literature and philosophy internal to Romanticism's origins, that makes Romantic writing continually illuminating to read with.

The incipience of literary modernity in China in the early twentieth century likewise gave rise to a critical disposition in practices of writing that offer critical reflections on their own status as imaginative writing while situating themselves in relation to a tradition of Chinese letters undergoing reclassification and revaluation. Like English Romanticism, the writing of early twentieth-century China gains impetus from philosophical claims informing political revolution. Like late eighteenth- and early nineteenth-century England, early twentieth-century China was a period in which questions of literary modernity were entwined with questions of political modernity.

The writings I study in this book stage quests for modernity. They ask what it is to be modern and how to address others as modern, enacting modernity as a set of questions rather than as the fulfillment of preconceived and programmatic definitions. In so doing, they take orientation from a framework of world literature as a condition of connection and comparison between languages and cultures. They take orientation also from the principles of freedom, equality, and mutuality pronounced explicitly as ideals in the turns to republicanism and democracy in the revolutions of the eighteenth century. If the Enlightenment articulates the equal authority of human beings everywhere to make laws for themselves as users of reason, the punctual, rationalist conception of modern subjectivity therein, it has often been noted, fails, often catastrophically, to acknowledge the complexity of human beings in their existences in language and history. As universal sociopolitical principles of humanity, freedom, equality, and mutuality are by themselves empty. They have substance only in the actuality of language or, more precisely, of languages that serve as vital mediums of inhabitation and imagination and thus operativity and efficacy. The efforts to write literary modernity in England and China at issue in this study reckon with how to be modern by grappling insistently with the question of how to address others as free and equal subjects in evolving configurations of mutuality. This ethical and philosophical endeavor is at the heart of their (self-)critical disposition.

Crucial for this endeavor and for this study is the fact that these writings do not pursue the quest for modernity in isolation. Rather, they receive articulation from and within histories and traditions that they variously repeat, displace, unwork, renew, and reevaluate. In these various operations, the texts in question evince critical awareness of their own implication within textual traditions and cultural configurations whose terms and conditions they test and revise. With this critical self-consciousness, these texts demand for their own reading the rereading also of the histories and traditions in which they are inscribed. By making such demands, these texts demonstrate how their own claims to modernity issue from and establish themselves by activating potentialities inherent in aspects of heterogeneous pasts.

Walter Benjamin has used the figure of the "constellation" to characterize the workings of a recursive temporality, in contrast to the articulation of historical meaning within the terms of consecutive chronology. In Supplement A to the theses "On the Concept of History," he distinguishes between a historicism that tells "the sequence of events like the beads of a rosary" and a historicism that would involve instead the historian grasping "the constellation into which his own era has entered, along with a very specific earlier one," and thus establishing "a conception of the present as now-time shot through with splinters of messianic time."[36] I invoke the figure of the constellation from Benjamin to designate the operations whereby the English and Chinese writers in question establish alike the nowness (the modernity) of their own times in relation to earlier eras within different cultural configurations.[37] Both sets of writers find sidereal orientation in the task of writing as subjects of modernity and of addressing their readers as modern subjects, but their constellatory historiographies take place in the mediums of different languages that carry within them the legacies of different metaphorics and logics of messianism and redemption.

Each chapter is dedicated to a literary form ostensibly common to both sets of writings. Instead of assuming the priority of the Western iteration as standard for imitation by non-Western writers, a fallacy attending the presumption of monoculturalism, each chapter investigates how the form in question derives from and renews antecedents in separate traditions. Each chapter focuses on uses of the form by select writers and performs close readings of these specific cases rather than broadly surveying uses of the form in the periods in question. Through close reading, each chapter analyzes how the particular literary form serves as the testing ground and site for enactments of modern sociopolitical forms of life. Each chapter traces the way the texts in question establish their nowness through critical and creative activation of the potential of textual practices from earlier eras in separate traditions. If close reading involves a shuttling back and forth between poetics and theory, comparative close reading of cross-cultural scope involves shuttling back and forth between different traditions of poetics and theory.

Chapter 1 approaches the literary manifesto as an exemplary form of literary modernity, which writers everywhere have used to declare bold new conceptions of literature and aesthetics. The form's global flourishing in the late nineteenth and early twentieth centuries, charted by Martin Puchner in *Poetry of the Revolution: Marx, Manifestos, and the Avant-Gardes*, was preceded by the wave of new definitions of poetry and declarations of new poetics by Romantic writers in an earlier age of political revolution.[38] In the later moment, coinciding with the end of the Qing dynasty and the beginning of the Republican era in China, Chinese writers composed various calls and proposals, very often nationalistic and programmatic, for a new Chinese literature. In the context of a radical and comprehensive reorganization of knowledge, these calls engage with the definition and institution of literature deriving from the European eighteenth century while participating in a classical category of writings on literary thought, the *wenlun*. My chapter focuses on literary manifestos by two major writers whose critical sophistication and wide-ranging erudition have made their work both sources of literary influence and forces in ongoing legacies of cultural critique. It reads together Percy Bysshe Shelley's 1821 *A Defence of Poetry* alongside two 1908 essays by Lu Xun, "On the Power of Mara Poetry" and "Toward a Refutation of Malevolent Voices." The two sets of texts are internally connected by the claim of solidarity Lu Xun makes with the "Mara poets," a coinage with which he renames Southey's "Satanic School" and that he extends to include, besides Byron and Shelley, the Russian poets Pushkin and Lermontov, the Polish poets Mickiewicz and Slowacki, and the Hungarian Sándor Petőfi. Lu Xun, who read Japanese, German, and perhaps a smidgen of Russian but not English, Polish, or Hungarian, relied on a variety of secondary sources to write his essay calling for the spirit of Mara poetry to renew literature and culture in China. While Byron and Byronism play a prominent role in his organization of the essay, it is, strikingly, with Shelley that Lu Xun, unbeknownst to himself, shows the most profound affinity. Both Shelley and Lu Xun figure poetic voice as an event of emancipatory newness throughout their writings, showing sustained critical preoccupation with the question of how an emancipated poetic voice may function as an emancipating poetic force in separate but connected fields of utterance and address.

This chapter analyzes the claims for the emancipatory power of the poetic voice in Shelley, which emanates from inhuman sources through the poet as medium, and it performs an exegesis of the "voices of newness" and "voices of the soul"—homophonous as *xinsheng* in Chinese—that Lu Xun attributes to the European Mara poets, calls for among his Chinese contemporaries, and derives from classical Chinese poetics. The chapter compares how Shelley and Lu Xun both espouse in their critical texts literary historiographies that involve cyclical return, with newness emerging not within a scheme of linear progression but out of the ashes of traditions that may contain sparks of renewing power. Hence, Shelley can use Aeschylean tragedy to allegorize cosmic renewal and the reorigination of language in *Prometheus Unbound*, and Lu Xun can write his two 1908 treatises not in the vernacular, which he would later promote as national and literary language, but in a stylized form of classical Chinese. He conducts a philological experiment, writing in a style that mixes contemporary neologisms with archaisms that predate the standardized classical Chinese of late imperial times that he associates with the ossifications of state orthodoxy. He responds to new political concepts by activating heterodox potentialities in classical poetics to advance his interpretation of modernity.

Chapter 2 moves from the high register of the literary manifesto, with its claims to inaugurate and emancipate, to the middling register of the tale collection, whose aim is to enchant and entertain. The form of the tale collection has long held popular appeal across cultures, serving as a vehicle for the recounting of adventures in faraway places or supernatural events in everyday life. In eighteenth-century Europe, the introduction of *The Arabian Nights* through processes of translation and redaction kindled an interest in "oriental tales" among European readers, for whom the encounter with the foreign was mixed with elements of the exotic and the fantastic.[39] In late Qing and early Republican China, toward the end of the nineteenth century and the beginning of the twentieth, collections of tales by such writers as Rider Haggard and Jules Verne ranked among the most popular texts in translation and entertained readers with stories of adventures that featured more than small doses of the improbable.[40]

This chapter approaches Charles and Mary Lamb's 1806 *Tales from Shakespeare* as a variation on such a form. Commissioned for the Juvenile Library of William and Mary Jane Godwin, the Lambs's *Tales* consist of prose redactions of twenty plays by Shakespeare: fourteen romances and comedies, six tragedies, and none of the histories. The collection had the distinction of being not only widely read in Regency and Victorian England, playing a role in the literary education of English children, but widely circulated, reprinted, anthologized, and translated in the British Empire and beyond in the nineteenth and twentieth centuries. In this latter capacity, the collection played a role in transmitting internationally the literary canonization of Shakespeare that had started taking place in England at the end of the eighteenth century. The *Tales* were translated into Chinese in 1904 with the title *Yinbian Yanyu* by Lin Shu, who was on his way to becoming the sociopolitically and culturally transitional era's most widely read and acclaimed translator of foreign, primarily Western, literature. Attributed to Shakespeare instead of the Lambs, *Yinbian Yanyu*—a title with literati cultural connotations loosely translatable as *A Poet Reading from Afar*—was the first Shakespearean text of any sort to appear in Chinese.

Lin was a translator who famously did not know any foreign languages, relying on collaborators who would interpret the literal meaning of texts he would then render in vivid and stylized classical Chinese. While he effectively did more than any other man of letters in his generation to expose Chinese readers to foreign literature, Lin was also, curiously, a political and cultural conservative who stood out in the reformist climate of his time for his Qing loyalism and adherence to Confucian classicism. His success and influence consisted in his rendering of Western novels and story collections in an idiom and form uncannily recognizable to his Chinese readers. He adapted the Lambs's *Tales* to the classical narrative form of the *chuanqi* (literally "transmission of the strange"), with its episodic structure and association with supernatural and exotic content. As the prose fiction form of *chuanqi* served also as the basis for theatrical adaptations, Lin found a resonant cultural counterpart for his retelling in Chinese of the Lambs's prose adaptation of Shakespeare's theatrical texts, themselves retellings of borrowed stories.

This chapter examines how each set of retellers manipulates the form of the tale collection to address and fashion an imagined "common reader"— that quintessentially nineteenth-century character of global literary and cultural history whose ascendancy in various locales is predicated on the spread of literacy and the increasing accessibility of printed matter. I focus on retellings of one play, *The Tempest*, to analyze how the characters of Miranda and Prospero emerge in the respective texts as figures or surrogates for the emergent common reader as a middling, imaginative subject in times of social enfranchisement and cultural change. While the literary manifesto functions as a form through which writers can self-consciously undertake the task of interrogating what it means to be modern, the tale collection affords, at the more modest eye-level of storytelling, a perspective onto modern configurations of social structures that are less perceptible because more local and gradual.

Chapter 3 examines the form of the familiar or informal essay, which flourished in Republican China from the early 1920s until the outbreak of the Second Sino-Japanese War in 1937, facilitated by the vibrant periodical press in metropolitan areas. In a 1921 essay in the Beijing *Chenbao* or *Morning News*, Zhou Zuoren, younger brother of Lu Xun and a leading figure in the New Culture or May Fourth Movement of 1919, points to a line of Anglo-American essayists from Addison to Chesterton as inspiration for his Chinese contemporaries. What characterizes the familiar or informal essay, as distinct from the critical or polemical essay, is a casual, informal tone with which the author simulates conversation with the reader as peer and uses occasions in ordinary life as points of departure and topics for reflection.

Among the English and American writers Zhou highlights is Charles Lamb, whose *Essays of Elia* had been serialized with great success in the *London Magazine* in the 1820s. An alter ego of Lamb, Elia is a clerk in the South Seas Office who, like Lamb, a clerk for a quarter century with the East India Company, writes in his leisure hours of the uncanniness of ordinary life in an increasingly globally connected and commercialized England. Without using a quasi-fictional character as a persona, Zhou wrote a century later of how seemingly trivial matters like comestibles and tea-drinking can serve as things that tease readers out of habitual contexts and ways of thought.

This chapter studies how Lamb and Zhou use the medium of the familiar essay to explore the strangeness of the everyday in writings that subtly position London and Beijing within a global network of multiple other locations, metropolitan and otherwise. At the same time, the aesthetic techniques of these writings show very different cultural derivations. In a close reading of Lamb's "Old China," this chapter analyzes Lamb's ironic use of an aesthetics of dioramic realism to express the pleasures and discontents of average bourgeois citizenship. It examines, in contrast, how Zhou practices a poetics of taxonomic lyricism in the essay "Wild Vegetables of My Hometown." In his capacity as a literary historian and theorist—and not just practitioner—of the familiar essay form, Zhou traces the form's predilection for the idle and idiosyncratic to late Ming dynasty or late sixteenth- to seventeenth-century practices of informal prose writing and elucidates the sociopolitically heterodox and dehierarchizing impulses and potential of such practices. While participating in different genealogies for the writing of the ordinary, Lamb and Zhou both attempt to address and unsettle, with gentle irony, the reader as a peer in the incremental and everyday task of rediscovering the ordinary.

Chapter 4 investigates the domestic novel as a literary form in which the woman as protagonist and the site of the household come to the fore as subject and scene of modernity. It concentrates on novels by two of the form's preeminent practitioners in English and Chinese, Jane Austen and Eileen Chang, who have drawn comparisons to each other for their clear, even cold-eyed, depictions of social and economic constraints on femininity and the complexity of feminine interiority. These writers share also a general narratorial position of ironic detachment vis-à-vis their female protagonists. They are each perhaps at their most mercilessly dissecting in their portrayals of their least likable heroines, Fanny Price in the 1814 *Mansfield Park* and Cao Qiqiao in the 1943 novella *Jinsuo ji*, which Chang herself translated into English as *The Golden Cangue*. This chapter reads together Austen's *Mansfield Park* and Chang's later bilingual rewriting of her 1943 novella as the novel-length *Yuannü* and *The Rouge of the North* (1967) after Chang's emigration to the United States in the 1950s. From a diasporic perspective, in the turbulent first decades of the People's Republic of China, Chang revisits her earlier Republican-era text in novelistic form. She renames the heroine "Yindi" and incorporates a dimension absent from the novella—sustained references by the protagonist to the Peking opera as well as the inclusion of a private performance as an event in the narrative.

Austen and Chang's novels show how changes in the articulation of femininity in different historical and cultural contexts take place in correlation to redefinitions of the status of the household itself as a site of modern life. Traditionally the domain of femininity and processes of production and reproduction that sustain ordinary life, the household emerges in political economic redistributions of authority in modernity as a site wherein questions of what it means to pursue a meaningful life may be raised anew. Both Austen and Chang incorporate the medium of theater into their narrations in ways that facilitate reflection on the shifts in consequence of the household. While Chang weaves the Peking opera into *Yuannü* and *The Rouge of the North*, Austen features in *Mansfield Park* the rehearsal of one play, Elizabeth Inchbald's 1798 *Lovers' Vows*, and the reading aloud of another, *Henry VIII*, attributed in Austen's time to Shakespeare but today to Shakespeare and John Fletcher. On the level of plot and character development, the medium of theater works in these novels to mediate the heroines' reflections on their own positions and identities within larger sociocultural frameworks. On the literary historiographical level, the incorporation of theater into the domestic novel allows the latter to define itself genealogically as a modern literary form in relation to theatrical traditions, which appear in both works as historically changing and culturally specific frameworks for the aesthetic mediation of community. Each novel displaces and takes on aspects of the work of theater by restaging "woman" as modern agent and spectatorial subject on the plane of the ordinary.

Quests for Modernity, Inhabitations of the Ordinary

Liberté, egalité, fraternité. Liberty, equality, fraternity: these are the terms that form the slogan of the French Revolution and that democratic modernity appeals to as sociopolitical principles of a shared humanity. But these principles have substance only within the languages and sociocultural configurations in which human beings as historical beings have their existence, and they can have operativity only within the terms and conditions of languages that sustain their meaning. Their universality is not a presupposition but rather, then, a promise whose actualization and reactualization take place in languages. My contention is that it is only on the basis of detailed and rigorous reading of these languages, as they encounter each other and enter into conversation, that we can begin to ask the question of what such principles as liberty, equality, and fraternity might mean—what modernity might mean within the specific terms and conditions of different lifeworlds. It is for this reason that this book examines practices of writing in Romantic England and Republican China that launch literary modernities by orienting themselves toward the task of actualizing these principles as attributes of being modern across different lifeworlds.

The valence of each term, the significance of the sequencing of terms, and the relationship between them all remain questions for ongoing consideration and deliberation, questions that become both more enigmatic and more precise when read comparatively and cross-culturally. "Liberty," for instance, is located among a cluster of terms including "freedom" and "emancipation" in English. To translate "liberty," Japanese and Chinese scholars in the late nineteenth century retrieved a term of previously minor currency and consequence, *ziyou*, from the Confucian classics as an approximation for a globally circulating concept with local instantiations.[41] That the term "fraternity" falls short as a principle of universality is evident in the way it takes a part—men or brothers—for the whole. In place of "fraternity," I prefer throughout this study "mutuality," which designates more properly a condition of interdependence and cooperation that would obtain between human beings as equals.

In my reading of the way the practices of writing in question explore what it means to be modern, I have found instructive the work of two contemporary North American philosophers, Charles Taylor and Stanley Cavell. In his 2004 book *Modern Social Imaginaries*, Taylor proposes the notion of an affirmation of ordinary life that is constitutive of modernity across cultures and regions.[42] This affirmation, according to Taylor, involves the valorization of those aspects of human life concerned with production and reproduction, with labor and work, activities that in the Aristotelian tradition of political thought had long been considered infrastructural for the higher task of living well, which was available only to the leisured few. The modern democratic revolutionary values of freedom, equality, and mutuality are in accord with such an affirmation of ordinary life, with the question and task of living well displaced into the locus of the ordinary as a possible pursuit for the many. Affirmations of ordinary life across multiple modernities involve what Taylor calls, after economist Karl Polanyi, "disembeddings" from traditional hierarchical orderings of societies and communities, processes of reform and revaluation that include, for instance, the complex transformation of Confucianism from state orthodoxy to way of thought and textual tradition beginning in the early twentieth century. Such disembeddings do not involve a clean break between pasts and presents, as in a linear conception of temporality. They involve acknowledgments and reckonings with the complex afterlives of traditional ordering systems as these undergo dehierarchizing rearticulation. If classical Chinese lost its operativity along with the dismantling of the Confucian administrative apparatus in early twentieth-century China, it survives within both the national vernacular of Mandarin Chinese and the regional vernaculars in which it had become embedded on all levels of linguistic use, from the official to the literary to the everyday, as *scripta franca* of empire. Elements of classical thought and literary expression inhabit both Mandarin as present-day *koiné* or *lingua franca* of the Sinophone world and the ordinary languages in which ordinary life continues always already to take place and evolve in the linguistic-political aftermath of empire and empires.

While Charles Taylor addresses questions of multiculturalism in a broad sense with his notion of modernity as a turn everywhere toward the affirmation of ordinary life, Stanley Cavell is a philosopher whose focus on skepticism as a problem staged in moral thought and aesthetics has taken place intensively and intimately in relation to European and Anglo-American texts. Where Taylor hypothesizes an affirmation of ordinary life, Cavell reads in a corpus of philosophical, literary, and cinematic texts processes well described by the punning title of his 1987 book *In Quest of the Ordinary: Lines of Skepticism and Romanticism*.[43] The ordinary stands here for both lived, everyday existence and the medium of ordinary language in which that experience of living is understood. Skepticism and Romanticism contest the terms and conditions of both ordinary life and ordinary language as a medium of thought, a process of questioning whose paradoxical character is, according to Cavell, essential to our being human. The ordinary is thus subject necessarily to both quest and inquest in the vitality of a process that, experiencing language as dead, seeks to renew and recover it, not by establishing a meta-language for higher thought, but immanently, within the unacknowledged intimacies of ordinary language itself. Cavell's thinking, which has not traveled as readily beyond the sphere of Euro-American letters as Taylor's or, even more widely, John Rawls's, opens up ways of thinking about and reading the operations of legacies of skepticism, in, say, Daoist and Zen Buddhist aesthetics, in the work, or play, of inhabiting and reimagining the ordinary as structurally universal yet locally and historically lived scene of modernity.

In summary, this book examines the literary and aesthetic means by which the question and task of living well as pursuit for the many is explored and enacted in connected moments of incipience for literary modernity in England and China. It aims to offer a complex perspective on the global legacy of conceptions of literature developed in the European Enlightenment and Romanticism as this legacy is activated across linguistic and cultural boundaries and interacts with local textual traditions and social systems. Beginning with the higher, more heroic register of Shelley and Lu Xun's manifestos, it moves toward middling registers of literary forms and forms-of-life associated with popular storytelling, quotidian leisure, and feminine domesticity, in which affirmations and interrogations of the ordinary involve thick evocation of the sensuous particulars of lifeworlds that are not readily available and recognizable to one another. My study traces culturally heterogeneous antecedents that inform and animate comparable creative practices and attends as well to the ways the English and Chinese texts in question register the promises and perils of mechanisms of technoeconomic homogenization that were likewise reorganizing human life in the global long nineteenth century. With the attentiveness it seeks to perform and to encourage, this book aims to open up ways of inhabitation and imagination to one another in a plurally shared and intimately lived world modernity.

1 Literary Modernity and the Emancipation of Voice

Defenses of Poetry by Percy Bysshe Shelley and Lu Xun

In 1908, a few years before the revolution that ended the Qing dynasty and initiated the Republican era in 1911, a young Chinese writer published a literary manifesto titled "On the Power of Mara Poetry" in a journal run by expatriate students and dissidents in Japan.[1] In this essay, he calls for powerful "new voices" to regenerate Chinese language and culture. With the binomial term for "new voices," *xinsheng* (新聲), he plays with homophones denoting "voices of the soul" (心聲) and "new life" (新生). With this trio of homophones, he suggests that the "new voices" in question would emanate from *xin* (心), a keyword in classical Chinese thought that designates the seat of both affect and cognition and that, resisting easy equivalence, is often rendered "heart-mind" by philosophical translators. "New voices" emanating from the "soul" or "heart-mind," the wordplay of the essay implies, would have the power to bring "new life" to a language and culture in danger of stagnation and voicelessness among the nations of the world. With this essay, the young writer would begin his career-long preoccupation with the poetics and politics of voice in his literary critical, fictional, and cultural-polemical writings. Ten years later, back in China, the writer would adopt the pen name of "Lu Xun," by which he would become known already by the time of his death in 1936 and emphatically after 1949, through the dubious blessing of state canonization, as modern China's greatest, or at least most sharply powerful, writer.[2]

"On the Power of Mara Poetry" calls for "new voices" that speak from the "soul" in early twentieth-century China by situating this very call in relation to the international or even internationalist legacy of European Romanticism. With the term "Mara poetry," Lu Xun renamed the "Satanic School," the term Robert Southey coined in 1821 for his younger contemporaries George Gordon, Lord Byron, and Percy Bysshe Shelley.[3] *Mara*, rendered *moluo* in Chinese, is Sanskrit for "demon" and Japanese slang for "penis." Lu Xun, who was fluent in Japanese, was very likely aware of the additional potency the latter connotation brought to his advocacy of the spirit of youthful rebelliousness.[4] Among the Mara poets, Lu Xun surveyed the lives and works of Byron, Shelley, Aleksandr Pushkin, Mikhail Lermontov, Adam Mickiewicz, Juliusz Slowacki, and Sándor Petőfi. This chronological ordering shows also a geographically eastward movement from Western Europe to East Asia, where Lu Xun called for a new generation of Chinese writers to heed the voices and join the ranks of the Mara poets. Written toward the end of a long nineteenth century bookended by revolutions and punctuated by uprisings—a timeline explicitly invoked within the essay itself—"On the Power of Mara Poetry" would seem to enact, extend, and comment on the legacy of European Romanticism.

"On the Power of Mara Poetry" consists of a critical-polemical prefatory section and epilogue that frame a survey of the European Mara poets. The survey gives exemplary status to Byron, not just as chronologically the first but as the iconic leader and prototype in relation to which the other six poets appear as followers. Each subsequent poet is presented and evaluated according to his adherence to the anti-patriarchal, anti-tyrannical heroism of Byronic themes and Byronic deeds. The entry on Shelley, for instance, selects works in which the principal characters—Alastor, Laon, Prometheus, Beatrice Cenci—double the image of Shelley doubling Byron in their defiance of convention and tyranny even unto death. At first glance, Byronism would appear to characterize a solidarity that arises from a pattern of emulation and imitation between poets of different nations writing in different languages. Fascinatingly, beyond this imitative solidarity that manifests itself on a thematic level, it is Shelley, rather than Byron, whose writings most echo Lu Xun's in their self-conscious and critically sustained engagement with the question of voice. The resonances between the writers suggest a logic of solidarity whose complexity exceeds identification and imitation.

The privileging of Byron results from the sources and procedures Lu Xun used to compose his essay. His sources were all secondary. Lu Xun had learned Japanese and German for the medical studies he famously abandoned for literature in 1906.[5] But he did not read English, or Polish and Hungarian, although he may have had rudimentary knowledge of Russian from studying it briefly in 1907. For the writing of "On the Power of Mara Poetry," he relied on Japanese and German translations of the various texts in their original languages and on the mediation of literary histories and biographies, likewise in translation. He may have turned to his younger brother, Zhou Zuoren, who was also studying in Japan, for consultation on texts in English. But his access to all the European Mara poets in question was mediated by such sources as the Danish literary critic Georg Brandes and the philosopher Friedrich Nietzsche, whom Lu Xun was reading studiously while writing the essay. The research of Japanese scholar Kitaoka Masako reveals the numerous secondary sources Lu Xun used.[6] For his entry on Shelley, he relied principally on a Japanese translation of J. A. Symonds's 1878 biography, which made the case that Shelley's life and work were "indissolubly connected" and promoted the image of Shelley as an effete and otherworldly aesthete, in contrast to the "radical Shelley" that had also emerged in the splitting of Shelley's reception in Victorian England.[7] Lu Xun's entry on Shelley combines elements of the ethereal aestheticist Shelley with the convention-defying aspects of the Byronic hero. His version of Shelley was mediated through Symonds, Japanese translation, and the narrative of European Byronism. While much of the particular appeal of Byron's poetry may have survived a mobile army of translation, paraphrase, and summary, Shelley thematized would involve refigurations that cover and elide the ambiguities, subtleties, and nuances that distinguish his writing and that issue the demand to read closely. Ironically, according to Lu Xun's own strict criteria for *xinsheng* as the emancipatory "voice of the soul" in "On the Power of Mara Poetry," Shelley would be "voiceless," or *wusheng*, in "On the Power of Mara Poetry."

In this chapter, I will examine how Shelley and Lu Xun both conceive, in connected yet separate ways, of literary modernity in terms of an emancipation of voice. In the first section, I investigate the indirect connection of their poetics and politics of voice in terms of a "desire for resonance" that motivates their claims to internationalist solidarity. This desire for resonance and the claims to solidarity are underwritten by the shared affirmation of freedom and equality as universal attributes of human beings. The universalism of these attributes is abstract, predicated on the Enlightenment philosophical conception of human beings as free and equal entities in their capacity to give laws to themselves as users of reason.[8] In its actualization, this abstract universalism involves the density and historicity of different linguistic traditions and cultural configurations and attains expression in the nineteenth century within the organizational structure of internationalism. The claims to internationalist—or what perhaps would be called in other contexts cosmopolitan—solidarity enacted in texts by Shelley and Lu Xun express a desire for resonance and activate universalism as promise. In the second section, I examine how Shelley and Lu Xun's poetics and politics of voice work to enact emancipations of voice within the context of distinct textual traditions and cultural configurations of operativity. Simply put, they take place in and issue their demands to be read not just in language, but in different languages. I turn to Shelley's 1821 *Defence of Poetry* to analyze how he figures the emancipatory capacity of poetic voice as an event that emerges from, acts on, and extends preexisting discourse within a recursive, cyclical structure. In another 1908 essay, "Toward a Refutation of Malevolent Voices," Lu Xun develops insights in "On the Power of Mara Poetry" to show how poetic voice can only emancipate itself from not just old but also new doxa by availing itself of the resources and potential of the Chinese language and poetic tradition itself. That modernity does not start wholly new, as if on a tabula rasa, but new *again* is an argument Lu Xun enhances by continuing in this essay the critical philological experiment he had conducted stylistically in "On the Power of Mara Poetry." The literary manifestos of Shelley and Lu Xun thus show in common a philosophical skepticism vis-à-vis language as an unstable medium whose noncoincidence with itself—or the capacity of words to mean several and even opposing things, or to remain ambiguous—issues the demand for attentive reading. In this stance, they orient themselves in common toward world literary modernity as a poetically shared modernity in which plural and separate literary modernities, inhabited within languages, may coexist and come into contact with each other. Such a poetically shared modernity constitutes an alternative to a modernity construed in terms of the ascendancy of instrumental rationality and the privilege of mathesis, which denies the thickness and historicity of languages and cultures in its confusion of the punctual subject of reason with the culturally embedded subject of history. If Shelley counters and critiques the latter version of modernity, ascendant in eighteenth-century Europe and spreading globally in the nineteenth century, so too does Lu Xun in his critique of the malevolent voices imitating and propagating scientific new doxa, purportedly against the old doxa of Confucian doctrine, but fundamentally, like the old doxa, against poetry itself. In a way, then, though both writers operate in distinct cultural and political traditions, they identify an analogous problem in trying to modernize and revolutionize the conditions of their times. In conclusion, I reflect on the implications of the resonances between Shelley and Lu Xun—strikingly unheard by one another, and curiously unheard, in turn, by readers of Shelley and readers of Lu Xun—for the work of reading comparatively and inhabiting a shared modernity.

Internationalism, Poetic Solidarity, and the Desire for Resonance

As is familiar to readers of English Romanticism, Shelley foregrounds the figure of voice in many of his poems. In the 1816 "Mont Blanc," the poet-speaker bears witness to and aims to transmit the voice of the eponymous mountain, which is said to have the power to repeal "large codes of fraud and woe" (l.81).[9] In the 1819 "Ode to the West Wind," the poet implores the Wind to scatter his words among mankind by being through his lips the trumpet of a prophecy.[10] In the "Ode to Liberty," likewise from 1819, the poet-speaker claims that the very poem records "a voice out of the deep" (l.15). In "The Mask of Anarchy," the speaker recalls being addressed by a "voice from over the Sea" to "walk in the visions of Poesy" and heralds, toward the end of the inset song supposedly issuing from Earth, the emergence of an oracular eloquence that would be like "a volcano heard afar" (l.363). Here are just a few examples from the many texts by Shelley that allegorize and look forward to their own participation in the language of left internationalism in the way they trope voice as agent and medium of transmission.

Beginning with "On the Power of Mara Poetry," Lu Xun calls for the emergence of poetic voices that would disturb the doxa that have everywhere, from England to China, sustained repressive traditional hierarchies and *anciens régimes*. By establishing this international link, he can focus on the question of how "new voices of the soul" may arise in China and participate in the international context. In a later essay of 1908, "Toward a Refutation of Malevolent Voices," he turns his focus on China as the site for the emergence of "voices of the soul" that would refute the authority of "malevolent voices" (*esheng*) both old and new. The figure of voice would feature prominently in his later writings, such as the Preface to his breakthrough 1922 collection of stories, *Outcry* (*Nahan*), in which he famously likens the emancipatory aims of his own writing to cries that may awaken sleepers in a locked iron house. Stories in that collection, such as "The Diary of a Madman" and *The True Story of Ah Q*, feature complex, polyphonic techniques that parody and expose the workings of "malevolent voices" and open up thereby the question of what a "new voice" might sound like. The 1927 lectures, "Voiceless China" and "The Old Tunes Are Finished," are polemical texts that show Lu Xun's continued preoccupation with the question of voice in the culturally tumultuous period of Republican China.

That there are fascinating resonances between Shelley and Lu Xun's poetics and politics of voice should be evident; that there is no direct connection between them is remarkable and worthy of more careful consideration. A slack explanation may account for their resonances by situating their rhetorics in a global context that saw the general diffusion of tropes of voice in left internationalist rhetoric through the circulation and translation of Chartist and socialist texts since the second half of the nineteenth century.[11] But such a slack explanation would not account for the finer affinities evident in the tropings of voice by the two writers. These affinities extend beyond their actual historical moments backward to elements of textual and cultural traditions and forward in the continued critical impact of their writings in separate but connected domains of reading as well as literary and cultural critique. Both writers remain good to think with, in English and in Chinese—and, potentially, *between* English and Chinese.

In this section, I examine how Shelley and Lu Xun figure the emancipation of voice at thresholds of the national and the international. For the emancipation of voice to take place within one political and cultural context entails for each author the emancipation taking place in relation to other emancipations in other political and cultural contexts. Therein consist their mutual claims to modernity. These political and cultural contexts involve jostling categories of political aspiration and organization, including peoples, nations, and empires. Insofar as late nineteenth-century left internationalism involves the struggles of peoples, variously defined, against imperial forms of control, the republican model of the nation serves as the de facto formation through which anti-imperial sentiment gets expressed in Shelley and Lu Xun, as well as the other European Mara poets. It is through internationalism that the abstract universal principles of freedom, equality, and fraternity receive historical concretization. I turn to passages in "The Mask of Anarchy" and "On the Power of Mara Poetry" to pay closer attention to how Shelley and Lu Xun express a desire for resonance while working at nexuses of nationalism and internationalism.

"The Mask of Anarchy" is an occasional poem that Shelley wrote in response to the massacre of peaceful protestors by militiamen and cavalrymen at St. Peter's Field in Manchester on August 16, 1819. It would not be published until 1832, after the passage of the First Reform Bill in England had, as editors Donald Reiman and Neil Fraistat phrase it, "won the battle for which Shelley had intended his poem as a kind of rallying hymn" (315). This posthumous publication contributed to the image of a "radical Shelley" that stands in contrast to Symonds's effete aesthete in Victorian reception history. The history that "The Mask of Anarchy" addresses and the history of its publication are both inscribed in the timeline of nineteenth-century uprisings and reforms that Lu Xun threads through the nine parts of "On the Power of Mara Poetry." Ironically, this poem is not mentioned in Lu Xun's entry on Shelley. Unlike *The Necessity of Atheism, Alastor, The Revolt of Islam, Prometheus Unbound,* and *The Cenci*, it lacks a character that can be easily personified and thematized as a Byronic figure of defiance.[12] Like "On the Power of Mara Poetry," "The Mask of Anarchy" was written abroad—from Italy—and addressed primarily to the author's countrymen. How does this poem raise and allegorize anew the question of voice at the nexus of the national and international?

"The Mask of Anarchy" is divided into two main parts: following the one-stanza prologue, the first part plays with the masque as a form of European early modern aristocratic entertainment and the procession as a public display of power; the second part consists of the song that emerges after the sequence of events following the maid Hope's interruption of the pageant of Anarchy. This song is sung "as if" by Earth and is addressed to the men of England. It has a rousing quality that has led to its being detached and circulated separately.[13] This song and the entire poem in which it is embedded both conclude with the following three stanzas:

> "And that slaughter to the Nation
> Shall steam up like inspiration,
> Eloquent, oracular;
> A volcano heard afar.
>
> "And these words shall then become
> Like oppression's thundered doom
> Ringing through each heart and brain,
> Heard again—again—again—
>
> "Rise like lions after slumber
> In unvanquishable number—
> Shake your chains to earth like dew
> Which in sleep had fallen on you—
> Ye are many—they are few." (ll. 360–72)

Considered closely, these last three stanzas pivot around the deictic "these words" in line 364 to look in two directions. They seem to look forward to how the final stanza, the rousing refrain that "these words" constitute, shall be heard. But they may also be taken to look back upon and to comment on what precedes—namely, aspects of the song that transmit out of the trauma of unjust murder the emergence of precisely the oracular, volcanic voice. The ambiguity of the referent of "these words" opens up both possibilities. One possibility is internationalist; the other offers a reading of English history.

Looking forward, "these words" point to the final stanza, which is a refrain that repeats verbatim the second stanza of the song. While in its first sounding the refrain had been addressed specifically to "men of England," there seems to occur in its return a shift in addressee. As the referent of "these words" in the penultimate stanza, the final five verses would seem to constitute the very words that, as the couplet prophesies, shall ring "through each heart and brain, / Heard again—again—again." These words, with the catchphrase detachability of their parts and whole, would accompany the transformation of the slaughter at St. Peter's Field into a sign of promised meaningfulness, like "a volcano heard afar." With the final refrain, the song and the poem in which the song is embedded gesture, then, toward addressees other than men of England, enacting an aspiration toward internationalism and expressing a desire for resonance. Strikingly, with the phrase "a volcano heard afar," these last three stanzas hearken back also to the prologue of the poem, when the poet-narrator recalls being "addressed" by "a voice from over the sea." Fascinatingly, insofar as that earlier voice had come to the poet while he "lay asleep" to lead him to "walk in the visions of Poesy," the very poem that earlier voice had occasioned tells the dream or vision of the emergence, in turn, of yet another voice (l.1, l. 4).

If they are taken to refer back to what precedes, the deictic "these words" and the entire penultimate stanza would seem to describe alternately a structure of reverberation that Shelley uses to compose the song embedded in the poem. Within this song, Shelley uses variations of the word "echo" three times, notably to mark stages in the attempt to answer one specific question—namely, "What is Freedom?"

> "What is Freedom?—ye can tell
> That which slavery is, too well—
> For its very name has grown
> To an echo of your own." (ll. 156–59)

> "Thou art not, as impostors say,
> A shadow soon to pass away,
> A superstition, and a name
> Echoing from the cave of Fame." (ll. 213–16)

> "The old laws of England—they
> Whose reverend heads with age are grey,

> Children of a wiser day;
> And whose solemn voice must be
> Thine own echo—Liberty!" (ll. 331–35)

These separate stanzas, which remarkably group together as a coherent unit, show the processual nature of evolving an answer to the question. The dashes in the first stanza may mark the temporal deferment of this answer. Earth's answer substitutes, rather, the statement of a condition of nominal enslavement that attends the catalogue of inequalities that ensues in the following stanzas of the song, in lines 160–212. Answering the question of freedom, that first stanza implies, is predicated on liberation from the echo of voices of domination. The second stanza likewise answers the question of freedom negatively by denying that freedom is merely a name echoing from the cave of Fame. The third stanza moves toward a positive definition in a future imperative formulation that crescendos in the extra fifth line in the word "liberty!" The actualization of liberty would come about when the voice of the laws coincides with the voice of the assembled men of England. These three stanzas mark a process that involves the emergence of a new voice whereby men of England may become heirs of the glory of England as land of the Magna Carta and the rule of law.

These three stanzas chart a process of individual and national self-deliberation whereby the emergence of the voice of the assembly as the voice of the laws would supplant the tautological echoing of "Thou art God, and King, and Law" among Anarchy's murderous crew. Together, they seem to address the "men of England" as both individual subjects and a collective body of resonant interiority, whose capacity to hear the echo of voices of domination and deception in relation to and within their own voices is necessary, though not sufficient, for the achievement of freedom.

Let us take one more look at the penultimate stanza of the poem. If the deictic "these words" are taken to refer to the final stanza, the second couplet would seem to anticipate a numerical proliferation of auditors through whose hearts and brains the exhortatory five verses would ring one after another, as these five verses may be recited repeatedly one time after another, as well. Yet, if the deixis refers back to what precedes, the penultimate stanza may indicate a process of reverberation in which the event of hearing anew, differently each time, takes place for and within the same subjects. Such a hearing anew is not incompatible with a numerical proliferation of auditors or recitations. Such a hearing is inscribed likewise as a possibility within the shift of addressee that seems to mark the poem's ending at the threshold of nationalism and internationalism.

At this threshold, the poem gestures toward the transmission of a voice that would be heard by "ye many" beyond the "men of England." This voice seems to profess itself as the very expression of liberty; it is a voice that emerges from a process of self-examination and deliberation, in which the assembly as a collective national body seems to consist of individual subjects of resonant interiority. By hearkening back to the "voice from over the Sea" in the prologue, the final stanzas, with the reference to an eloquence that would be like "a volcano heard afar," implies that the poem participates in a relay of voices that reach those in slumber. That it remains unclear whether the poet-speaker of the prologue ever awakens contributes, on one level, to a sense of uncertainty over whether the narrated developments will ever take place. On another level, the ambiguity seems to bespeak a skepticism inherent within the poem's very gesture toward internationalism.[14] It suggests that the poem, as itself the dream or vision of a voice, has as its primary condition of transmission and reception, curiously, the unconsciousness rather than the wakefulness of "ye many" beyond England.

What does it mean for the desire for resonance to be addressed to the unconsciousness of the many others? By specifying the oneiric and unconscious character of its own transmission, the poem demonstrates skeptical self-knowledge concerning its ontological status as poem rather than as self-consistent statement of knowledge. It shows thereby an awareness of the limits that condition and constrain the immediate transmission and reception of its own voice. This voice does not simply travel across seas and borders as agent of emancipation that speaks the conscious language of knowledge as power. Its transmission involves, rather, encounter with the languages of others as likewise mediums in which wakefulness entails slumber and dream—languages that remain partly, indeed, unconscious to and of this voice itself.

In turning to "On the Power of Mara Poetry," I reiterate first that Lu Xun locates the power of Mara poetry centrally in its capacity to release *xinsheng*, or the "voice of the soul." In the second sentence of the essay, he claims that "civilization's most potent legacy to later generations is the voice of the soul" and that it is poetry, above all forms of speech and writing, that has the greatest capacity to emit, record, and transmit *xinsheng* (97). The latter phrase is repeated throughout the essay, reverberating with homophones meaning "new voice" and "new life." Mara poetry, for Lu Xun, has the power to regenerate languages and cultures through the release of voices of newness that are likewise voices of the soul. It is this capacity that he seeks to activate among a new generation of Chinese writers at a time when, as he claims at the very beginning of the essay, Chinese civilization is afflicted with a desolation he glosses as a crisis of voicelessness. From the vantage point of the early twentieth century, such a crisis seems to afflict other ancient civilizations also, including India, Egypt, and Persia. The silence or voicelessness of contemporary China becomes, paradoxically, audible as an absence within a new international system denominated by the term "world," *shijie*, for China a new term that had begun only in the late nineteenth century to displace the traditional cosmological term of *tianxia*.[15] It is in the epistemic framework of this new "world" that Lu Xun raises the question of what it is for a Chinese writer to have a voice.

How might Lu Xun's concern with voice in the essay be understood as an enactment of solidarity with—if not as a conscious and direct response to—Shelley's voice? The "world" in question for Lu Xun, in which having a voice is such an urgent task, is one in which the criterion for participation is specifically the pursuit of freedom and equality. This pursuit he identifies—and identifies with—on a thematic level in the works and lives of the Mara poets, beginning with Byron. And the process of identification in relation to a common pursuit may contribute to the structure of a shared modernity, a new "world" that emerges beyond hierarchical orderings at work in various, heterogeneous traditions. Yet, this structure remains purely formal without attention to the difference that language makes—and the differences that languages make—in the very pursuit of freedom and equality. This latter self-consciousness informs a sustained concern with the poetics and politics of voice that Lu Xun begins in "On the Power of Mara Poetry." Such self-conscious attentiveness to language supplements an otherwise simply formal structure of imitative and identificatory solidarity and opens up a more complex understanding of the conditions of internationalism.

Lu Xun raises the question of how a Chinese writer is to have a voice in the world both by turning abroad and by turning to his native land. Significantly, he raises the question not just at the level of content but by performing a stylistic experiment. Under the influence of his mentor, the philologist and political revolutionary Zhang Taiyan, he writes his literary manifesto calling for cultural renewal, ironically, in a stylized form of classical Chinese.[16] He uses arcane and archaic phrases whose currency dates back to the Han dynasty (202 B.C.E.–220 C.E.) alongside recent coinages—for instance, *ziyou* for "freedom" and *shijie* for "world."[17] He departs thereby from what had come to be standardized as classical Chinese following the expansion in administrative scope of the imperial civil service examination system in the Song dynasty (969–1279). It is such standardization of language through the effects of state regulation that Lu Xun implicitly critiques by experimenting with an archaic style. This experiment takes place at a time of radical transition in the very status of the Chinese language itself and in the context of heated polemics concerning the status of a modern national and literary language.[18] Lu Xun decides here not to use the vernacular, for which he would later become acclaimed as a master stylist, but an archaic language. This stylistic decision serves as a corollary to the content of his essay's call for cultural and discursive renewal in relation to the Mara poets and informs his complex and temporally nonlinear view of Chinese literary and cultural modernity.

In an untimely style that calls attention to the density and historicity of language itself, Lu Xun pursues the question of what it is for a Chinese writer to have a voice in this new world first by looking abroad. He situates this question at the very threshold of the national and the international. In Part 1 of his essay, right before he defines Mara poetry, explains the Sanskrit etymology, and identifies Byron as head of the group, Lu Xun writes:

> It seems a small thing when poets become extinct, till the sense of desolation hits. To praise the true greatness of your native land takes introspection and knowing others—awareness comes from careful comparison. Once awareness finds its voice, each sound strikes the soul, clear, articulate, unlike ordinary sounds. Otherwise tongues cleave to palates, the crowd's speech founders: the advent of silence redoubled. How can a soul steeped in dreams find words? Yet to be driven forward by external shocks leads not to strength but only to greater sorrow. So I say that taking a nation's spirit forward depends on how much one knows of the world.
>
> I let the past drop here and seek new voices from abroad, an impulse provoked by concern for the past.[19]

> 詩人絕迹，事若甚微，而蕭條之感，輒以來襲。意者欲揚邦之真大，首在審己，亦必知人，比較既周，爰生自覺。自覺之聲發，每響必中於人心，清晰昭明，不同凡響。非然者，口舌一結，眾語俱淪，沉默之來，倍於前此。蓋魂意方夢，何能有言？即震於外緣，強自揚厲，不惟不大，徒增稀耳。故曰國民精神之發揚，與世界識見之廣博有所屬。

> 今且古事不道，別求新聲於異邦，而其因即動於懷古。[20]

This passage presents the audition and knowledge of voices from other nations and cultures as condition of possibility for the awareness of the ownness of one's own voice, and it demonstrates the extent to which Chinese literary modernity begins as comparative literature. The relation between nations seems to be figured in terms of a hearing that gives rise to a new way of hearing or overhearing oneself. It is only on the basis of such self-hearing that voicelessness might be overcome. Such self-hearing can be considered a self-overhearing insofar as it entails a predicament of self-estrangement in which one does not simply hear oneself speak but, as if estranged from oneself as speaking subject, hears oneself being spoken by language. While expressing the desire for resonance with "new voices from abroad," the sentence across the paragraph break expresses also a new orientation toward resonances from the Chinese past. By letting the past drop here and turning to "new voices from abroad," Lu Xun does not reject the past but shows, rather, concern for the past. The term *huaigu*, which the translators Shu-Ying Tsau and Donald Holoch render as "concern for the past," begins with the character *huai*, used verbally here in relation to *gu*, the past, as direct object. If *huai* connotes "concern," it connotes a concern of a specifically commemorative nature. The "concern for the past" that motivates the search for new voices from abroad is one that involves critical work in cultural memory. With such critical revaluation, the past gets differentiated in its complexity as a source of both repressive dogma and renewing potentiality. The latter serves as the source of emancipatory potential whereby the condition of voicelessness might be overcome in differentiated resonance with, rather than reproductive imitation of, "new voices from abroad."

In Part 2 of the essay, Lu Xun turns to the tradition of classical Chinese poetics to pursue the question of voice as one whose renewal takes place necessarily within the context of this tradition, as in the medium of the Chinese language. The following passage reconfigures terms in classical poetics as it aims to open up space for voices of newness.

> Poets are they who disturb people's minds. Every mind harbors poetry; the poet makes the poem, but it is not his alone, for once it is read the mind will grasp it: everyone harbors the poet's poem. If not, how could it be grasped? Harbored but unexpressed—the poet gives it words, puts pick to strings, mental chords respond, his voice pervades the soul, and all things animate raise their heads as though witness to dawn, giving scope to its beauty, force, and nobility, and it must thereby breach the stagnant peace. Breach of peace furthers all humanity. (102)

> 蓋詩人者，攖人心者也。凡人之心，無不有詩，如詩人作詩，詩不為詩人獨有，凡一讀其詩，心即會解者，即無不有詩人之詩。無之何以能解？惟有而未能言，詩人為之語，則握撥一彈，心弦立應，其聲澈於靈府，令有情皆舉其首，如睹曉日，益為之美偉強力高尚發揚，而汙濁之平和，以之將破。平和之破，人道蒸也。(69)

Lu Xun reiterates in this passage key concepts in classical Chinese poetics, the *locus classicus* of which is the "Great Preface" to the *Shijing* or *Classic of Poetry*. This Han-dynasty text, dating no later than the first century C.E., systematizes scattered earlier texts on poetry while providing a guide to interpreting the poems anthologized in the *Shijing*.[21] The statements concerning poetry and poetics in the "Great Preface" have served as the basis of numerous reiterations, both orthodox and heterodox, since the canonizing practices of the Han dynasty. Lu Xun reformulates the relations between key poetic and philosophical terms, including *shi* (which may denote the substantive "poem," serve as shorthand for the *Shijing* itself, or, for Lu Xun, connote more abstractly the very capacity for poetry itself), *xin* ("heart-mind," "mind" or "soul"), and *yan* (language as externalization).

Lu Xun advances in the previous passage the idea of poetry as a potentiality inherent in all human beings. Because of this principle, poetry as object and poiesis as activity cannot be the sole possession or property of the poet, and it is owing to this principle that there is communicability at all. That a poem may be understood by others attests to the capacity for poetry in the minds of others. Language or words function to actualize the potentiality for poetry and externalize it as a manifestation communicable to others. Communication is figured in terms of responsive reverberation. In this responsive reverberation, extension is achieved, such that poetry performs a function of collective enlivening. It is in this conception of poetry's extensive, collective function that Lu Xun deviates from the orthodox position of conceiving of this extension as productive of peace or harmony—connoted by the term *pinghe*, which conjoins balance and harmony—ending this scenario of the emergence of voice, *sheng*, on a note of violent breach as a repeated event of growth-inducing change.

In this scenario, the event of voice phenomenalizes poetry-as-potentiality. This event would seem, for Lu Xun, to be in itself an act of freedom that originates from the poet as a singular source among plural equals capable of comprehending the utterance. One could say, indeed, that it is the act of utterance itself that singularizes and establishes the poet as free. And the newness of this act occasions an expansion of the sensory and expressive capacity of the collective body, which dynamically reorganizes itself in relation to the new voice. Iconoclastically, Lu Xun puts into question the homeostasis of harmony as the tonal condition toward which the plural energies of a polity should aim, privileging rather the moment of breach or rupture as the moment of utmost vitality for both the poet and the polity.[22]

By expressing the desire for resonance with "new voices from abroad," Lu Xun turns to the task of eliciting "new voices from the soul" among modern Chinese writers. Such newness derives, seemingly paradoxically, from classical articulations of poetic origination. Undertaking the work of critical revaluation, Lu Xun situates the emancipation of voice in the reinterpretation and reconfiguration of an existing linguistic and poetic medium that is not just that which the poet speaks but that which speaks through the poet. Such work makes possible the conditions for a new logic of deliberation and new conditions of resonance to emerge on both individual and collective levels. In the critical self-consciousness with which Lu Xun tropes and reflects on tropings of voice in the Chinese language, he manifests, unwittingly, the most momentous poetic solidarity with Shelley.

Defenses of Poetry:
Promises of Modernity, Critiques of Modernity

Shelley wrote in 1821 his *Defence of Poetry* as the first of a two-part essay, but he died in 1822 before he could either see the publication of the first part or write the second. The *Defence* would not be published until 1840, when Mary Shelley included it in her edition of *Essays, Letters from Abroad, Translations and Fragments*. It now ranks as one of the most important critical and theoretical texts about literature in the modern age. In the European Romantic period, it joins such texts as Wordsworth's 1800 Preface to the second edition of *Lyrical Ballads*, Friedrich Schlegel's *Athenäum* fragments (1798–1800), and Coleridge's *Biographia Literaria* (1817), among numerous instances of literary criticism that reflect philosophically on the very nature of poetic language itself. It shows a concern with poetic originality and newness that anticipates the explicit thematization of revolutionary newness in literary manifestos of the late nineteenth and early twentieth centuries. In this later period, the literary manifesto would reach the height of its popularity as a global form. Critical writings of the Romantic period anticipate this popularity insofar as they inaugurate and prompt reflection on redefinitions of literature and aesthetics in the European Enlightenment that would have complex repercussions on organizations of knowledge and redefinitions of literature around the world in the nineteenth and twentieth centuries.

In his book *Poetry of the Revolution: Marx, Manifestos, and the Avant-Gardes*, Martin Puchner argues for the impact of Marx and Engels's 1848 *Communist Manifesto* on the self-definition of both avant-garde and arrière-garde literary and artistic movements in late nineteenth- and early twentieth-century modernisms.[23] He charts Jean Moréas's "Symbolist Manifesto" of 1886 as an early, self-styled example of a modernist manifesto. By the time Marinetti's *Manifesto of Futurism* was published in 1909, it was part of a wave of literary and artistic manifestos appearing in Russia, England, France, Latin America, and East Asia.

In the context of late Qing and early Republican China, this wave took the form of numerous critical-polemical texts calling for a new literature and a redefinition and revaluation of the tradition of Chinese letters within a new, Western-derived epistemic structure that replaced the classical Confucian organization of knowledge. The year 1905 serves as a landmark year in this radical reorganization of knowledge, as it is the year in which the Confucian examination system was abolished. While the numerous texts calling for a new literature did not necessarily declare themselves as manifestos, they feature the concern with programmatic newness typical of the form. And many of these texts, such as Liang Qichao's "On the Relationship between Fiction and the Government of the People" (1902) and Hu Shih's "Some Modest Proposals for the Reform of Literature" (1917), carried markedly nationalist overtones. Lu Xun's 1908 "On the Power of Mara Poetry" takes its place among such texts.

As I have previously established, Lu Xun's essay figures literary modernity in terms of an emancipation of voice that invites comparison with writings by Shelley. Later in 1908, Lu Xun would expand his consideration of the poetics and politics of voice in another essay, "Toward a Refutation of Malevolent Voices," which he had planned as the first part of a longer composition he did not complete. Together, the two 1908 essays form companion pieces that advance a complex account of modernity and literary modernity that puts into question trends within reformist and nationalist discourses. "Toward a Refutation of Malevolent Voices" takes as one of its two principal targets "malevolent voices" that promote a chauvinistic and jingoistic nationalism, with the other being voices that champion the eradication of "superstition" with the aim of achieving a disenchanted modernity. As its title indicates, this essay aims to refute or interrupt, *po*, contemporary voices that claim to offer a program for Chinese modernity in imitation of a Western model. In contrast to such a scientific conception of Chinese modernity, Lu Xun argues for the alternative of a poetic modernity that would emphasize the originative, emancipatory, and revitalizing potential of poetic voice.

In this section, I compare how Shelley in *A Defence of Poetry* and Lu Xun in "Toward a Refutation of Malevolent Voices" give poetry a radical role in their respective conceptions of a modernity in which freedom and equality are activated as principles of universal humanity. Both define poetry as a capacity inherent in all human beings, rather than the practice or property of a select group. While poetry may take phenomenal and durable form in written language, it is not ontologically reducible to a stable substance but acts also dynamically as an event. Shelley and Lu Xun both figure the event-status of poetry as voice and situate this event within heterogeneous linguistic and cultural contexts. Within these contexts, poetic voice does not emerge as entirely new but performs the work of linguistic and discursive renewal according to recursive, cyclical structures. Shelley and Lu Xun's defenses of poetry show thereby how poetic voice as emancipatory event takes place not in the same way everywhere but within languages as historical and culturally specific—that is to say, lived and inherited media. With these conceptions of a radically poetic or literary modernity, Shelley and Lu Xun counter and critique the ascendancy of a model of modernity that privileges instrumental rationality and fails to acknowledge the difference of language to itself and the differences of languages to one another.

Like Lu Xun in his reinterpretation of classical poetics in "On the Power of Mara Poetry," Shelley defines poetry in the *Defence* as a capacity inherent in all human beings, rather than as the sole possession of poets as writers of literature or verse per se. The latter he distinguishes as those in whom the universal capacity for poetry is more pronounced and exists "in excess" (512). At the very beginning of the essay, he associates the capacity for poetry with the faculty of imagination, which he contrasts with the faculty of reason. Imagination is the faculty of mental action that creates new thoughts and values from the relations it discerns between thoughts. Reason is the faculty that involves the contemplation of "the relations borne by one thought to another, however produced" (510). Shelley explains the action of the imagination in terms of the Greek infinitive *to poiein*, etymologically at the root of "poetry" and its cognates in English and other European languages. *To poiein* designates an act of linguistic making that involves the principle of synthesis. Every human being as an experiential subject is capable of apprehending new relations and generating in language new thoughts and expressions that change or add value to understandings of the relations between parts and the way the parts constitute a whole. Reason, in contrast, involves the work of analysis, *to logizein*, and "the enumeration of quantities already known" (510). Imagination has priority over reason insofar as it is the former that generates and creates objects for the operations of the latter.

Imagination necessitates the medium of language for the generation and communication of its new thoughts and ideas. In his remarks on language, Shelley anticipates insights of the linguistic turn of twentieth-century critical thought. Rather than serving simply as tool or instrument, language functions, according to Shelley, as "at once the representation and the medium, the pencil and the picture, the chisel and the statue, the chord and the harmony" (511). Language has the power to signify by drawing upon an available "treasure of expressions" and acting upon and augmenting itself as the very "medium of signification" (511). While poetic language is vitally metaphorical and augments language with signs for new thoughts and associations, language can also "become through time signs for portions or classes of thoughts instead of pictures of integral thoughts" and thus "dead to all the nobler purposes of human intercourse" (512). To prevent such stagnation, new poets are required to revitalize language through the generation of new thoughts and expressions.

As mentioned previously, Shelley repeatedly foregrounds the figure of voice in his poems. Significantly, I underline here, the voices that are foregrounded are not those of the poet-speakers but inhuman or impersonal voices that these speakers claim to transmit: those of Mont Blanc, the West Wind, and the Skylark, among other voices that emanate from the heights or the depths. The poet-speakers serve as witnesses or vehicles, rather than agents, of voices they hear or that sound through them. Shelley repeats this displacement of the authority of poetic voice in the penultimate sentence of the *Defence* when he compares poets to "the words which express what they understand not, the trumpets which sing to battle and feel not what they inspire" (535). The poets themselves do not so much speak but are spoken through. The event of poetic voice as an emancipation and revitalization of language involves an abeyance of consciousness and will. In this abeyance, language may originate anew for the nobler purposes of human intercourse.

As an event that acts upon and augments preexisting language, poetic language seems to take place for Shelley as reorigination. Its action is interminable, insofar as language, in its temporal existence, always runs the risk of stagnation and is in need of revitalization. In the context of literary history, Shelley shows in the *Defence* how poetic language operates likewise according to a logic of renewal and reorigination. In his review of European intellectual and literary history that constitutes much of the essay, Shelley both theorizes and performs a cyclical theory of poetic rewriting. "Every original language near to its source," he writes, "is in itself the chaos of a cyclic poem" (512). He treats instances of Greek bucolic and erotic poetry as "episodes to that great poem, which all poets, like the co-operating thoughts of one great mind, have built up since the beginning of the world" (522). In its individual, episodic instances, poetry, as original and originating language, participates in the rewriting of a cyclic poem.

Shelley's claims for the world-expansive reach of this cyclic poem notwithstanding, his multiple examples in the essay and his own poetic practice indicate that the parameters of this cyclicity remain by and large European and perhaps, with a stretch, Indo-European. A sphere of operativity that includes Confucianism, Daoism, and Buddhism remains outside of the cultural logic of this cyclicity, even if Shelley may gesture toward other contexts. The principle of cyclicity Shelley mentions in the *Defence* manifests itself in his poetic practice in multiple instances of cyclical rewriting that allegorize on multiple levels how poetry takes place as reorigination. In *Prometheus Unbound*, for example, he rewrites Aeschylus's *Prometheus Bound* and reconstructs the lost sequel of *Prometheus Unbound*. On the level of individual utterances within the play, he shows how Prometheus can begin the process of his own unbinding only by repeating the very curse he had used against Jupiter. It is only by hearing anew in this repetition the words that had locked him in a symmetrical relationship with the language of patriarchal domination that the emancipatory process of repealing such language can begin for Prometheus. On the level of the overall plot of the play, Shelley shows how the repeal of the curse initiates a process that includes Asia's visit to Demogorgon, the rise of Demogorgon, the fall of Jupiter, and cosmic liberation. On the macro-level of literary history, the play constitutes a rewriting of Aeschylean tragedy as an allegory of poetic emancipation in the context of revolutionary modernity.

The *Defence* itself can be said, indeed, to rewrite the Judeo-Christian tradition of prophecy itself in a secular register. It reinterprets the divine from the secular perspective of a theory of poetic language. If secularization is constitutive of modernity in the West, with the authority of reason displacing the authority of God and God's intermediaries, Shelley puts into question the centrality of reason by supplementing reason with language as necessary, yet unstable grounds of historical meaning. Prophecy has an afterlife in Western secular modernity, for Shelley, as the creative force of the imagination that phenomenalizes itself in the form of a poetic language that never quite coincides with the language of reason and cognition. To be modern, it is not enough to know. Knowing must be supplemented by reading.

The *Defence* is a theoretical text that began as a polemical response. Shelley wrote the essay in response to his friend Thomas Love Peacock's tongue-in-cheek 1820 essay "The Four Ages of Poetry." After offering a seriocomic analysis of the history of European poetry in analogy to the mythical notion of the four ages of man in Hesiod and Ovid, Peacock concluded by urging intelligent men to stop wasting their time writing poetry and to apply themselves instead to the useful new sciences of moral thought, political science, and economics. These new human or social sciences, as Peacock acknowledges, have the advantage of utility and offer new instruments for government and reform as they convert human life into quantifiable forms and objects of cognition and administration, such as "populations."[24] Shelley does not object unequivocally to these new sciences altogether. In the Preface to *Prometheus Unbound* (1812), he professes to share the very "passion for reforming the world" that proponents of the new sciences display and devise methods to undertake (208). He objects, rather, to the overvaluation of these new sciences and the forgetting of poetry such overvaluation produces: "The poetry in these systems of thought is concealed by the accumulation of facts and calculating processes" (530). He identifies the dangers consequent upon the overvaluation of science and the sciences. The conquest of the "external world" by means of instrumental rationality captures human beings, ironically, within the world become technologico-scientific empire and subjects their valuation to the criterion of money. The invention of machines "for abridging and combining labor" has led to the unintended result of new inequalities (531). And the valorization of instrumental rationality has promoted a conception of selfhood in unitary terms to which money corresponds as "the visible incarnation" (531). Shelley's defense of poetry counters and critiques the ascendancy of a model of modernity that Peacock likewise describes in the emphatically nonprophetic tone of jesting semi-affirmation.

In 1908, in "Toward a Refutation of Malevolent Voices," Lu Xun would seem to enter into conversation with Shelley in his conception of modernity in terms of an emancipation of poetic voice and in his critique of a model of modernity that privileges instrumental rationality. The essay is divided into two parts. In a prefatory section, Lu Xun elaborates on the key notion of *xinsheng* he had advanced in "On the Power of Mara Poetry." Bracketing the homophones that denote "new voices" and "new life," Lu Xun focuses in the later essay on *xinsheng* as "voices of the soul" or "heart-mind." In "On the Power of Mara Poetry," he had claimed that it is poetry, above all other forms of speech and writing, that has the greatest capacity to emit, record, and transmit such voices of the soul. In the later essay, he continues to claim that it is only with the release of such voices that cultural revitalization can take place and the crisis of voicelessness in China be overcome. In the possibility of such release Lu Xun rests his hope for the future. In the longer section of the essay that follows, he polemicizes against "malevolent voices" in contemporary reformist discourse that would block or deny the release of *xinsheng*. Among these voices, he identifies two sets: one that advocates the eradication of "superstition" or folk culture and popular religion in China, and another that clamors for a chauvinistic nationalism. In the former he identifies an effort to deny the capacity for and erase the legacy of poetry itself among common people (*pusu zi min*). In both sets of voices, he identifies the slavish imitation of a Western-derived model of modernity, misappropriated and misadapted for the purpose of competitive expediency. Such self-congratulatorily modernizing reforms, he criticizes, institute only new orthodoxies and hierarchies of power.

What is *xinsheng*? Shu-ying Tsau and Donald Holoch render the term in their translation of "On the Power of Mara Poetry" as "voice of the soul," while Jon von Kowallis renders it as "voice of the heart" in his translation of "Toward a Refutation of Malevolent Voices."[25] As mentioned, *xin* is a keyword in classical Chinese thought for which there is no exact equivalent in the lexicon of European philosophy. Lu Xun's usage consistently situates this term in a position of interiority. *Xinsheng*, as "voices of the soul" or "voices of the heart," externalize what Lu Xun calls *neiyao*, "inner brightness," in which the character *yao* connotes the verbal dynamism of a "shining" in excess of the substantive "brightness." He associates the attributes of *zhen*, "genuineness," and *cheng*, "sincerity," with the voices of the soul or heart. Critics have traced *xinsheng* to a passage in the *Fayan* or *Exemplary Figures* of Yang Xiong (53 B.C.E.–18 C.E.), the Han-dynasty thinker and commentator on the *Analects* and Sima Qian's *Records of the Historian*. Yang writes in the passage, "Speech is the voice of the heart [*xinsheng*], and writing, its images" (言，心聲也。書，心畫也。).[26] The voice of the heart, *xinsheng*, attains phenomenal and thus legible form in speech and writing. It externalizes what issues from within.

As the externalization and activation of an "inner brightness," the voice of the heart has the power to emancipate on multiple levels: on the cosmic and, in the human or mortal domain, on individual and collective levels. Lu Xun writes:

> Once the voice [of him who speaks from the heart] arises, the whole land under heaven will reawaken, and that strength could well prove greater than any other natural force, stirring the human realm and startling it into an awakening. This awakening will mark the beginning of our rise out of the

present situation. Only when one speaks from the heart, does one speak as one's own master, and the human can begin to have a self; only when each human being has a self will the grand awakening of the collectivity be nigh. (Modified from translation of Jon von Kowallis, 42)

是故其聲出而天下昭蘇,力或偉於天物,震人間世,使之瞿然。瞿然者,向上之權輿己。蓋惟聲發自心,朕歸於我,而人始自有己;人各有己,而群之大覺近矣。[27]

The voice of the heart has an impact on both nonhuman and human domains, exerting its force on the "whole land under heaven" and stirring the "human realm." The event of this voice initiates the very process of individuation whereby the speaker or subject of utterance can begin to have a self. Selfhood as property of the speaker seems to begin with, rather than to preexist, the very event of enunciation. The implication is that the persistence of this selfhood depends on the continued repetition and renewal of the very event of enunciation. The process of individuation serves as the condition for the grand awakening of the collectivity. In this formulation, the category of the collectivity does not precede the category of the individual. Rather, the collectivity results anew from a multiplicity of individuals who constitute and reconstitute themselves as such by speaking from the heart. In this formulation, Lu Xun reverses the traditional order of precedence between the collectivity and individuals. In such an orthodox configuration, "everyone leans in the same direction and ten thousand mouths sing the same tune," such that "this singing cannot come from the heart, it is mere chiming in with others, like the meshing of gears in a machine" (42). The uniformity and conformity of such a chorus make it tantamount, according to Lu Xun, to voicelessness.

Xinsheng, the voice of the heart, thus serves as the externalization of singular and original interiority. Such originality has heterodox potential, as it is not predetermined in its content or direction by conformity with existing and external doxa. The event of *xinsheng* activates a momentary autonomy or sovereignty, as expressed in the striking phrase *zhen gui yu wo*, which I render "speak as one's own master."[28] Each character stands alone as a signifying unit in the combination of four characters, instead of entering into binomial combinations to create the effect of symmetry or stable apposition. The staccato effect of the articulation brings the phrase into rhythmic relief. Grammatically, *zhen* and *wo* both function as first-person pronouns among the multiplicity of pronominal shifters in classical Chinese. Etymologically, as Wang Hui, one of present-day China's leading intellectuals, explains in his 2007 close reading of Lu Xun's essay, "the word *zhen* used to mean 'I,' but after the Qin and Han dynasties, it became the exclusive appellation by which emperors referred to themselves. [The entire phrase] thus means returning the self to myself, thereby freeing the self from the hierarchy characteristic of the monarchial regime."[29] By conducting the philological experiment of writing in a classical style less regulated than the standard classical Chinese of later periods, Lu Xun plays with looser effects of syntax and etymological connotations to stage an allegory of the emancipatory workings of *xinsheng* or the voice of the heart. Every speaking subject is capable of activating the principles of freedom and equality in the event of speaking from one's own singular interiority. The act of such utterance itself is what constitutes one's autonomy or sovereignty, whose extension is not guaranteed, however, but renewed in repeated acts of speaking from the heart. The density of allusions to Confucian, Daoist, and Buddhist terms and concepts throughout Lu Xun's text situates the emancipatory event of voice within the complexity and thickness of a textual and intellectual tradition that the event of voice unworks and renews from within.[30] The heterodox potential of such an event gains significance from the specificity of a linguistic and cultural medium.

If Lu Xun bemoans ossifying tendencies within traditional Chinese culture while calling for the emancipation of voices of the heart, he discerns the dangers of stultification in "malevolent voices" that establish new doxa. Instead of working with a simplistic divide between old and new, tradition and modernity, he finds in both classical and contemporary discourses false voices that promote orthodoxy and suppress the voice of the heart. The loud clamor of such contemporary voices threatens to sustain, paradoxically, the voicelessness Lu Xun finds imposed by mainstream classical culture. He targets, as mentioned, two sets of malevolent voices—those advocating the eradication of "superstition" in folk culture and popular religion and those promoting a nationalism whose chauvinism displays itself in the slavish admiration of powerful nations and the denigration of weaker and conquered nations. Both sets of voices claim to speak in the name of modernization and reform. However, Lu Xun finds such claims hypocritical and self-interested. One set denies the poetry inherent in folklore and mythology as cumulative and collective productions of the imagination of the common people. Another champions the development of military technology, industry, and commerce, operating with wealth and power as the guiding principles for their conception of modernity. Both sets propound a model of modernity they purport to derive from the West, one that privileges instrumental rationality and an aculturalist scientism. Against such a model of modernity, on the rise in his contemporary early nineteenth-century Europe, Shelley had offered in *A Defence of Poetry* a critical counternarrative. Against such a model of modernity in its adaptation and iteration in early twentieth-century China, Lu Xun aims likewise to articulate a counternarrative of a poetic modernity oriented not by wealth and power but by freedom and equality as guiding criteria.

As companion pieces, "On the Power of Mara Poetry" and "Toward a Refutation of Malevolent Voices" both argue but show even more effectively in their style and textuality how *xinsheng*, the voice of the soul or heart, derives the power to actualize freedom and equality, abstract in their universality, in language as a historical medium. Together, the essays elaborate a conception of poetic or literary modernity that critiques and supplements a conception of modernity that privileges scientific knowledge. By giving his 2007 reading of "Toward a Refutation of Malevolent Voices" the subtitle "What Is Enlightenment?," Wang Hui may shed light on the complexity inherent in the global circulation of philosopher Immanuel Kant's pathbreaking question. Wang alludes to Kant's 1784 essay with the same title, suggesting that Lu Xun raises the question anew in the context of China. Kant famously defines enlightenment in terms of a "daring to know" predicated on a passage out of one's own immaturity, or *Unmündigkeit*, "the inability to use one's understanding without guidance from another."[31] The word *Unmündigkeit* is based on the word *Mund*, "mouth," and the situation of *Unmündigkeit* implies the inability to speak, a voicelessness that is, moreover, *selbstverschuldet*, "self-incurred." Instead of defining enlightenment in positive terms, Kant defines enlightenment as a process of coming to speech that entails release from the guidance of others. Lu Xun may be said to repeat such a work of negative definition in making way for *xinsheng*—to which, it is important to note, he never gives positive content—by releasing it from the malevolent voices that would speak in its place. Among such voices are those that would profess to answer the question "What is enlightenment?" in positive terms and thereby to offer a programmatic modernity. If Lu Xun can be said to repeat the question "What is enlightenment?," his stylistic practice in his 1908 texts shows further that the process implicit in the question and quest thereof takes place necessarily in language as an unstable medium and, moreover, in languages in the plural. In the awareness of the differences within language and languages, Shelley had shown similar insight. That poetry necessarily supplements the project of Enlightenment—and that reading supplements the work of knowing—is the shadowy knowledge Romanticism brings to the task of being modern.

Literary Modernity 47

For the epigraph of "On the Power of Mara Poetry," Lu Xun quotes from Part 3 of Nietzsche's *Thus Spake Zarathustra*. He translates the quote into the archaic style of classical Chinese in which he writes the rest of the essay. I provide, in order, Lu Xun's translation, Nietzsche's German, and my translation of the German text.

求古源者將求方來之泉，將求新源。嗟我昆弟，新生之作，新泉之湧於淵深，其非遠矣。(63)

Wer über alte Ursprünge weise wurde, siehe, der wird zuletzt nach Quellen der Zukunft suchen und nach neuen Ursprüngen.—

O meine Brüder, es ist nicht über lange, da werden neue Völker entspringen und neue Quellen hinab in neue Tiefen rauschen.[32]

Whoever searches after the ancient wellsprings will seek at last the sources for the future and discover new wellsprings.—

O my brothers, it will not be long before new peoples spring up and new sources murmur in new deeps.

Lu Xun remains semantically and even, to a certain degree, syntactically faithful to Nietzsche's prose, but he deviates from Nietzsche's wording by substituting the term *xinsheng*, here denoting "new life," for *neue Völker*, literally "new peoples." Instead of rendering *neue Völker* as *xinmin* (新民), Lu Xun begins with this substitution the chain of reverberations of *xinsheng* throughout his essay. With this epigraph, Lu Xun also establishes affinity or, as the epigraph suggests, fraternity with Nietzsche in the latter's capacity as poet-philosopher-philologist. Just as Nietzsche turns to the Persian Zarathustra to put into question and subvert conventional Western morality, Lu Xun plays with the Sanskrit *mara* as a primal signifier for the various iterations of Satanic and other subversions he brings together in resonant poetic solidarity. With his stylistic experimentation, he pursues critical philology in the spirit of Nietzsche and with the influence of his mentor Zhang Taiyan. His two 1908 essays on *xinsheng* as emancipatory voice enact Nietzsche's genealogical method by—as the metaphor in the epigraph intones—searching after the ancient wellsprings to seek new sources for the future.

Unbeknownst to Lu Xun and, for the simple reason of chronology, to Shelley, Nietzsche may serve as the intermediary between the two figures, whose resonance with one another was imperceptible to each of them. If Lu Xun was influenced by Nietzsche to undertake, with rigorous attention to the letter, a genealogy of the voices of good and evil in the Chinese tradition, Shelley can be said to anticipate Nietzsche in his protocritical-genealogical approach to European literary history, both in his poetic practice and in the *Defence of Poetry*, in which he abstracts the vitality of rewriting as renewal from the pious reproduction of tradition as mere repetition. Shelley, Nietzsche, and Lu Xun all display likewise critical-philosophical and philological approaches to language as an unstable medium and condition for the production of thought and meaning and to languages as phenomena in history. It is this vigilance toward language that has given Shelley's writing originative force for later theories and practices of reading—most significantly, deconstruction. And it is this vigilance that has made Lu Xun, the propagandistic manipulations of state canonization notwithstanding, such a powerful figure to read with in Chinese letters. Wang Hui, for one, is such a reader in and of Lu Xun's legacy. If the resonance between Shelley and Lu Xun was inaudible to one another—because of the banal fact of chronology, on the one hand, and the refigurations of mediation, on the other—the resonance between them remains likewise largely unheard by readers of Shelley and readers of Lu Xun.

This resonance, which manifests itself as a non-hearing, marks precisely, I argue, deep veins of what remains unthought and therefore demands to be read between them. The task of hearing and reading between them is displaced, then, upon the comparative reader. Upon this reader befalls the task of undertaking the critical philological work of reading between projects of poetic renewal that involve complex processes of destruction and recovery and that confront their addressees with irony and ambiguity. What this reader faces, then, is a world literary modernity that consists of heterogeneous literary modernities that enact in common, but necessarily within the thickness of different languages and spheres of operativity, the shared principles of freedom and equality. The inhabitation of such a poetically shared modernity demands the work of reading plurally and acknowledging the multiplicity of traditions of poetics and theory. Such an inhabitation of a poetically shared modernity goes beyond opening readers up to the voice of the other or the voices of others. Most significantly, it opens readers up to the irony within the voice of the other and within the voices of others, the irony without which others cannot appear in their freedom and singularity.

The *Defence of Poetry* and "On the Power of Mara Poetry," along with "Toward a Refutation of Malevolent Voices," are literary manifestos that articulate respectively a conception of literary modernity in English in a European context and a conception of literary modernity in Chinese in an

East Asian context. In the way these texts and other writings by their authors express a desire for resonance by gesturing beyond their linguistic and cultural spheres, they disclose the promise of a world literary modernity for which reading is the method of activation. The form of the literary manifesto serves as a site of connection through which the definition and inception of new literatures can be seen in their orientation by a common definition of literature emerging within the epistemic shift of the European Enlightenment. While Shelley and Lu Xun both define poetry as a capacity inherent in all human beings, rather than the property or practice of a select few, each still inclines toward a vanguardist conception of the process of poetic renewal. For Shelley, such vanguardism expresses itself in the figure of the prophet-poet; for Lu Xun, in the "one or two scholars" with whom he speculates the awakening of the collectivity would begin.[33] The "Mara poets" are, of course, a vanguard. For both Shelley and Lu Xun, the activation of freedom and equality entails a vanguardism of the third term in the French Revolutionary slogan—namely, fraternity.

As a term for the aspiration toward universal humanity, fraternity is a flawed because partial term. Beyond leaving out a biological or sociological category, it leaves unacknowledged entire aspects of existence and lived experience, which I would call the experience of ordinary life. "Mutuality" is the comprehensive term for which fraternity is a partial expression and more fittingly accompanies freedom and equality as universal attributes of the human. The question of the relationship among freedom, equality, and mutuality and of their priority in relation to one another continues to be a vital question for modern thought.

In the high and self-consciously theoretical register of the literary manifesto, Shelley and Lu Xun make legible how poetic voice may perform the work of emancipatory renewal within and across literary modernities, thus opening up traditions of poetics and theory to be read in relation to one another. They shed light on a pattern and even logic of connection whereby writings in other registers and other forms may be read in their reflections on and renewals of the grounds of mutuality that serve as sites for the enactment of freedom and equality.

2   Shakespearean Retellings
    and the Question of the
    Common Reader

    Charles and Mary Lamb's *Tales
    from Shakespeare* and Lin Shu's
    Yinbian Yanyu

This chapter examines two texts of Shakespearean retelling in the long nineteenth century that participate in the emergence, in local and global contexts, of that quintessentially nineteenth-century character of literary and cultural history, the "common reader." In 1806, at a historical juncture that saw the growing popularization of Shakespeare in various media in England, including the 1807 publication of Thomas and Henrietta Bowdler's notorious, expurgated *Family Shakespeare*, there appeared the *Tales from Shakespeare* by Charles and Mary Lamb.[1] This specimen of Romantic storytelling, still in print two decades into the twenty-first century, had the distinction of being read not only in Regency and Victorian England but widely circulated, reprinted, anthologized, and translated abroad in the nineteenth and twentieth centuries.[2] It exercised effects beyond both British colonial and semi-colonial contexts, beyond the semiosphere of what is termed today the "Anglophone," becoming the first text of Shakespeare in any form to be translated into Chinese. It appeared in 1904 as *Yinbian Yanyu*, translated by Lin Shu in collaboration with his interpreter Wei Yi—one in a line of younger collaborators with whom Lin, who famously did not know any foreign languages, would carry out his translations.[3] In 1904, after the enormous successes of his versions of *La Dame aux camélias* in 1899 and *Uncle Tom's Cabin* in 1901, Lin was in the process of attaining practically *auteur* status in China as a translator and literary figure.[4] Although *Yinbian Yanyu* would not enjoy the immense popularity of the novels by Dumas *fils* and Stowe, it still went through a robust eleven printings by the 1930s, even after Lin Shu's cultural influence had waned in the aftermath of the New Culture, or May Fourth Movement, of 1919.

The *Tales from Shakespeare* was commissioned for the Juvenile Library, under the imprint of Thomas Hodgkins, the pseudonym of the political philosopher William Godwin and his second wife, Mary Jane.[5] It consisted of adaptations of twenty plays by Shakespeare—fourteen romances and comedies by Mary and six tragedies by Charles. Upon first publication, the volume was attributed only to Charles and not to Mary—an omission not because of her femininity but because of the scandal of her history of madness and matricide.[6] As is well known to Romanticists but not perhaps beyond Romanticist circles, the older Mary had stabbed their mother to death in 1796 in a fit of insanity. To keep her from being institutionalized, Charles agreed to serve as her guardian—a situation that resulted in his dividing his time between writing and working as a clerk for the East India Company. *Yinbian Yanyu*, like other volumes that would eventually constitute *Lin's Library of Translated Fiction*, was published by Shanghai Commercial Press. Lin and Wei translated all twenty of the tales but gave them new titles and reordered them in a new sequence. The title page attributed the tales to Shakespeare, omitting mention altogether of the Lambs as mediating authorial entities.

Lin's work as a translator took place at a time of radical cultural change in China involving the accelerated assimilation of Western or new learning—an epistemic restructuring that subtended reformist movements at the end of the Qing dynasty and China's transition from empire to nation-state. The tumultuous period from the late Qing dynasty to the early decades of the Republic saw an unprecedented surge in translation, one in which the criteria, conventions, and methods for the practice itself were undergoing reinvention, dovetailing with debates over language reform itself.[7] It is in this context that Lin translated the *Tales* and other Western literary works into not vernacular but classical Chinese—and specifically *guwen*, "ancient-style prose"—which constituted a stylistic alternative to the extant standard style for the Confucian civil service examinations that ended in 1905. Indeed, Lin's use and continued advocacy of *guwen* would account for his marginalization in the 1920s as a casualty of cultural wars that favored monolithic interpretations of nationalism and a developmentally linearist understanding of modernity.[8]

My basic claim is simple: these two texts of Shakespearean retelling constitute efforts to imagine and fashion a "common reader" in heterogeneous, asynchronous, but connected scenes of global literary modernity. But what is a "common reader"? Let us turn to a few sources for a provisional definition. In his pathbreaking, now-classic study *The English Common Reader: A Social History of the Mass Reading Public, 1800–1900*, Robert Altick approaches the term "common reader" interchangeably with the notion of the "reading public." The latter is "composed of what the Victorians were fond of calling 'the million.' It is *not*," he writes, "the relatively small, intellectually and socially superior audience for which most of the great nineteenth-century authors wrote. . . . Here we are concerned primarily with the experience of that overwhelmingly more numerous portion of the English people who became day-by-day readers for the first time in this period, as literacy spread and printed matter became cheaper. The 'common reader' studied in these pages may be a member of the working class, or he may belong to the ever expanding bourgeoisie."[9] In his sociological approach to the rise of print culture in England, Altick defines the common reader in quantitative terms: the common reader is one of the many, "the million," units of which became enfranchised not just year by year, but measurably in the increment of "day by day" over the course of the nineteenth century. Within the parameters of the long nineteenth century itself, in his 1903 essay on Robert Browning, G. K. Chesterton implicitly situates the abstraction of the English "common reader" among "a race of young men like Keats, members of a not highly cultivated middle class, and even of classes lower, who felt in a hundred ways this obscure alliance with eternal things against temporal and practical ones."[10] The period following the French Revolution saw "the first beginning of the aesthetic stir in the middle classes which expressed itself in the combination of so many poetic lives with so many prosaic livelihoods. It was," Chesterton writes, "the age of inspired office-boys."[11] Chesterton's remarks here underline the extent to which numbers among those who would be designated "great nineteenth-century authors" (he enumerates Ruskin, Carlyle, Keats, Dickens, and Browning as examples) themselves began as "common readers," had their starts in relation to the image of the new median captured in the phrase "inspired office-boys."

Let us spin the globe—or swipe the screen—and turn the clock ahead. In a 1963 essay, Qian Zhongshu, one of twentieth-century China's most cosmopolitan men of letters, offers his recollection of first reading Lin Shu's translations in the 1920s as a boy in Wuxi County, Jiangsu:

> The two boxfuls of *Lin's Library of Translated Fiction* were a great discovery to me at age twelve; they led me into a new world [*xintiandi*], a world [*shijie*] other than that of *The Water Margin*, *The Journey to the West*, and *Strange Stories from a Chinese Studio*. Prior to this I had read such works as *Fifteen Little Heroes*, translated by Liang Qichao, and the detective stories translated by Zhou Guisheng, and invariably had been bored by them. It was not until I came into contact with Lin Shu's translations that I realized how captivating Western fiction could be. I tirelessly perused the works of Haggard, Washington Irving, Scott, [Dickens, and Swift,] in the Lin translations. If I was in

any way self-consciously motivated toward learning English, it was so that one day I could gorge myself on the adventure stories of Haggard and company without hindrance.

Forty years ago, in the small county that was my hometown, we rarely had the chance to see moving pictures[; we could only see travelling performers put on monkey shows or travelling salesmen hawking potions with a limping camel in tow.] The kind of recreation children of later days enjoyed in watching animal movies, or in a visit to the zoo, I was able to seek only from adventure stories.[12]

Qian's sketch here of boyhood in a provincial county town in early Republican China offers a different, decidedly nonmetropolitan, non-office-space backdrop for the emergence of a Chinese common reader, not unlike himself, that *Lin's Library of Translated Fiction* was instrumental in helping fashion. Before easy access to a new technology of entertainment such as moving pictures and a global form of municipal recreation, the zoo, adventure stories served as entertainment and diversion. Lin's translations provided stories different from, yet strikingly mentioned in contiguity with, the stories of heroes and bandits, exotic sights and adventures, and occurrences of the supernatural in *The Water Margin*, *Journey to the West*, and *Strange Stories from a Chinese Studio*: they revealed, on multiple levels, worlds beyond both the actual world of everyday Wuxi in the 1920s and the worlds disclosed in these well-known works of vernacular and classical Chinese fiction. What the Jacobean translator of Homer George Chapman was to John Keats in London in 1816, Lin was to Qian in Wuxi in 1922. Chesterton's demographic of "inspired office-boys" have their counterparts in the growing formation of middle-class readers and "petty urbanites," or *xiao shimin*, of early twentieth-century China.

The English common reader and the Chinese common reader have heterogeneous, asynchronous, and yet connected histories. Part of what makes each "common" requires a numerical explanation: Altick's social historical approach from the 1950s presupposes what historians and philosophers of science such as Lorraine Daston and Ian Hacking have explicitly theorized more recently—namely, that the modern subject is socially and politically organized as a statistical subject.[13] This subject's condition of being one—singular and individual—necessitates being counted as equal as any*one* among the many that together constitute the democratic masses, however conceived and collectivized. As demographic quantities, the English common reader and the Chinese common reader are inscribed, however, in different linguistic and cultural systems and histories, ordered within different regimes of typicality and normativity as well as fields of contestation. As such, they are alike in being subject to number as a condition of their modernity, but the structure of their subjection—and subjectivity—is culturally and historically distinct.

The Lambs were most active in the first decades of the nineteenth century; Lin Shu was most active as a translator at the cusp of the late imperial and modern periods in China. The Lambs wrote in advance of the Victorian period, which was demarcated by the Reform Act of 1832 (which extended the power to vote from one adult male in ten to one in five) and was marked by the gradual implementation of compulsory public education in the 1830s and beyond. The "common reader" the Lambs imagined and addressed in the Regency period, with its burgeoning popular press, was proleptic insofar as it would acquire new content with the extended enfranchisements of the later, Victorian period. In early twentieth-century China, the reading public grew alongside the burgeoning of the press, the circulation of popular fiction, and the widening of elementary and middle school education.[14] Lin Shu's translations both anticipated and were situated within this process of accelerated enfranchisement of readers, exerting proleptic influence on the emergence of a new popular audience.

In *The Making of English Reading Audiences, 1790–1832*, Jon Klancher describes this period in England as "a particularly poignant moment of cultural transformation" because "perhaps for the last time, it was still possible to conceive the writer's relation to an audience in terms of a personal compact."[15] Following the watershed year of 1832, Klancher implies, the writer's conception of the reader in terms of a personal compact faces mounting pressure to subjection to the power of number. Perhaps, instead of the irreversible finality Klancher finds, what literary texts perform in the context of the global rise of quantitative determinations of common readers in various parts of the world are reconfigurations of traditionally conceived relations of kinship and friendship and cultural logics of subjection. It is my wager that considering the *Tales from Shakespeare* and *Yinbian Yanyu* alongside one another may shed light on the logic of each text's enactment of the question of the common reader.

Shakespeare for Beginners

Simply put, the *Tales from Shakespeare* and *Yinbian Yanyu* are texts for beginners. Each imagines and addresses the "common reader" as a beginner. Let us unfold the subtle and intricate implications of this basic, seemingly obvious observation.

The *Tales from Shakespeare* was addressed primarily to English children. It positions this category of readers in front rows behind which adults are implicitly situated as onlookers and overhearers. *Yinbian Yanyu* was addressed primarily to Chinese adults interested in the distant and the foreign, here specifically in the work of a foreign writer reputed to be England's national bard, the equivalent of Du Fu in the West, as Lin takes care to note in his translator's preface. The texts in question thus function fundamentally as introductions or primers, retelling Shakespeare to readers conceived of as beginners. How does each text perform this task?

To retell Shakespeare for children, the Lambs chose the form of the tale collection, a form long associated in various traditions with oral storytelling and popular entertainment. Around the time of the Lambs's redaction, the tale collection was linked with European translations of the *Arabian Nights* and volumes of regional folklore such as the Grimms's *Kinder- und Hausmärchen*, which would appear in Germany in 1811, a few years after the *Tales*' publication.[16] Each tale is relatively short and presents to a newcomer the story of a play in a form that lends itself readily to retelling and retransmission. As the Lambs explain in their Preface, they aim in their abridgement to initiate the young reader to Shakespeare to prepare him or her for future reading of the plays themselves.

In converting the plays into narrative form, the Lambs simplified the multiple plot structure of Shakespeare's plays, focusing on the main plots. Certain minor characters and subplots disappear: Caliban's conspiracy with Sebastian and Trinculo gets omitted from Mary's version of *The Tempest*, Malvolio altogether from *Twelfth Night*, and the scene with the gravediggers from Charles's retelling of *Hamlet*. The Lambs simplified and updated Shakespeare's language by trimming, though not eliminating, Elizabethan diction and using more straightforward syntax in transforming Shakespeare's verse into prose. Selected passages in Shakespeare get quoted and modified as dialogue in both direct and indirect speech. Significantly, the Lambs chose to retell a selection of only twenty plays rather than to aim at comprehensiveness and retell all of them. They chose fourteen comedies, six romances, and six tragedies, omitting the histories and Roman plays altogether. What results, then, is a remarkably unheroic collection: a version of Shakespeare from which English national history is curiously absent, in which Britain as an explicit dramatic setting features only in *King Lear* and *Macbeth*. In terms of sequencing, the Lambs do not follow the chronology of Shakespearean composition and performance or group the tales according to dramatic genre. Instead, they present the *Tales* in an order that begins with *The Tempest* and ends with *Pericles*, interspersing comedies, romances, and tragedies in between.

The storytelling voice in the *Tales* is that of an unidentified omniscient narrator of avuncular or aunt-like disposition. This voice is heard first in the Preface, commenting on the aims and methods of the collection for young readers before it shifts from referring to such readers in the third person to addressing them directly in the second. At the end of the Preface, the narrator states directly how he or she hopes the *Tales* will delight and instruct as "enrichers of the fancy, strengtheners of virtue, a withdrawing from all selfish and mercenary thoughts, a lesson of all sweet and honourable thoughts and actions, to teach you courtesy, benignity, generosity, humanity: for of examples, teaching these virtues, [Shakespeare's] pages are full" (5). The didactic persona of this narrator is maintained throughout the collection, though not obtrusively, appearing usually at the end of a tale to offer moral commentary on the lesson learned.[17] For instance, this narrator comments at the end of *The Winter's Tale*—"Thus have we seen the patient virtues of the long-suffering Hermione rewarded. That excellent lady lived many years with her Leontes and her Perdita, the happiest of mothers and of queens" (40)—and at the end of *Romeo and Juliet*—"So did these poor old lords, when it was too late, strive to outgo each other in mutual courtesies: while so deadly had been their rage and enmity in past times, that nothing but the fearful overthrow of their children (poor sacrifices to their quarrels and dissensions) could remove the rooted hates and jealousies of the noble families" (226). Strikingly, the narrator's voice loses its externality and fuses with the world of the Shakespearean text—specifically, Puck's epilogue—at the end of *A Midsummer Night's Dream*, playing with the very liminality between waking and dreaming at the heart of that play: "And now, if any are offended with this story of fairies and their pranks, as judging it incredible and strange, they have only to think that they have been asleep and dreaming, and that all these adventures were visions which they saw in their sleep: and I hope none of my readers will be so unreasonable as to be offended with a pretty harmless Midsummer Night's Dream" (29).

In keeping with the declared intention in the Lambs's Preface that "for young ladies . . . it has been my intention chiefly to write," the *Tales* give heightened attention to female characters in their retelling of Shakespeare. The very preponderance of comedies and romances among the tales ensures the preponderance of heroines—and heroines who operate within the ensemble constraints of comedic convention—as the absence of the history plays ensures the paucity of rousing stories of bands of brothers. Beginning with *The Tempest* and ending with *Pericles*, the *Tales* opens by spotlighting the character of a daughter, Miranda, who listens to her father's story of who she is and how she came to the island, and concludes by giving emphatic attention to another, Marina, who tells her long-lost father her story of who she is.

Implicit in this sequencing is a movement from the daughter as listener to the daughter as storyteller. The avuncular or aunt-like voice of the narrator chaperones this development, which may be seen to parallel and mirror the desired development of the young reader, whose accession to storytelling is predicated on her attentive listening to stories herself. The sequencing of the *Tales* may be said to simulate the arc of a typical female *Bildungsroman* in which the Lambs present a variation by substituting a concatenation of linked heroines for one individual heroine.

What kind of reader does this retelling of Shakespeare imagine, address, and promote? What kind of reading practice does it encourage? As a collection, it presents a multiplicity of characters, extending the *dramatis personae* of each play across twenty plays, redacting a Shakespearean world on the feminine bias. The serialization of heroines in permutations of predicaments encourages readers to discern doublings, patterns, and types, as if inviting Proppian morphological readings *avant la lettre*. While the shift toward femininity highlights the interest in the complexities of femininity in Shakespearean texts themselves, in the context of Regency England, it betokens a shift for which "femininity" does not just designate biologically women readers but functions synecdochally to mark a fundamental cultural-historical shift. In *Desire and Domestic Fiction*, Nancy Armstrong has argued influentially that this shift is symptomatic of modern Western culture and bespeaks the emergence in the West of a new form of political power since the end of the eighteenth century. Such power, according to Armstrong, "emerged with the rise of the domestic woman and established its hold over British culture through her dominance over all those objects and practices we associate with private life."[18] The reader the *Tales from Shakespeare* imagines, addresses, and promotes seems to be one whose space of action was being redefined by a shift from public to private life as a quasi-dioramic locus of distributed power.

In his ingenious book *Exemplarity and Mediocrity: The Art of the Average from Bourgeois Tragedy to Realism*, Paul Fleming traces in eighteenth-century European debates about the aesthetic-pedagogical function of the theater in public life the emergence of compassion—over pity and admiration—as privileged affect in the education and improvement of average and common persons. The dramatist Gotthold Ephraim Lessing is a key spokesperson for the value of compassion in what Fleming precisely terms "a democratic-majoritarian aesthetic project premised on a mimetic relationship not to 'what is' but more decidedly to 'what is the majority.'"[19] Pity and admiration depend on social hierarchy and, as responses to heroic greatness, can only inspire improvement via emulation. "Compassion, on the other hand," writes Lessing in a letter to his friends Nicolai and Mendelssohn, "improves immediately; it improves without us having to add anything to the process; it improves the man of reason as well as the idiot."[20] In an age when statistical normativity mediates the very mimetic project of Western representation, compassion promotes an egalitarianism among types that is oriented by the average; and it does so more effectively than admiration, which promotes rather a heroism resituated in relation to the law of the average as extreme or exception.

The common reader that the *Tales from Shakespeare* addresses is an unheroic or post-heroic subject. She may be considered the sister of the "inspired office-boy." In relation to the character-system presented in the collection, she is prompted to find likeness between and with the contiguous and mutually auxiliary heroines showcased in different predicaments in the tales. As a "young reader," she is cued to recognize and read positions within a structure that orders loci of power and action.

It is this decidedly nonheroic or post-heroic version of Shakespeare that reaches Lin in its nineteenth-century global itinerary and that Lin, in turn, retells in translation as an introduction to Shakespeare for adult Chinese readers. Let us now consider general linguistic and formal features of Lin's retelling.

In using the *Tales* to introduce Chinese readers to Shakespeare, Lin uses *guwen* instead of vernacular Chinese as the language of retelling. Indeed, he would use *guwen* for all 180–200 of his translations of works of Western literature, beginning with his breakthrough 1899 version of *La Dame aux camèlias*. For a collection such as the *Tales*, specifically, the use of *guwen* befits Lin's transposition of the Western text into the traditional Chinese form of the *chuanqi*, literally "transmission of the strange" or "marvelous." As a generic term, *chuanqi* sustains a curious generic duality, designating both a genre of narrative fiction since the Tang Dynasty (seventh to tenth centuries) and drama of the Ming-Qing period (late-fourteenth to nineteenth centuries).[21] Indeed, many Chinese traditional operas or musical dramas, including Ming-Qing *chuanqi*, derived from stories in earlier tale collections. Lin's choice of style and manipulation of form work together to produce a text that would appear oddly familiar and evocative to contemporary Chinese readers. As Michael Gibbs Hill analyzes in *Lin Shu,*

Inc., Lin's use of *guwen* is not "pure" but includes neologisms and loanwords from the recent surge in Japanese and Chinese translations of Western texts.[22] The use of the term *ziyou*, for instance, for Ariel's liberation at the end of *The Tempest*, derives from this wave of translingualism in East Asia. Lin's *guwen* carries kernels of cultural hybridity, traces of the foreign within an otherwise ostensibly traditional Chinese medium.

Significantly, Lin arranges the tales in a new sequence in *Yinbian Yanyu*. He begins with *The Merchant of Venice* and ends with *The Tempest*, and he renames the titles of the plays (which the Lambs used directly as titles for their tales) altogether. Each of Lin's retold tales receives a two-character title naming a knot or conflict in the plot (for instance, "*Rouquan*," or "A Bond of Flesh," for *The Merchant of Venice*, "*Nübian*," or "Daughters' Mutiny," for *King Lear*), an object that serves as a plot device (for instance, "*Huanzheng*," or "Ring Evidence," for *Cymbeline*), or a pivotal scene or situation (for instance, "*Linji*," or "A Gathering in the Woods," for *As You Like It*).[23] The use of two characters as titles has significant precedent in Ming *chuanqi*, with a work like *The Peony Pavilion* divided into acts with two-character titles such as *Youyuan* ("Wandering in the Garden") and *Jingmeng* ("The Interruption of a Dream") that designate situations and plot developments. Lin repackages the *Tales* in a form that effectively created for the Shakespearean corpus a Chinese counterpart in *chuanqi* literature.

In this repackaging—be it entirely Lin and Wei's doing or a project involving the intervention of Shanghai Commercial Press—Shakespeare's name acquires a prominence on the title pages of all editions, with the Lambs elided altogether as intermediaries. Lin was credited as the translator, with Wei acknowledged in different ways in the paratextual matter for his assistance, with both emerging as the substitute for the Lambs in retelling Shakespeare to Chinese readers. For the Lambs's Preface Lin substitutes, in most but not all editions, his translator's Preface. The avuncular or aunt-like narrator of the Lambs's *Tales* disappears from this Preface, replaced by Lin's voice addressing *in propria persona* adult Chinese readers in an effort to articulate Shakespeare's significance for them. If the Lambs's narrator reappears throughout the *Tales*, in *Yinbian Yanyu*, the narratorial voice withdraws beyond the translator's Preface to a reticent third-person perspective throughout.

Speaking *in propria persona* and signing, dating, and locating his writing of the Preface, Lin situates for his readers his translation and retelling of Shakespeare in the context of late-Qing debates concerning cultural and scientific reform. It is in this reformist historical context and with polemical intent that Lin presents *Yinbian Yanyu* as a version of Shakespeare for adult Chinese beginners. Lin's quarrel is with young reformers (*xinxuejia*), who subscribe to a linear model of enlightened historical progress that entails the obsolescence of folk superstition and interest in the supernatural, literally "gods and spirits" (*shenguai*).[24] The drive toward newness necessitated a vilification and abandonment of the old and past as superannuated. For "our country" (*wuguo*), a category increasingly imbued with an aspirationist nationalism, the attainment of such newness involves programmatic emulation of and catching up with the "advanced civilization" of the "great Western nations," whose very own modernity, it is supposed, depended on an eradication of the supernatural in their own pasts. Against such a simplistic understanding of time and progress, as a linear movement from old to new, enchantment to disenchanted rationality, Lin points out the preponderance of "gods and spirits" in Shakespeare's works.

In resonance with received ideas concerning Shakespeare's reputation as a national and, by 1904, even "world" poet, Lin compares Shakespeare for his readers to Du Fu in terms of equivalence in national prestige: 莎氏之詩直抗吾國之杜甫. However, *Yinbian Yanyu* fashions, in effect, a Shakespeare that warrants comparison less with Du Fu and more with Gan Bao and Pu Songling as transmitters of the strange in their tale collections or a Tang Xianzu in dramatic form. In a classificatory gesture hardly imaginable outside of the context of late Qing and early Republican China, Lin joins Shakespeare and Rider Haggard in apposition—哈氏莎氏—as writers whose incorporation of varieties of the "strange" in their texts shows that an interest in the mysterious and supernatural is not incompatible with national strength and civilizational sophistication.

In *Yinbian Yanyu*, Lin produces, like the Lambs, a prose text that unfolds a multitude of characters within the covers of one book. Changing the Lambs's sequence, he begins with *The Merchant of Venice* and ends with *The Tempest*, with Prospero giving up his magic books and returning from the unnamed enchanted island to the identifiable site of Naples, as if he were a version of a literatus hermit-scholar leaving a site of retreat for a return to worldly administration. What is lost in this resequencing is the Lambs's emphasis on female characters. What is maintained—and fascinatingly assimilated to a traditional Chinese typology—is a multiplicity of characters among whom readers are prompted to discern doublings, patterns, and other morphological resemblances. The focus shifts away from the strategies and struggles of Rosalind and Celia, Hermia and Helena, and other heroines to the marvelous encounters of Macbeth, Hamlet, Prospero, and others who resemble ambitious generals or hapless scholars who reckon with temptations and dangers in the form of witches, ghosts, or animal spirits as they take transformative detours from a normal or normative order.

In his Preface, Lin uses multiple generic terms to designate Shakespeare's writings, including *shi* (poetry), *biji* ("random jottings"), and *jishi* ("records" or "chronicles"). Significantly, he also gestures toward drama: after remarking that Shakespeare's verses are recited household to household in England, he states that such verses form the basis of scripts (*yuanben*) for the theater (*liyuan*) and conjures up the striking image of gentlewomen (*shinü*) moved to tears while sitting in audiences joined sleeve to sleeve next to each other—聯襼而聽，欷歔感涕. Lin effectively describes Shakespeare as what would today be termed a "transmedial" author. What might this position of Shakespeare at the nexus of genres and media show us?

Insofar as many Chinese traditional operas or musical dramas derived from earlier narrative *chuanqi*, Lin's positioning of Shakespeare between poetry, prose, and theater suggests his intuition of a cultural doubling. If classical Chinese tales of the marvelous have served effectively as a transmedial cultural repertoire, then the retelling of Shakespeare in *Yinbian Yanyu* intimates to adult Chinese readers that comparable operations may be at work in relation to the Shakespearean corpus. Lin's intuition brackets out, of course, Shakespeare's own sources in Ovid, Greek and Roman drama, and Italian *novelle*, among other texts. In retelling the Lambs's retelling of Shakespeare, he introduces, wittingly or unwittingly, a Shakespeare not so much in the key of a poet-sage like Du Fu, the source of lofty thoughts about conditions of national scope and epic sentiments conveyed in a lyrical vein; rather, he transmits a Shakespeare whose cultural function and register of expression are closer to the key of writers of marvelous tales or plays exploring the uncanniness of the ordinary on the smaller stages of private life.

This version of Shakespeare, like the text it retells in translation, is a nonheroic or post-heroic one, from which English sovereigns and English national history are absent. As I have proposed earlier, the Lambs's *Tales* addresses its imagined reader as an average and common reader and promotes in her the capacity to discern morphological likenesses between characters and situations and how these characters are defined and act in relation to others within an intelligible shared social order. The *Tales* appeal to her intellectual capacity to discern likeness and her emotional capacity for compassion. *Yinbian Yanyu* finds for the *Tales* analogies in traditional Chinese literature. How might it, in doing so, imagine and address for its time a "Chinese common reader"?

What *is* its time? According to the terms of Lin's Preface itself, this time is perched between new (*xin*) and old (*jiu*), and it is a time when what is Chinese is undergoing redefinition in an expanded sense of the world and in relation primarily to the West. Against contemporaries who embrace the new as a rejection of the Chinese past, Lin seems effectively to approach the new as a particular and selective renewal of elements of the Chinese past in correlation, if not direct conversation, with Western culture. In his enactment of such a recursive newness becomes perceptible what Jonathan Hay has dubbed as a useful heuristic, an "otherly modernity," one that has heterogeneous antecedents and distinct cultural traits and that is not simply a belated version of a standardized Euro-American model.[25] *Yinbian Yanyu* can be said to serve as the curious site of encounter between two modernities that operate according to distinct cultural logics.

This site serves as the site for the remaking of a Chinese common reader. This making may be said to be a remaking insofar as it harks back to tales and plays of the strange as antecedents. *Yinbian Yanyu* introduces Shakespeare to readers capable of recognizing the stock characters that populate classical *chuanqi* and musical dramas *and*, through the mediation of such recognition, being open to the wonder and surprise of the strange. The Shakespeare it fashions from the Lambs is the poet of a system of stylized roles that constitute a shared world, one whose "aesthetic project," to tweak Paul Fleming's formulation, "is premised on a mimetic relationship not to 'what is'" but to a sociocultural order that, while undergoing transformation, nevertheless serves to scaffold and mediate social relations and interactions.

Figures of the Common Reader: Miranda and Prospero

In the Lambs's and Lin's respective retellings of Shakespeare, *The Tempest* enjoys a prominent position. The Lambs begin with the play; Lin ends his collection with his rendition of the Lambs's tale, renamed "*Juyin*," or "Storm Ruse." In her redaction of the romance, Mary Lamb subtly but unmistakably shifts the weight of attention to the character of Miranda. In his retelling of Mary's tale, Lin reallocates attention to Prospero. In these respective allocations may be discerned differing conceptions of the common reader. The respective characters may be seen to function as figures or surrogates for a common reader that each collection aims to address, imagine, and fashion.

Let us turn first to Mary Lamb's redaction of *The Tempest*. Simplifying the plot, she foregrounds the story of Miranda's formation, aligning other characters in relation to this central concern. Prospero figures prominently insofar as the father-daughter relationship serves as a vehicle for Miranda's growth. Ariel, as the instrument of Prospero's orders, plays an important role in the tale. And Ferdinand receives attention as a love match for the heroine. While Prospero's reconciliation with Antonio and Naples forms part of the tale's happy ending, that story retreats to the background, with Gonzalo playing a much lesser role in the tale than he does in Shakespeare's play. Caliban is likewise diminished as a character, with Sebastian and Trinculo omitted altogether.

How is Miranda recast as the heroine of *The Tempest*? Remarkably, Mary Lamb repositions Miranda as the heroine by making her not so much the principal actor in the story but the principal listener, spectator, and thereby actor in the play-within-the-play "directed" by Prospero. The liminal position she had already occupied in this most meta-theatrical of Shakespeare's plays gets amplified in transposition to the medium of narrative. She is portrayed, on the one hand, listening to her father's stories and, on the other, looking at, commenting on, and becoming absorbed in the spectacles Prospero stages with the aid of Ariel, his stage manager, who remains invisible to her throughout. Insofar as this spectacle is directed toward multiple ends, including Miranda's marriage with Ferdinand and Prospero's restoration as the Duke of Milan, Mary Lamb places the emphasis on the achievement of the former, spotlighting the process of Miranda's coming-into-the-world and leaving the home of her childhood. Miranda's progress is here predicated on her being a listener and spectator, and thereby an actor—a subject who becomes a subject through engagement with illusion.

In a letter to his childhood friend and schoolmate Samuel Taylor Coleridge dated October 23, 1802, several years before the writing of the *Tales*, Charles Lamb writes of a visit with Mary to a London bookshop, Newberry's, where he saw that Anna Letitia Barbauld's books for children had "banished all the old classics of the nursery."[26] "Knowledge insignificant and vapid as Mrs. Barbauld's books convey," he continues,

> must come to a child in the *shape of knowledge*; and his empty noddle must be turned with conceit of his own powers when he has learnt that a horse is an animal, and Billy is better than a horse, and such like; instead of that beautiful interest in wild tales, which made the child a man, while all the time he suspected himself to be no bigger than a child. Science has succeeded to poetry no less than in the little walks of children than with men. Is there no possibility of averting this sore evil? Think what you would have been now,

if, instead of being fed with tales and old wives' fables in childhood, you had been crammed with geography and natural history![27]

In contrast to the "powers" that positive knowledge can give a child, Charles affirms the alternative power that "wild tales" may impart in feeding the imagination of a child. A diet of wild tales makes the child what is not yet but could and would be—that is, "a man," opening up a difference between "what is" and what could or would be through the mediation of the "as if." If science teaches knowledge of "what is," poetry opens up futures and possibilities by teaching through the dimension of the "as if." Such teaching is "wild" insofar as the future it opens up cannot be known in advance in tame conformity with the laws of "what is."

Miranda figures in Mary's retelling of *The Tempest* as such a child made woman through the mediation of wild tales. Let us consider more closely how Mary's interpretive retelling of Shakespeare's play shows this mediation at work.

The first paragraph of the tale introduces the setting and Prospero and Miranda as the two main characters. The first sentence mentions Prospero first, introducing Miranda in relation to him and elaborating in the final clause on her attributes:

> There was a certain island in the sea, the only inhabitants of which were an old man, whose name was Prospero, and his daughter Miranda, a very beautiful young lady. She came to this island so young, that she had no memory of having seen any other human face than her father's. (7)

Miranda emerges as the grammatical subject of the second sentence from her subordinate position at the end of the first, where she is positioned within a larger structure and given attributes. The island will serve as the setting and stage of her development. Mary Lamb elaborates in the next few paragraphs on the setting of the island, introducing Ariel and Caliban (notably and problematically omitted in the first sentence from the count of the inhabitants of the island), and referring to Sycorax and the history of the island before Prospero's arrival. This exposition ends with the mention of the violent storm that Prospero conjures up with the aid of his spirits. This storm is the catalyst of the actions that will unfold in the rest of the tale. And this storm is presented to Miranda as a spectacle for her to behold: Prospero "showed his daughter a fine large ship, which he told her was full of living beings like themselves." In response to this sight Miranda speaks for the first time in the tale:

O my dear father . . . if by your art you have raised this dreadful storm, have pity on their sad distress. See! the vessel will be dashed to pieces. Poor souls! they will all perish. If I had power, I would sink the sea beneath the earth, rather than the good ship should be destroyed, with all the precious souls within her. (8)

She speaks here in the capacity of a spectator, responding to the distress of the souls on the ship with compassion while soliciting from her father the affect of pity, which implies his holding a position of power in relation to the wretches he is making toss and turn on the waters.

Assuring Miranda that "no person in the ship shall receive any hurt," Prospero proceeds to tell Miranda for the first time of their past. He prefaces his story with questions: "Can you remember a time before you came to this cell? . . . Tell me what you can remember, my child." To this demand Miranda answers, "It seems to me like the recollection of a dream. But had I not once four or five women who attended upon me?" (8) More than that she does not remember, but dream-like recollection functions in the listener like innate knowledge that gets awakened and activated in this occasion of storytelling.

In the process of Miranda's education through storytelling and spectacle, she is variously—or ambiguously—active and passive. Prospero and Ariel conspire to present Ferdinand to her gaze as a wondrous spectacle. Through indirect speech, Mary Lamb reports Miranda's feelings about this wondrous sight—"Miranda, who thought all men had grave faces and grey beards like her father, was delighted with the appearance of this beautiful young prince"—and continues to describe Ferdinand's reciprocal response to Miranda's attractions. After the young couple fall instantly in love, Prospero is portrayed shifting to the position of spectator, testing Ferdinand's honesty and spying on Miranda's shift in loyalties. From spectator, Miranda in turn becomes an actor in the scenario her father has initiated and set in motion.

Ironically, Miranda's acting in what is, in effect, Prospero's play entails her disobedience of her father's strictures. She takes the side of Ferdinand as he is submitted to the test of hard labor by Prospero, showing her love for the former by forgetting to heed the latter's commands. Miranda begins to depart from his script and to speak her own lines. Mary Lamb portrays Prospero taking pleasure as the hidden spectator of his child's disobedience. Overhearing Miranda tell Ferdinand her name "against her father's express command," Prospero "smiled at this first instance of his daughter's disobedience . . . he was not angry that she showed her love by forgetting to obey his commands" (13). Hearing her then say, "I fear I talk to you too freely, and my father's precepts I forget," Mary Lamb's Prospero "smiled, and nodded his head, as much as to say, 'This goes on exactly as I could wish; my girl will be queen of Naples'" (14). Prospero's pleasure at signs of his daughter's dawning independence and display of a separate identity is not made explicit in Act III, Scene 1 of Shakespeare's play. Mary Lamb accentuates this possibility in her interpretive retelling.

It would seem, then, that Prospero's play-within-the-play functions in Mary's retelling as a jointly improvised script. The story of Miranda's formation depends on a tacit and delicate collaboration between father and daughter, a collusion, so to speak, contingent upon the actor's willing participation in the co-illusion that the dramaturge/director creates and shapes in relation to unfolding circumstances. Miranda's independence is portrayed here not in terms of an absolute, sovereign individualism but as one constrained by interaction with interdependent others. Miranda forms thus the first in the distribution of heroines in the tales to follow whose progress involves receptivity to stories and illusions that mediate their own actions and interactions with others.

In his retelling of Mary Lamb's tale as "*Juyin*" (颶引) or "Storm Ruse," Lin allocates attention back to Prospero.[28] Lin takes obvious delight in embellishing the character of Prospero. Where Mary Lamb describes Prospero simply in her first sentence as "an old man," Lin adds details: 髮禿齒危，一衰翁也 (148). In Lin's retelling, Prospero becomes a wobbly greybeard who is losing his hair and his teeth and a variation of a scholar-hermit whose move to the island is termed 大隱, or a "great retreat" (148). Lin accentuates the account of Prospero's book-lined study in Lamb's exposition and has Miranda tell Ferdinand that her father studies Daoist texts (*daojing*). Prospero gains color and details as a Daoist or magician in Lin's text. The kind of power Prospero wields is clearly heterodox to the power operative in the normal order of things from which he has gone into exile and retreat.

The very title, "*Juyin*," foregrounds the element of artifice or illusion. *Yin* can be translated as "ruse," "trap," "lure," "ploy," or "stratagem." Prospero operates in collusion with Ariel, who is cast as *guidong* 鬼董, in managing by the indirect means of ruse changes in the status of characters and in the relations between them. Prospero delights in watching as a spectator the processes initiated by the ruse of the storm. Lin translates the pleasure Mary Lamb attributes to him in watching and overhearing his daughter disobey his precepts. Besides arranging for the marriage of his daughter, Prospero hears from Ariel as a consequence of their ruse the penitence of

Antonio and Naples, which leads to the reconciliation of the estranged brothers and harmony among the soon-to-be fathers-in-law. Whereas Mary Lamb spotlighted the story of Miranda's coming-of-age, Lin distributes interest to the other storylines—besides that involving Antonio, Naples, and Gonzalo, most notably that leading up to the emancipation of Ariel. If Mary Lamb's tale culminates with the setting-free of Ariel, followed by a quotation of Ariel's song, "Where the bee sucks," and a summarizing coda, Lin twists this conclusion by giving more weight to the scene of emancipation. In Lamb, Prospero's role as father has clear priority over the other roles he plays in a nexus of relationships. In Lin, the role of father takes its place alongside his roles as brother and master. Indeed, Lin may even be said to emphasize the master/servant relationship over the other relationships in which changes are effected and relations modified by means of the storm ruse.

In the coda, Mary Lamb tells of how Prospero buried his books and wand and renounced his magical arts. The penultimate sentence summarizes the conclusion and reaches an expansive crescendo in the description of the marriage of Miranda and Ferdinand, and the last sentence directs the reader to Naples as the setting for the wedding:

> And having thus overcome his enemies, and being reconciled to his brother and the king of Naples, nothing now remained to complete his happiness, but to revisit his native land, to take possession of his dukedom, and to witness the happy nuptials of his daughter Miranda and prince Ferdinand, which the king said should be instantly celebrated with great splendour on their return to Naples. At which place, under the safe convoy of the spirit Ariel, they after a pleasant voyage soon arrived. (17)

Instead of translating this coda faithfully, Lin condenses it, after mentioning Prospero's renunciation of his magical arts, to simply:

> 迨及國，即行婚禮，明日果一帆風順，抵奈百而司矣。(156)
>
> Once they reached land, the nuptials would be held. Indeed, there was smooth sailing on the morrow as all arrived in Naples. (Translation mine.)

The brevity of this conclusion shifts attention back to the final scene of Ariel's emancipation. Mary Lamb, taking license and departing from Shakespeare, parses Ariel's freedom thus: "to wander uncontrolled in the air, like a wild bird, under green trees, among pleasant fruits, and sweet-smelling flowers" (17). Lin dispenses with this idyllic embellishment altogether and gives Ariel a speech found neither in Lamb nor in Shakespeare:

愛里而感翁次骨，因曰：「吾雖以忠爲職，然愛其自由實重於愛主人。主人恩重，聽我自由，我無以報貺。明日群作一程，風送主人歸舟」。且言曰：「今得自由，自由之樂，安有極者。」(156)

With deep gratitude toward the old man, Ariel said, "Although loyalty is the virtue attached to my position, my love of freedom outweighs my love of the master. For the master to give, with profound grace, hearing to my freedom, I have nothing to give in requital. For the journey tomorrow, I will accompany the winds to provide safe convoy." And then he added, "Today, I receive freedom. Is there a joy greater than the joy of freedom?" (Translation mine.)

Lin introduces in this passage the notion of a love of freedom that outweighs his love of his master and consequently the specific kind of loyalty that attends the latter category of love. Lin retells the "safe convoy" Ariel provides the crew to Naples in terms specifically of *bao*, or requitement, which, as Patrick Hanan points out, serves as "the moral grammar of interactions among men or between men and gods."[29]

In Lin's retelling, Prospero is shown occupying a nexus of roles and negotiating via illusion a nexus of relationships, including father/child, older brother/younger brother, master/servant. If these relationships belong to the domain of the human and constitute variations on recognizable Confucian bonds, the human/spirit relationship—indeed partnership—operative throughout the text serves as a supplement to the normative human models. The human/spirit relationship exists outside of the social domain but works to occasion changes within this domain. The human/spirit relationship may thus be seen as the means whereby the dimension of the "as if" estranges and opens up the workings of the "what is."

If Miranda functions as a figure or surrogate of the reader in the Lambs's retelling of Shakespeare for children as beginners, Prospero can be seen to perform that function as an adult making a new beginning through the mediations of the "strange"—in the senses of both the foreign and the supernatural—in Lin's retelling of Shakespeare to Chinese adults as re-beginners at a transitional period for Chinese history and culture. The crux of strangeness at which the foreign and the supernatural converge is, precisely, freedom. *Ziyou* is in "*Juyin*," or "Storm Lure," a neologism like other terms—for instance, *gongli*, that Lin had used in his previous 1901 translation of Harriet Beecher Stowe's *Uncle Tom's Cabin*.[30] As both linguistic and narrative event, freedom takes place on the ground of the supernatural as an inhuman site of potential transformation of the very terms of human community.

Miranda and Prospero may be taken as figures or surrogates of the common reader that the Lambs's and Lin's respective retellings of Shakespeare address, imagine, and fashion. The *Tales from Shakespeare* addresses the reader as one capable of growing through receptivity to stories and complicity in illusions that mediate their own actions and interactions with others. The text positions this reader among others like her in the collection of tales that teach a grammar of social interaction. *Yinbian Yanyu* addresses the reader as one capable of recognizing and negotiating a repertoire of cultural roles that scaffolds social interactions and that remains open to change and renewal through the mediating effect of illusion. Indeed, in Lin's retelling of Shakespeare, there emerges a model of change that takes place through mechanisms within—rather than simply against—traditional structures, tested for tensile resilience, and that entails a more gradual and gradualist pace. The Lambs's and Lin's retellings of Shakespeare each present a dioramic vision of social life and may be said curiously to double one another by situating characters and readers—and characters as reader/spectators—on a distinctly unheroic, indeed middling plane as agents of a decentralized, distributed power.

Finally, as a coda, let us turn to paratextual matter—passages in the Prefaces—to consider how these texts are inscribed in processes of global production and circulation that subtend their distributions to culturally distinct, local readerships. The very existence of these texts is predicated on the late eighteenth-century European notion of aesthetic education that received content and currency throughout the long nineteenth century through an array of institutional practices and textual technologies. It is through such practices and technologies that Shakespeare emerged in the course of that century as a global canonical figure. The Prefaces to *Tales from Shakespeare* and *Yinbian Yanyu* allegorize the texts' own participation in this process.

In their cowritten Preface, the Lambs compare their own tales to "small and valueless coins ... pretending to no other merit than as faint and imperfect stamps of Shakespeare's matchless image" (3). The metaphor connects Shakespeare specifically to the site of the market, conceiving of Shakespeare as a form of cultural capital with which young readers may gain access to a cultural economy. Notably, the form it takes here seems to be the small change of what today has been formalized as "microfinancing." Fascinatingly, the following passage develops the Lambs's story of textual production and mediation, telling of a "minting process," as it were:

For young ladies too it has been my intention chiefly to write, because boys are generally permitted the use of their fathers' libraries at a much earlier age than girls are, they frequently having the best scenes of Shakespeare by heart, before their sisters are permitted to look into this manly book; and therefore, instead of recommending these Tales to the perusal of young gentlemen who can read them so much better in the originals, I must rather beg their kind assistance in explaining to their sisters such parts as are hardest for them to understand; and when they have helped them to get over the difficulties, then perhaps they will read to them (carefully selecting what is proper for a young sister's ear) some passage which has pleased them in one of these stories, in the very words of the scene from which it is taken; and I trust they will find that the beautiful extracts, the select passages, they may choose to give their sisters in this way, will be much better relished and understood from their having some notion of the general story from one of these imperfect abridgements:—which if they be fortunately so done as to prove delightful to any of you, my young readers, I hope will have no worse effect upon you, than to make you wish yourselves a little older, that you may be allowed to read the Plays at full length (such a wish will be neither peevish nor irrational). (4)

Remarkably, this one long sentence is itself the result of labor jointly undertaken by the Lambs as brother-and-sister collaborators: Mary begins the sentence, and Charles picks up, as he relates to William Wordsworth in a letter, after the dash "—" with the words, "which if they be fortunately so done...."[31] The collaboration on this sentence reproduces the story of collaborative reading narrated by the sentence itself. In its first leg, the sentence situates the mise-en-scène of reading in the private, domestic unit of the household with its evocation of "their fathers' libraries." After the first semicolon, the second leg asks the brother to serve as a more experienced guide in providing selection and annotation; the third section recommends reading aloud as an occasion for the transmission of choice passages; the last two sections anticipate the effects of such a collaborative reading. The sentence describes a process of reproduction of what the *Tales from Shakespeare* itself performs and, to an extent, the reproduction process that the Lambs themselves performed in retelling Shakespeare. The text inserts itself, then, as a medium in a chain of mediations, in which brother-sister matrices function as agents for the production and reception of Shakespearean retellings. This lengthy sentence would seem to link together, then, stages of a production process of Shakespearean retelling itself. In assuming authority over and in their fathers' libraries, the brother-sister matrices turn the library unit into a decentralized workshop of retelling.

Turning now to Lin Shu's Preface to *Yinbian Yanyu*, we see that, in Lin's recounting of the translation process, he seems unwittingly to participate in aspects of the very production process of Shakespearean retelling that the Lambs allegorize. In the second half of the Preface, Lin turns to the topic of the occasion and production of *Yinbian Yanyu* itself. Instead of a brother-sister matrix, the reader-retellers are a pair of friends from two generations. Lin calls Wei Yi "dear friend" (挚友) and "the honorable younger brother Wei" (魏君春叔). The principle of friendship promotes an equality that works across the generational divide. It is Wei that occupies here the position of the brother in Lamb: it is Wei who—"young and learned, steeped in Western languages" (年少英博，淹通西文)—can read the Shakespearean text "in the original" and offer his "kind assistance" in explaining to Lin Shu "those parts that are hardest to understand." Wei and Lin collaborated on this, as on other texts, using the method of *duiyi*, or face-to-face translation: "The honorable Wei would interpret, while I would commit it to narrative prose" (魏君口譯，余則敘致爲文章). The two of them had already translated three or four different kinds of texts, with the "grandest" (最鉅本) being John Gibson Lockhart's *History of Napoleon Buonaparte*. Significantly, it is during idling breaks at night from the grand labor of translating this heroic and monumental biography that Lin would hear Wei speak about Shakespeare's continued appeal, in spite of his use of the supernatural, among contemporary social and political reformers in England.

If the father's library turns into a workshop for textual production and reproduction for the Lambs, this library finds its counterpart on the other side of the globe in a kind of literatus studio turned workshop in Lin. The very title *Yinbian Yanyu* 吟邊燕語—"Recitations Heard from Afar"—that Lin chooses, with its connotations of literati leisure, seems to situate the very occasion of the text in a locus of receptive hearing, a locus that serves also as the site of writing. When the Lambs's text travels to China, it passes from the father's library to the literatus studio as a workshop for retelling and transmission, for exchange into another currency and passage through another distribution system for the potential microfinancing of middling imaginative readers, connecting "inspired office-boys" and their sisters to dreaming *xiao shimin*.

Undoubtedly, such processes of global circulation and connection exert homogenizing effects, appealing to writers and readers in their capacities as producers and consumers in elevating markets as sites of exchange and workshops as sites of production over court, church, temple, and halls of learning as sources of authority.[32] The elevation of markets and workshops is symptomatic of the ascendance in the nineteenth century of the political economic as the dominant culture of global modernity. In varying modalities of local opposition to this homogenizing dimension of modern life, residual and emergent cultures interact dynamically with currents of standardization. Lin's retelling of the Lambs's retelling of Shakespeare turns to what was already at the time in the process of becoming a residual culture in China and makes it staging grounds for the emergence of the new. According to Raymond Williams, who coined the very term "emergent culture," that term is, strictly speaking, a misnomer, for "what we have to observe is in effect a *pre-emergence*, active and pressing but not yet fully articulated, rather than the evident emergence which could be more confidently named."[33] This condition of pre-emergence, whose very dynamism resists conceptual solidification, Williams famously theorizes as "structures of feeling," which he defines precisely as "social experiences *in solution*, as distinct from other social semantic formations"—for instance, worldviews or ideologies— "which have been *precipitated* and are more evidently and more immediately available."[34] The linguistic and narrative event of freedom in Lin's retelling of *The Tempest*, as it emerges between Prospero and Ariel, marks the potential articulation of a new social bond within a given yet pliable system of social relations. Such an event opens up, without fully naming, the promise of new passions, new feelings, and ways of being among others.

3 Estrangements of the World in the Familiar Essay

Charles Lamb and Zhou Zuoren's Approaches to the Ordinary

The familiar essay eludes rigid definition. In the lexicon of literary terms in English, correlatives from different periods and cultural contexts include the "informal essay" and the "personal essay."[1] In his 1818 lecture "On the Periodical Essayists," William Hazlitt, one of the form's best-known English practitioners, claimed the sixteenth-century French writer Michel de Montaigne as the "father of this kind of personal authorship among the moderns, in which the reader is admitted behind the curtain, and sits down with the writer in his gown and slippers."[2] As Hazlitt's definition dioramically illustrates, the familiar essay typically involves a casual, conversational style, with the writer expatiating on matters from his or her subjective point of view and simulating an address to the reader as a peer or friend in conditions of private, sartorially specific leisure.

In a 1921 essay in the literary supplement of the Beijing *Chenbao* or *Morning News*, Zhou Zuoren includes this category of writing under the broader rubric of the now-dated term "belles lettres," distinguished as "artistic" rather than "critical and scholarly" prose.[3] Zhou sees such writing flourishing abroad most of all in Anglo-American letters, naming a line from Joseph Addison, Charles Lamb, Washington Irving, and Nathaniel Hawthorne to John Galsworthy, George Gissing, and G. K. Chesterton as key exponents. After listing these writers in quick survey, Zhou suggests that "in China, the prefaces, jottings, and anecdotes written in ancient-style prose can also be called a kind of belles lettres. But in modern literature in the national language, we have not yet seen this kind of essay. Why don't those planning the new literature," he suggests, "try their hand at it?"[4] Zhou's proposal constituted a gentle but unmistakable nudge among the forces that gave impetus to the flourishing in Republican China in the 1920s and '30s of essayistic writing in general and prominently the familiar essay. He himself would become one of the leading writers and promoters of the genre, which would, in part because of his efforts as a literary historian and theorist, come to be called in its modern instantiation *xiaopin wen* or "little prose pieces."[5] While the term was mentioned as early as the fifth century in the *Shishuo Xinyu*, or *The New Account of the Tales of the World*, it came primarily to designate late Ming-dynasty or sixteenth- into seventeenth-century informal essays on everyday pleasures. Zhou would identify this corpus in the early 1930s as important antecedents for the modern, Republican-era familiar essay.

This chapter examines a nexus in the implicit conversation between traditions of writing Zhou adumbrates in his 1921 essay. It juxtaposes texts by one of the writers on Zhou's list, the English Regency–era essayist Charles Lamb, and by Zhou himself. This conversation between traditions is an oblique and uneven one. The point is obvious but needs to be noted. In his essayist's pose as master of ceremonies, Zhou shows, however lightly, a more systematic knowledge of literature in English than any writer on his list, past or present, could or did of literature in Chinese. As a professor of European literature at Peking University, Zhou writes in 1921 against the background of a century of literary histories and anthologies, genres in a corpus of knowledge *about* literature that had accumulated and circulated globally since the late eighteenth century, when literature as such became a separate domain and object of knowledge in the West. The aforementioned 1818 lecture by Hazlitt is one such text in this voluminous corpus of knowledge. Zhou's casually learned reference to Western literature is predicated on such knowledge. In his own iteration, he performs a gesture repeated so often it may be said to be constitutive of modern Chinese literature itself. Modern Chinese literature comes into self-awareness by responding in a deliberate and often programmatic way to the task of reevaluating itself as modern and as literature—in the broader context of the epistemic shift at the end of the nineteenth century toward a Western post-Enlightenment organization of knowledge.[6] This shift may be seen, in one light, as the advent of Chinese modernity but also, in another, as a node of long-durational encounter between what the art historian of late imperial China Jonathan Hay has called "double" or "otherly modernities."[7]

In gesturing toward a tradition of Anglo-American familiar essay writing, Zhou was not importing a Western model: he was initiating, rather, an oblique conversation between traditions of writing. From being steeped in more than one literary tradition, Zhou was able to articulate a historiography in which the late Ming flourishing of *xiaopin wen* had resonance for his own Republican moment. He would locate in the late Ming corpus a radically nonconformist and democratizing potential that contests blatantly ideological tendencies among his fellow Chinese writers and intellectuals in the 1920s and '30s. The genealogy of his essayistic practice does not derive from but compares to that facilitated by the Anglo-American line from Addison to Chesterton.

The familiar essay practices of Lamb and Zhou are part of asynchronous moments in separate, heterogeneous, and intertwined modernities. They are minor exercises that simulate casual forays into the informal, the personal, the ordinary, and the everyday. As such, they render perceptible on a small and intimate scale tremors occasioned by major cultural shifts. In this chapter, I juxtapose texts by these authors to analyze how each uses the medium of the familiar essay to register the estrangements of a world in flux and thus performs the task of reapproaching the ordinary. In conclusion, I reflect on the question of what it means to read these writers as distant peers in oblique conversation with one another.

After the Revolutions: Two Lives

Given cultural differences and compounded by the effects of compartmentalization in literary studies, those who know the work of Charles Lamb will not be likely to know the work of Zhou Zuoren, and those familiar with Zhou Zuoren are not likely to be familiar with Charles Lamb. Highly popular from the 1820s into the Victorian period in England, Lamb is no longer read widely outside of specialist circles, despite the efforts of such lay admirers as the contemporary English psychoanalyst and public intellectual Adam Phillips, who edited the Penguin volume of Lamb's *Selected Prose*. To many students of Romanticism, Lamb is primarily known as the "gentle-hearted Charles" to whom the major Romantic poet Samuel Taylor Coleridge addresses his famous conversation poem "This Lime-Tree Bower my Prison" (1800). Within the Chinese-speaking world, Zhou Zuoren is hardly an obscure name. Along with his older brother Lu Xun, he is one of the most important and influential figures of modern Chinese literature. Selected writings have been anthologized in translation, and David Pollard has edited and translated selected essays in a Chinese-English edition.[8] Zhou has not, however, circulated much beyond specialist circles outside of Sinophone areas. Brief introductions are thus in order here.

Charles Lamb was born in London in 1775 and died there in 1834. He studied on a scholarship at Christ's Hospital, a charity school where he met his fellow pupil Coleridge, with whom he would become lifelong friends. Like Coleridge and other members of a generation self-consciously ambitious about redefining the status of literature in the millenarian atmosphere of the French Revolution, Lamb too wrote poetry in the 1790s. He tried unsuccessfully also to write a few plays. He would turn primarily to prose in the 1800s, cowriting with his sister Mary the *Tales from Shakespeare*, among other works for children commissioned by William and Mary Jane Godwin for their Juvenile Library; and he wrote in his own name literary and dramatic criticism for the *Reflector* and *Quarterly Review*. In the 1820s, he started writing essays featuring a semi-autobiographical and semifictional character named Elia for the *London Magazine*. These essays were collected in 1823 in the book *Essays of Elia*, and in 1833 further essays appeared as *The Last Essays of Elia*. He is best known for these essays.

At a time when fellow writers of his acquaintance, including Coleridge, Wordsworth, Southey, Hazlitt, and younger contemporaries such as Byron, Shelley, and even Keats, could claim or aspire to writing as a sole vocation, Lamb notably worked for over thirty-five years as a clerk. He spent thirty-three of those years in the accountant's office of the East India Company. As mentioned in Chapter 2, a family tragedy kept him at this job: Mary had killed their mother in a fit of insanity. To keep Mary from being institutionalized, Charles agreed to serve as her guardian. Just as Lamb's employment at the East India Company informs the portrayal of Elia as a clerk in the South Seas Office, the figure of Mary informs to some degree the portrayal of Bridget, the cousin with whom the bachelor Elia shares a household.[9] In Elia, Lamb created a double of himself, toying with the line between fiction and nonfiction. As Marilyn Butler observes in *Romantics, Rebels, and Reactionaries*, "Lamb's ordinariness made him in the 1820s, for, as Hazlitt discerned, his variant of the man of letters was the figure with which the middle-class readership could empathize."[10]

Zhou Zuoren was born in 1885, in the eleventh year of the Emperor Guangxu. He was in his twenties when the 1911 revolution ended the Qing dynasty, and he died in 1967, the eighteenth year of another republic, the People's Republic of China. He was born to a gentry family in decline in Shaoxing, in the eastern part of Zhejiang, one of the coastal provinces south of the Yangtze River that had become mercantile and cultural powers during the late Ming and Qing dynasties. Along with Lu Xun, Zhou was part of a class and a generation that received a private classical education that would have prepared him for the Confucian state examinations that were abolished in 1905. He received also a utilitarianized version of a Western education at the Jiangnan Naval Academy, one of a series of institutions set up in the late nineteenth century for Western-style scientific and technological training. And, like many in their generation, the Zhou brothers received government scholarships to study in Japan, Lu Xun for medicine and Zhou Zuoren for civil engineering. Abandoning these paths, they became writers instead. The Zhou brothers spent their time in Japan from 1906 to 1911 reading voraciously, writing and translating, and participating in expatriate anti-imperial, revolutionary groups. They returned to China in 1911, at the crux of its transition from empire to republic, Zhou with his Japanese wife Habuto Nobuku. Zhou worked as an inspector of schools in Zhejiang before assuming a position teaching European literature at Peking University in 1917, where he was a prominent figure in the reformist May Fourth or New Culture Movement of 1919. Throughout the 1920s and into the '30s, he wrote, translated, taught, and edited a literary magazine in the context of increasing political turmoil and imminent war. After the Japanese invasion in 1937, Zhou's decision to remain in occupied Beijing and eventually to accept positions in the puppet government has long clouded his reputation. After the war and the 1949 revolution, Zhou continued to write, at a reduced pace in relation to reduced demand, and when on demand, often about Lu Xun, who had died in 1936 and from whom he had become estranged in the 1920s. He continued to work also during this time as a translator from English and ancient Greek. He died in Beijing in 1967, apparently after multiple beatings by Red Guards.[11] It would be an understatement to say that his was a complex history, whose complexity seems symptomatic of the complexity of Chinese modernity itself.

A few parallels emerge from these biographical sketches. Lamb and Zhou were, at asynchronous moments, members of generations inspired to redefine literature and culture in relation to the claims of democratic revolution. While many of their peers adopted, in the case of English Romanticism, rhetorically prophetic and, in the case of modern China, self-heroically programmatic approaches to the task of defining a new literature, Lamb and Zhou were persistently understated. Both participated in the burgeoning periodical press of their times, addressing growing numbers of metropolitan, middle-class, and women readers. Each preferred to address their readers not from an elevated oratorical perspective but at eye level and from the middle distance. Marilyn Butler has called Lamb an "enemy of system," one who preferred the truth-telling potential of the fragmentary, occasional, and piecemeal to the elevation of a supra-perspective.[12] In their ambivalence toward the supra-perspective, stemming from skepticisms enacted on the plane of the ordinary, Lamb and Zhou write works that resonate evocatively across languages and traditions.

On the Way to the Ordinary

What do we talk about when we talk about the ordinary? On the way toward the ordinary in Lamb and Zhou, I turn to philosopher Charles Taylor, whose work engages not with the ordinary per se but centrally with the notion of "ordinary life." Taylor's thinking is especially useful here for the invitation it extends toward cross-cultural comparison. In his 1989 *Sources of the Self*, Taylor proposes the notion of the affirmation of ordinary life as constitutive of the history of modernity in the West. "Ordinary life," he writes, designates "those aspects of human life concerned with production and reproduction, that is, labour, the making of the things needed for life, and our life as sexual beings, including marriage and the family."[13] "Ordinary life" would correspond to "life" in Aristotle's classic distinction in the *Politics* between "life and the good life."[14] If ordinary life is traditionally regarded not as in itself a fully human life but merely the condition of possibility for the pursuit of the good life, modernity effects a definitive change in this hierarchy by displacing the locus of the good life from a range of higher activities to the domain of ordinary life itself. Modernity consists in the very affirmation of ordinary life, which entails, as Taylor argues, "an inherent bent towards social levelling"; "the centre of the good life lies now in something which everyone can have a part in, rather than in ranges of activity which only a leisured few can do justice to" (214). Replacing by and large an older aristocratic and heroic ethos, a "new model of civility emerges in the eighteenth century, in which the life of commerce and acquisition gains an unprecedentedly positive place" (214).

Taylor reiterates his formulation of modernity as the affirmation of ordinary life in later writings that extend the implications of his thesis toward the task of thinking about multiple modernities in a culturally complex, multiform world. He proposes in his 2004 *Modern Social Imaginaries* that an affirmation of ordinary life is operative across multiple modernities in their respective and asynchronous transitions or disembeddings from traditional sociopolitical hierarchies based on birth and wealth.[15] In reconstructing the emergence of what he terms a "modern social imaginary" in the West, Taylor refers centrally to John Locke and Hugo Grotius as proponents of a modern moral and social order based on the mutual benefit of equal participants. Mutual benefit and equality serve for Taylor as the prime criteria orienting not just the affirmation of ordinary life in the West but comparable affirmations in heterogeneous modernities. Thus Taylor's genealogy of the modern Western social imaginary invites, even requires, the retelling of the histories of other, non-Western modernities.

It is possible to abstract in schematic form an affirmation of ordinary life in a history of Chinese modernity in a series of lectures, *On the Sources of the New Chinese Literature,* that Zhou delivered in 1932.[16] Zhou traces the sources of the new or modern Chinese literature to currents in the history of thought and letters at the end of the Ming dynasty. He names two groups of heterodox writers and thinkers who embraced spontaneity and the expression of "innate sensibility" against the imitation of orthodox models. These were the Gongan School and the Jingling School, both of the late sixteenth to early seventeenth centuries. Members of the Gongan School wrote in a "fresh and limpid" (*qingxin liuli*), easily accessible style and, in terms of subject matter, avoided pompous generalizations about the proper conduct of state affairs. Members of the Jingling School wrote in a denser and more difficult style, next to which Gongan writing could appear superficial. Zhang Dai, a later Ming writer of informal essays on private and everyday matters, combined the strengths of both schools, Zhou argues.

In her extraordinarily fine monograph, *Zhou Zuoren and an Alternative Chinese Response to Modernity,* Susan Daruvala traces the emphasis on innate sensibility and spontaneity among these late Ming writers to the influence of the pivotal early sixteenth-century thinker Wang Yangming and his followers in the Taizhou school.[17] Wang prioritized interiority and subjectivity in a radical reinterpretation of key terms in Confucian thought. His followers in the Taizhou school located in this turn the basis for their claims concerning the originative potential of the "everyday uses" of "the common people" (*baixing riyong*) as sources for the generation of social and moral norms.[18] Such claims interpret the *dao* or Way as answering to the everyday uses of the people rather than the people to an orthodox determination of the Way.

These groups of sympathetically schismatic late Ming thinkers can be said, from a Taylorian viewpoint, to theorize an affirmation of ordinary life that involves an inherently leveling bent and that situates the cultivation of virtue and the good life immanently in the domain of labor, production, and reproduction itself rather than in a range of higher activities. Zhou charts a genealogy for the new or modern Chinese literature of the Republican era that taps into a set of ideas and a corpus of writings with radical sociopolitical implications from a specific late imperial moment. The newness he advocates as an attribute of the new literature does not belong to a temporally linear conception of modernity wherein Chinese modernity merely follows or imitates the West. Newness appears rather as a capacity for renewal within and of a shared culture that stems from everyday, local, and decentralized sources of normative potential whose expressive instrument *and* medium are language itself. The genealogy Zhou sketches in his 1932 lectures sheds light on the writing of his peers as well as on his own aesthetics as he seeks, in the Republican era, in oblique conversation with Western and foreign literatures, to practice a new writing of the ordinary.

The World Estranged in "Old China" and "Wild Vegetables of My Hometown"

Among the numerous essays by Lamb and Zhou, I select and pair for close analysis two of their best-known and most frequently anthologized pieces: Lamb's "Old China," which appeared in the *London Magazine* in March 1823, and Zhou's "Wild Vegetables of my Hometown," published in April 1824 in the Beijing *Morning News*. Each essay is typical of its author's wry interrogations of occasions that present themselves in ordinary and private life, away from scenes of public and national importance; each scrutinizes minutiae of daily existence. Lamb's essay reflects on and registers the mysteriously unsettling effects of the foreign on the ordinary life of an average middle-class London household. In terms of its investigation of the drawing-room or armchair uncanny, "Old China" is contiguous to such a minor masterpiece of skepticism as the 1822 "Dream Children: A Reverie." In terms of its thematization of things Chinese and its meditation thereby on economies of pleasure and pain, "Old China" would seem to form a companion piece to the 1822 "A Dissertation upon Roast Pig." In "Wild Vegetables of my Hometown," Zhou's reminiscences about forageable plants in eastern Zhejiang register and revaluate how the locus of the hometown has been discursively resituated in relation to an altered sense of the world. The perspective of the cosmopolitan observer of local customs informs likewise such famous essays as the 1924 "Tea-Drinking" and the 1926 "Dark-Canopied Boats."

While "Old China" and "Wild Vegetables of my Hometown" are well known to their authors' respective readers, they have not been analyzed together before. What emerges in their juxtaposition is how they both stage ways of looking at what may be called "Old China" and, in doing so, generate sensations of lingering though gentle disquiet. Not only do they stage ways of looking at "Old China," they offer, most remarkably, subtle critical reflection on the terms and conditions of the acts of looking inscribed in their acts of writing. Therein consists their aesthetic self-awareness. In discussing the essays, I aim to explain how each produces its effect of mild unease and argue that it is precisely through such effects that each opens up, within connected yet separate cultural contexts and in relation to different philosophical traditions, the possibility of reapproaching the ordinary.

As the title of Lamb's essay, "Old China" functions as an ambiguous term within the text's semantic field. On a literal, referential level, it designates the porcelain tea set that Bridget and Elia use one evening. Elia refers to it as "a set of extraordinary old blue china (a recent purchase) which we were now for the first time using."[19] The parenthetical term "recent purchase" qualifies the age of the tea set and has induced one recent reader, Elizabeth Chang, to ask about its provenance: was it imported by the East India Company, or was it made by Spode?[20] Lamb's parenthesis toys with the distinction. On another level, "Old China" designates a place or civilization, one that either produced the object or its method of making, traces of which are visible on the painted surfaces of the cups. On another level, the term alludes to the china trade as a condition of possibility for the tea set's appearance in Elia's drawing room.[21] And on yet another level, the term connotes an imaginative world private to Elia as he muses aside to the reader on how, since a time he was "not conscious of," he had been fascinated with the images of men and women on china teacups. In its very ambiguity, the title indicates the complex status of the term "Old China" as cause of the unease the essay produces.

The essay consists of two parts. In the prologue, Elia shares private musings in the modes of autobiographical recollection and ekphrastic description. In the second part, he recounts the tea-time conversation between him and Bridget the previous evening. This conversation consists of a lengthy monologue by Bridget, followed by a short response from Elia. An ekphrastic coda, in the form of a direct address to Bridget, returns to Elia's unspoken ekphrastic musings from the prologue.

My analysis considers first the conversation in the second part of the essay. At its beginning, Elia asks Bridget to look at the images upon their tea set, remarking "how favourable circumstances had been to us of late years, that we could afford to please the eye sometimes with trifles of this sort" (217–18). Refusing to look, she sighs, "I wish the good old times would come again when we were not quite so rich," and launches into a monologue of discontent about their newfound bourgeois comforts (218). Significantly, the monologue is bracketed from beginning to end by a refusal to look.

Curiously, Bridget's lament takes the form of a ledger. Against gains in convenience, easy luxury, and upward mobility, she counts losses in the purposiveness of frugal spending, the more intense pleasures of hard-earned delights, the camaraderie of the crowd in the gallery. She strings together vignettes of shared past purchases and pastimes—from a Beaumont and Fletcher folio to walks to Enfield to visits to the theater and treats of strawberries and peas when they were less common and thus more dear in affective value, if not in price. Her references to numerous places anchor her speech in a mappable London, as Lamb seems quasi-sociologically through her to list the habits and depict the habitus of the recently leisured classes.[22] Bridget's balance sheet of comparative pleasures ends, strikingly, with the image of an actual ledger. She recalls past New Year's Eve reckonings to "account for our exceedings," when they would review their expenditures and the balance of their capital and make adjustments and projections for the next year. "Now," she mourns, "we have no reckoning at all at the end of the old year—no flattering promises about the new year doing better for us" (220). Bridget's reckoning reaches a crescendo, ironically, in a reflection on how final reckonings themselves have expired as stable instruments of evaluation.

The mode subtending this mournful ledger is the idyll, whereby a simpler England and a simpler past, one that precedes the entanglements of global and imperial commerce, are defined in relation to a fallen present. Bridget speaks for a nostalgic middle-class English type still very well with us in the twenty-first century. In reply, Elia rebuts her balance sheet almost line by line, chiding the selectiveness of her memory. At the end of his disillusioning rebuttal, he offers his counter-version of a past visit to the theater. He remembers being "pushed about, squeezed, elbowed"; her "anxious shrieks"; the "delicious *Thank God, we are safe*" at the top of the stairs (221). From this elevation, where his recollection has taken both Bridget and the reader, his next figure of speech startlingly plunges both Bridget and the reader down through the house, through and beneath the stage, down to a descent so unfathomable as he "would be willing to bury more wealth in" than had the mythical King Croesus or the contemporary Rothschild to "purchase" that time back (221).

What is this fall? In response to Bridget's anxious pastoralism, Elia uses the figure of the fall to make a point about their living irredeemably in fallen time. Strikingly, he stages this fall in the space of the theater, creating a strangely destabilizing effect for both Bridget and the reader. He breaks this fall with a swerve to another view. He calls Bridget's attention back to a teacup, returning in the last sentence of the essay to the ekphrastic mode by asking her once again to look. "Old China" seems oddly to figure as both causal symptom and potential remedy for Bridget's anxious pastoralism.

Let us now turn back to the prologue. Elia begins with an autobiographical reminiscence, telling the reader semi-apologetically of his longtime and "almost feminine" partiality for old china. Such objects of everyday and domestic use and decoration rank low in a Western hierarchy of the arts it would take another half century for a William Morris to upturn.[23] In recounting his taste for old china, since the time immemorial of childhood, Elia moves between the perspective of the adult and the gaze of the child. The adult's perspective is a quasi-sociological, call it a realist, one. It frames the telling of a history of taste in England since old china started appearing in the china closets of great houses and later in the drawing rooms of the not-so-great. The adult's perspective is also a mathematizing one that figures as one of two modes interwoven in the ekphrastic descriptions that ensue. This perspective is apparent in Elia's reference to "our optics," in light of which the figures on the cup appear "lawless" and part of a "world before perspective" (217). In terms of content, these references all have to do with distance, scale, and calculability. As such, they resonate with Bridget's concern with the measurability of pleasures. On grammatical and stylistic levels, these references function not as ekphrastic description proper but as meta-ekphrastic interjections that are either contained within parentheses or set apart by dashes.

(so they appear to our optics)

. . .

—two miles off. See how distance seems to set off respect!

. . .

—which in a right angle of incidence (as angles go in our world)

. . .

—if far or near can be predicated of their world— (217)

These meta-ekphrastic interjections interrupt and comment on the descriptions proper, which feature saliently terms in Latin—*terra firma* and *speciosa miracula*—as well as archaisms that would more appropriately describe legendary or medieval imagery. The latter include "fairy boat," "dancing the hays," "a cow and rabbit couchant" (217). Strikingly, Elia uses language befitting pre-perspectival European pictorialism to describe the "world before perspective" he claims to see on old china (217). Obviously, none of this—as the essay itself wryly hints—can be taken seriously in a literal vein as knowledge of or about Old China.

Nestled within the adult's perspective, which vacillates between authoritative framing and parasitical interjection, is nothing other than a child's gaze. What is this gaze? It is one that motivates Elia, in at least semi-earnestness, to call the figures on the cups "my old friends—whom distance cannot diminish" (217). In complicity with these old friends, the child's gaze too belongs in another sense to a "world before perspective," insofar as a sense of scale and measure is what children acquire, rather than are born with, by entering formally ordered systems of value.[24] In *Perspective as Symbolic Form*, art historian Erwin Panofsky famously explains how perspectival pictorialism in the Renaissance West establishes a purely mathematical space that is "infinite, unchanging, and homogeneous" and that is distinct from, perhaps propped on, the "psychophysiological space" of perception.[25] Elia's efforts at pictorial description bespeak a somewhat comical struggle between the language of mathematical space and the anachronistic and culturally inappropriate language of "wild ekphrasis." What remains silent in this absurd internal dialogue is the language of psychophysiological space. Such language persists, however, negatively as a function of the struggle between languages itself, kept open as such by the mere percipience and drive-to-see of a child's gaze that sees but does not know. Operative in the struggle between languages, this drive to see puts the framework of the adult perspective out of joint, exposing the subject to the unpredictability of a sensing that does not coincide with knowing.

This unpredictability is manifest in the fall Elia conjures up in his figuring to Bridget the irredeemability of lost time. The theater is one among the multiple London spaces represented or mentioned in the mode of literary realism, which historically follows the invention of perspective in the West and which became the dominant symbolic mode of nineteenth-century Western European fiction. Remarkably, Lamb's essay participates in such realism with a wink. As paradigmatic space of representation, the theater joins the drawing room, with its "luxurious sofa," "well-carpeted fireside," little people, and miniature tea set, along with other sites enumerated in Bridget's speech, as spaces recognizable to the newly leisured, middle-class readers for whom Lamb's couple function as Lilliputian doubles. The fall in the space of the theater defamiliarizes and renders askew the very logic of dioramic realism that Lamb plays with in his familiar essay practice. "Old China" is an essay that registers an earthquake in the dollhouse of the ordinary. To soften the shock of this tremor, it offers as a remedy the injunction simply to look.

From another viewpoint, by other formal means, and in a different sociocultural context of address, Zhou Zuoren's "Wild Vegetables of My

Hometown" is also a familiar essay that raises the question of looking not just at but in Old China. Zhou's essay too divides into two parts: a conversational prologue and a second part consisting of a triptych of three consecutive paragraphs rich with visual details. In the prologue, the narrator speaks as if in address to the reader of having had multiple hometowns: eastern Zhejiang, Nanjing, Tokyo, and currently Beijing, the scene of writing. A few days ago, his wife had spotted the wild green known as *jicai*, or shepherd's purse, for sale at the local market. Not unlike Proust's madeleine in *À la recherche du temps perdu*, shepherd's purse functions as the device that transports the narrator to another place and time. The rest of the essay unfolds in that other place and time: eastern Zhejiang in an indeterminate spring or springs of the narrator's childhood. These springs parallel the present season of writing, April 1924 on the Gregorian calendar, or the third month of the lunar calendar. The latter serves as a calendar of reference for two festivals around which various details of the triptych are gathered. Each paragraph is taxonomically dedicated to a particular plant forageable in eastern Zhejiang: shepherd's purse, cudweed, and milkvetch. Each paragraph forms a discrete unit that resembles in scale a traditional album leaf painting and that mixes the expressivism of ink-and-brush painting with the figural and narrative detail of a finer brush style. Details repeat or appear only in one frame or another; motifs repeat and gather significance in repetition. At the very end of the essay, in what functions as a parting glance, the narrator draws the reader's eye to a focus wherein a subtle potentiality is released. I aim to explain in what follows how the effect of this moment of gentle restlessness is attained and to show the potentiality this kernel of restlessness holds.

In speaking of his hometowns in the prologue, the narrator shows himself to be a man whose sense of place and time involves a palimpsest of places in a personal history of displacement. He professes not to be too attached to his hometown. Or is it to *any* hometown, or is it to *the idea of* a hometown that he is so lightly attached? The formulation Zhou chooses in Chinese is not preceded by a genitive or demonstrative pronoun or any other qualification, so all the options mentioned, if not more, are possible. Hometowns are like neighbors rather than kin, he remarks: the habit of passing acquaintance gives rise to mild but real affections. Notably, the title in Chinese, *Guxiang de yecai*, also does not come with the genitive I have inserted in translation, "Wild Vegetables of *My* Hometown," primarily for metrical reasons.[26] The ambiguity of Zhou's formulation implies that the essayist's relationship to the local or what we would today call the locavore culture of eastern Zhejiang can be generalized to characterize any other's relationship to the terroir of their hometown. If, as mentioned, the hometown for the narrator is not one but plural, so is the relationship to the childhood hometown not direct but mediated. This mediatedness is apparent in the texture of references, quotations, and allusions that form the palimpsest of personal history, which itself overlaps with another, transindividual palimpsest of texts about the region from various authors and speakers from different times.

In what I have called the triptych, Zhou interweaves references and quotations relevant to each plant from a range of sources with sensorily detailed descriptions of human activities having to do with each plant. References and quotations include or derive from children's ditties; folk proverbs; a Ming-dynasty book of travel literature, *West Lake Sites*; and a Qing-dynasty almanac on local customs, the *Record of Qing Festivals*. Notably, these latter texts are cited as themselves citing local proverbs. Without citation, Zhou incorporates, as if in free indirect speech, language deriving from plant taxonomies as well as recipes. Beyond Chinese sources, he cites in the passage on milkvetch an entry from the *Japanese Haiku Dictionary* (*saijiki*) that groups the plant with dandelion in its commonness and its appeal to women and children. After this reference, he makes an offhanded archaeological-ethnographic remark that, since ancient times, the Chinese have not had the practice of making garlands, although children are fond of clustering balls of milkvetch for play. This offhanded remark subtly extends the geographical range of textual references in question to Greco-Roman pastoral poetry, where—he himself does not spell out but I annotate—garlands figure as a poetic convention linked to local practice. This cross-cultural allusion to an otherly pastoralism also discreetly indicates his sense of connection in this essay to a separate tradition of pastoral literature.

Through and in relation to this web of quotations, Zhou describes various human activities. In the paragraph on shepherd's purse, townswomen and children forage in backyards with scissors and baskets while peasants come to town to sell another kind of green. In the paragraph on cudweed, cakes are made by unseen hands out of the paste of cudweed leaves, children sing a ditty about how much they want to get their hands on the cakes and the cakes into their mouths, and families bring them to tombs of their ancestors as offerings. He zooms in on the shapes and sizes and mulls over the tastes of such cakes made in eastern Zhejiang as compared to Japan and Beijing. Besides direct description, Zhou selects quotations to open up more views onto these human figures. He uses details in the quotations themselves for "borrowed views" (the technique of *jiejing*) that add, from diverse angles, to the sensory richness of his narration.[27] The world of the hometown in spring opens up in the interplay between perspectives from a plurality of past and present sources. The quotation from *West Lake Sites* offers a first glimpse of men and women sporting flowers for personal adornment. The quotation from the *Record of Qing Festivals* opens up views of bunches of shepherd's purse on hearths to keep insects away, children selling foraged vegetables at dawn, and, in close-up, flowers adorning women's hairpins. Zhou's artful editorial use of these quotations suggests an affinity between their authors' connoisseurship of the common and ordinary in this landscape and his own eye, ear, and taste for local colors, folk rhymes and songs and the flavors of local confections. In these phenomena consist the pleasures of processes of labor, production, and reproduction. Notably, it is only in relation to such human activities in the foreground that views of the landscape open up: backyards, streets, and hearths in the first paragraph, hills or mountains in the second, fields and water in the third.

The dates of two spring festivals organize uses of the plants. The third day of the third month of the lunar calendar is one traditionally dedicated to love and romance. In relation to this date shepherd's purse flowers appear in the quotation from *West Lake Sites* as adornment on the persons of men and women. But it is the specific association of flowers with women that recurs across the triptych. The fifteenth day after the spring equinox, which can coincide with the third day of the third month, is the Qingming Festival, or Tomb-Sweeping Day, a major holiday dedicated to the honoring and remembrance of the dead. In relation to this date, cakes made of cudweed paste appear as offerings to be taken across water and up hillsides to the tombs. In relation to this day, flowers reappear as signifiers that hover in significance between erotic promise and the remembrance of death.

The essay ends with an image of flowers in a parting glance for both narrator and reader. The final sentence in Chinese divides into two parts around a semicolon. As it is difficult to translate this sentence as a single sentence in English, I render it as two, departing from aspects of the literal sense but conveying, I hope, the multiple syntactical appositions in the composition.

> In eastern Zhejiang, tomb-sweeping takes place with the banging of cymbals and blowing of horns, so in my youth, I'd follow the music to catch sight of "The Lovely Lasses on the Boats to the Tombs." Families with no money had

no wind and percussion, but a posy of milkvetch and azaleas peering from under the canopy over the prow would give sure proof that the boat was headed for the tombs.

浙東掃墓用鼓吹，所以少年常隨了樂音去看《上墳船裡的姣姣》；沒有錢的人家雖沒鼓吹，但是船頭上蓬窗下總露出些紫雲英和杜鵑的花束，這也就是上墳船的確實的證據了。(111)

This final sentence, two in my translation, guides the reader's eye in a scanning motion that follows the procession and then the youth following the procession toward the water. It next draws the reader's eye to a posy of flowers. With quiet precision, this image, I claim, occasions a lingering effect that has the capacity to continue moving the reader after the page is turned. How does it do so?

I offer two annotations of my translation. First, where I use the first-person pronoun and genitive in the first sentence, Zhou uses none in Chinese (although he had done so in the sentence immediately prior). The absence of the "I" here, a grammatical option with classical antecedents in his writing of the modern vernacular, opens up the referent of "youth," *shaonian*, beyond the particular youth in question to a generality of youths who may take his place in this rite of spring. Second, it is notable that "The Lovely Lasses on the Boats to the Tombs" is a phrase that derives from the third line of a folk rhyme on monthly festivities.

The first sentence offers images accompanied by what can be likened to diegetic sound until it enters, precisely at the moment the folk rhyme is quoted, the domain of interiority. The quotation, detached as an idiomatic expression, had entered the youth's memory: it may be ringing in his ears, or he may even be reciting it in anticipation, as he follows the processional music. Silence follows in the remark about the privation of money accompanying the privation of sound. Against the emergent quiet appears the posy of flowers. These flowers serve as a hint of femininity, betokening the anticipation of femininity becoming visible outside of gendered sequestration on a spring festival day. As such, they signify also the desire of the gentry youth, the past self of the narrator. Remembered here is the desire of the youthful self, directed toward a femininity that is here a femininity across class lines. I take this femininity to be metonymic of a more general, capacious sense of erotic futurity. The gaze of the youth looks forward in time, while the gaze of the adult narrator looks retrospectively back at—and also through—the youth's gaze. These gazes converge upon the image of flowers, a precarious signifier of both death and of erotic futurity as the potential survival of death. This object of sight is not static but moves in gentle undulation with the boat and the waves beneath the boat. In this very gathering, offered to the reader as a parting glance, futurity opens up as the potential for renewal.

This futurity is not just nostalgically located in the past but activated in the present of narration in 1924 Beijing and potentially reactivated in the present of reading. It originates where the gaze of the youth meets the gaze of the adult without merging into one. The difference between the outward- and forward-looking desirous percipience of the child and the knowledge of the adult is the condition for origination as *re*origination. Beyond its capacity to say directly, Zhou's essay performs an idea concerning origination reiterated in classical Chinese thought. With respect to the concept of *xin*, the term for interiority and subjectivity that comprehends what English separates as "mind" and "heart," a quote from Mencius says, "The great or virtuous man does not lose the mind-heart of the child" (大人者，不失赤子之心也).[28] In his "Discourse on the Childlike Mind-Heart," the late Ming heterodox thinker Li Zhi writes that "just as the child is the beginning of the human, the mind-heart of the child is the beginning of the mind-heart."[29] With the posy of milkvetch and azaleas, upon which the desirous gaze of the percipient child and the knowing gaze of the adult converge, Zhou allegorizes a principle of origination that depends upon the movement activated in the gap between percipient sensibility and ordered knowledge, or *daoli*.

Within the essay, Zhou's quotations from *West Lake Sites*, *Record of Qing Festivals*, the *Japanese Haiku Dictionary*, and his subtle allusion to Greco-Roman pastoral poetry do not quote simply for the sake of restating knowledge or information. Rather, they facilitate "borrowed views" onto the sensibilia of ordinary life that derive from a plurality of sources: flowers on a hairpin, local sayings, children plucking dandelions, making garlands out of flowers. With the authors and compilers of these traditional texts, he shares the taxonomic impulse of ordering knowledge. But, with them, the essay implies, he shares also a taxonomic lyricism wherein a childlike drive to percipience keeps the process of ordering the knowledge of the ordinary from reifying into an ordered knowledge of the ordinary. Insofar as the restlessness of this taxonomic lyricism is radically driven by mere percipience, it reverberates with the drive to see that keeps Lamb's dioramic realism from ever quite getting into balance.

Distant Peers

What does it mean, I ask finally, to read Lamb and Zhou as distant peers of one another? The words of a contemporary poet may help with the question. At a symposium for international writers in New Delhi in

December 2017, the Bengali poet Joy Goswami remained quiet in the final workshop, listening attentively to the discussion taking place in multiple languages—Spanish, Arabic, Mandarin Chinese—with English as the medium of translation.[30] He broke his silence by offering remarks at the end in Bengali, which the poet and the host of the symposium, Sharmistha Mohanty, translated approximately thus: "I have been so happy to listen in the last few days to poets speaking of their work in their own languages. I have heard rivers flow that seem to flow from inner rivers in them. I have been so happy to hear how those rivers come together."[31]

To read Lamb and Zhou as distant peers of one another is to listen to different rivers flowing from inner rivers. These rivers are in different languages. They bespeak lifeworlds that are shared in different ways. Each addresses his readers as peers in the form of the familiar essay. That is to say, each addresses them as equals within shared worlds at moments of transition from traditional sociopolitical hierarchies. Lamb figures his readers as average, middle-class subjects not unlike his persona Elia. The poetics of his dioramic realism emerges to reflect the very condition of these readers' averageness, a statistical concept that was part and parcel of the infrastructure of the ordinary emergent in the age of political economy. Remarkably, Lamb's writing also sheds light on the limitations and precarious provisionality of the realist construction of the ordinary. In its gentle subversiveness, this writing does not propose that the edifice should be torn down entirely but that it remains a work-in-progress whose improvement takes place in the increment of the everyday. Zhou Zuoren addresses his readers at a moment when a shared Chinese social world was undergoing radical reorganization in the direction of a standard global model that relies on building materials from the realist architecture of the ordinary. He uses the mode of taxonomic lyricism as a medium of address to the reader, recovering in the ordering tendencies of traditional Chinese thought and discourse terms for a decentralized and pluralist inhabitation of the ordinary.

While both Lamb and Zhou work in the medium of a similar form, their essayistic practices tap into different traditions of skeptical questioning. Such skepticism manifests itself negatively in the suspensive interrogation of the essays' own conditions of meaning and modes of expression. In this suspension, sheer percipience itself becomes manifest as that which activates and reactivates, inherits and regenerates, culturally and historically specific codes and logics of subjection. That these codes and logics of subjection are not the same makes the conversation between Lamb and Zhou as distant peers necessarily an oblique one. Lamb and Zhou may each seek to address their readers as peers, deranging the stability of their respective grounds of cohabitation; but the relationship between Lamb and Zhou as peers does not rest on the even grounds of what would be homogeneous, mathematical space.

To read Lamb and Zhou as distant peers is to listen to the heterogeneous sources of different rivers flowing. Doing so involves putting into question the prejudices of the satellitic supra-perspective that governs our everyday lives today, that forms and deforms our local modes of inhabitation while uniformizing our global sense of the ordinary for the expedient purposes of information and exchange. The question of the distant peer is the question of how to listen to the rivers today.

4 Between the Theater and the Novel

Woman, Modernity, and the Restaging of the Ordinary in *Mansfield Park* and *The Rouge of the North*

It is notable that more than a few general readers, as well as scholars of Eileen Chang, have sought to define her appeal beyond the Chinese-speaking world by comparing her to Jane Austen, cursorily if not systematically. In a 2018 article in the *New York Review of Books*, Louisa Chiang and Perry Link make the comparison on a thematic level when they write that Chang's "brilliant short novels . . . are reminiscent of Austen in their preoccupation with romantic and family relationships portrayed against a backdrop of upper-class dysfunction in a semicolonial world."[1] In his Introduction to a 2012 collection of essays on Chang, Kam Louie zooms in on a similarity of style: "Like Jane Austen, to whom she is often compared, [Chang] was . . . adept at dissecting in minute detail the mundane things in life that affect human relationships."[2] In a 2016 article in the *South China Morning Post*, an anonymous reviewer highlights tonal affinities that complement thematic ones, writing that Chang's "characters' tragic yet sometimes comical attempts to navigate unfair expectations and maintain illusions of proper manners resonate with all readers regardless of background. These experiences are even reminiscent of the struggles of Jane Austen's protagonists."[3] On thematic and stylistic levels, in terms of tone and characterization, Chang and Austen present resonances to their readers.

Chang and Austen wrote over a century and a quarter apart. Austen published her six major novels in the 1810s. Chang was most active at the beginning of her career in the 1940s, bursting onto the literary scene of wartime Shanghai with her essays, short stories, and novellas. She would continue writing into the 1990s. Her fifty-year career saw an extraordinary amount of mobility that bespeaks the turbulence of mid-century Chinese history. Before her death in Los Angeles in 1995, she had moved in the 1940s from Shanghai to Hong Kong and back, then after the Communist Revolution of 1949 to Hong Kong again in 1952. From Hong Kong she emigrated to the United States in 1955, where she would then move from the East Coast to the West. Motivated by war, revolution, and civil strife, Chang's itinerancy stands out in contrast to the relative placidity of Austen's life and circumstances, which would seem to have facilitated Austen in her famous, self-appointed task of working on "three or four families in a country village" in each of her novels.[4]

Having received a bilingual education, Chang wrote not just in Chinese but in English. She began publishing essays in English already in the 1940s, in English-language journals in Shanghai, around the same time as she was making a name for herself as a brilliant new talent in Chinese fiction. She would later translate her own work as well as that of others from Chinese into English.[5] While in Hong Kong from 1952 to 1955, she wrote two novels in English, *The Rice-Sprout Song* and *Naked Earth*, on commission from the United States Information Service as Cold War propaganda. After emigrating to the United States, she returned to her acclaimed 1943 novella *Jinsuo ji*, expanding it into a novel in English called *Pink Tears*, which she shelved after it was rejected for publication by Knopf.[6] She would return several times to her 1943 text by translating it into English as *The Golden Cangue* and expanding it into novels in Chinese and English concurrently in 1966–67 as *Yuannü* and *The Rouge of the North*.[7] This return to older material seems part of a general tendency in her post-exile or emigration writing to revisit the scenes and settings of Republican China. In a new and foreign land, confined by the rigid ideological divisions of the Cold War, Chang took to casting retrospective glances at the early twentieth-century Chinese past. Indeed, she would continue to train her gaze on the mundane details of romantic and family relationships in Shanghai and Hong Kong in ways evocative of Austen's working on "three or four families in a country village."

Already during her lifetime and even more so after her death, Chang has been considered one of the finest writers of modern Chinese fiction and one of the finest Chinese women writers *tout court*. So it is notable but not surprising that, while readers of Chang have repeatedly compared her to Austen in seeking to recommend her, readers and scholars of Austen have rarely, if ever, done the same. On an obvious level, this imbalance bespeaks general global asymmetries of cultural power and cross-cultural literacy that have persisted into the twenty-first century. However, there is an imbalance internal to Chang's own work that may accompany the imbalance between Chang's and Austen's statuses as world literary figures. If Chang's writings in Chinese devote themselves to the continued potential of a fractured and transformed Chinese literary and cultural tradition, her writings in English likewise continue to prioritize China as the primary ground of creative origination. She wrote as an exile and emigrant, not an immigrant. While her writings in Chinese make her a figure of major importance and vital influence in the Chinese-speaking world, her writings in English, her translations, and the translations of her work into English have resulted by and large only in her status as a niche curiosity in English-language letters. Attempts to classify her as a Chinese American writer in the immigrant model seem only to have further enhanced the awkward fracturing of her reception. The case of Eileen Chang puts to the test what is understood as a "woman writer of world importance." From another angle—one responsive to the vantage points that the works of Chang and Austen themselves present —the question may be put somewhat differently: what might it mean to read the category of the "world" itself through the category of "woman"? That is a critical question, I claim, that the works of Chang and Austen pose in radical and resonant ways to their readers.

I pursue this question in this chapter by focusing on two novels, Austen's 1814 *Mansfield Park* and Chang's 1967 *The Rouge of the North*, which she published in Chinese with the title *Yuannü*, literally "resentful" or "embittered woman." I approach them as cross-cultural instances of the "domestic novel," a form associated with the household as traditionally the domain of women's lives. In each novel, the principal site of action is the household: in *Mansfield Park*, the eponymous Northamptonshire estate, and in *The Rouge of the North*, centrally if not solely, the traditional imperial-bureaucratic Yao family compound in Shanghai. Both novels are told by omniscient third-person narrators and focalized through female protagonists. Strangely, these protagonists are widely considered improbable or unlikable, or improbable because unlikable, heroines. Fanny Price is not only considered meek and unassertive among the characters of *Mansfield Park*—"little more than an observant stillness," writes one critic—but is also the least animated among all of Austen's heroines.[8] Indeed, the peculiar blandness of her characterization has contributed to *Mansfield Park*'s reputation as the "problem novel" in Austen's oeuvre. And, as *Yuannü*, the Chinese title of *The Rouge of the North*, clearly indicates, Yindi is resentful and vindictive, a victim turned victimizer given to everyday acts of petty and ultimately futile sadism. It is safe to say that few readers want to be like Fanny or Yindi. Austen and Chang make use of these protagonists to displace readerly attention away from psychological identification and sympathy to notice instead shifting structures of authority and frameworks of meaning that condition the protagonists' inhabitations of their respective households.

Significantly, both novels incorporate elements of theater and theatricality in their examinations of women in households undergoing changing structural logics at moments of historical transition. *Mansfield Park* incorporates rehearsals of a recent play, Elizabeth Inchbald's *Lovers' Vows* (1798), and the reading of a Jacobean one, *Henry VIII* (1613), attributed in Austen's time to Shakespeare but today considered cowritten by Shakespeare and John Fletcher. *The Rouge of the North* notably incorporates into its narration an aspect absent from the earlier novella versions of the story: references to Peking opera as the source of lines, roles, and scenes that serve as analogues for characters to find meaning and orientation in their lives. Besides providing a cultural repertoire, Peking opera also functions offstage in the novel as a professional institution whose changes Yindi beholds with confused fascination. In each case, the novel defines itself as a modern literary form genealogically in relation to theatrical traditions, which appear in both works as historically changing and culturally specific frameworks for the aesthetic mediation of community. Both novels displace and take on aspects of the work of theater, I argue, by restaging "woman" as modern agent and spectatorial subject on the plane of the ordinary. The novels educate readers thereby in the work of accommodating the ordinary and shed light on the delicate task of cohabiting a shared modernity.

Households and Heroines: Sites of Revision, Subjects in Revision

Lionel Trilling begins his now classic 1972 book of European literary and intellectual history, *Sincerity and Authenticity*, with a sentence of magisterial ease: "Now and then it is possible to observe the moral life in process of revising itself."[9] The particular "now and then" he identifies for the focus of his study begins in the second half of the eighteenth century, with *Mansfield Park* featuring significantly for him as a key text of this period in which the aforesaid process of revision presents itself as legible and evident.[10] Trilling's argument bases itself on his observation that, during this time, the terms "sincerity" and "authenticity" emerged as salient criteria for the evaluation of selfhood, which was increasingly seen to be determined by immanent social forces rather than by a transcendentally located authority. Trilling historicizes this shift as modern, one accompanying the secularizing turn constitutive of the radical redefinition of the grounds of moral and political authority in Britain and Europe.

Following Trilling, I affirm that a revision of the moral life is indeed evident in *Mansfield Park* and that such a process of revision is, furthermore, an enactment of particular dynamics of British and European modernity, although I differ with specific aspects of his reading of the novel—to which I will return in a later section of this chapter. But Trilling's insight into the general literary and intellectual historical importance of *Mansfield Park* can also ground a comparative juxtaposition of Austen's novel with Chang's *The Rouge of the North*, which, I argue, represents another moment, another "now and then," when the moral life presents itself in processes of revision. In staging the revision of moral life, I furthermore claim, both novels enact asynchronous, heterogeneous transitions into modernity in England and China.

At issue, in other words, is the connection each work exposes, and the connections they expose in each other, between a historical experience and critique of modernity, on the one hand, and domesticity on the other. As domestic novels, *Mansfield Park* and *The Rouge of the North* take the household, traditionally the domain of both feminine and ordinary life in England and China, as the principal site of action. As has been amply established, the form of the domestic novel itself came to prominence in eighteenth- and nineteenth-century England as a form written by and for women. Overlapping with the mode of sentimental fiction, its emergence coincided with the rise of the novel itself.[11] Following such writers as Samuel Richardson and Frances Burney, Austen came to be known as a key practitioner of the domestic novel, with her novels and the manipulation of the marriage plot therein eventually taken to be exemplary of the form itself. In China, the early twentieth century saw a rapid increase in the number both of women writing and writing for women, a phenomenon made possible by the transformation of traditional, patriarchal practices of gender organization after the 1911 Revolution and the consequent liberalization of educational and professional opportunities for women. Shanghai, the most cosmopolitan and outward-looking of China's cities in the early twentieth century, afforded such opportunities in particular. By the 1940s, when Chang began to publish her writings, Shanghai had fostered a robust literary scene even during wartime where young women could become visible and active as writers, editors, and public intellectuals. Nicole Huang has traced, in *Women, War, Domesticity: Shanghai Literature and Popular Culture of the 1940s*, how "the distinctive trademark of women's cultural practices in occupied Shanghai is the focus on the realm of the domestic."[12] The writing of domesticity during this time had numerous sources, both Chinese and Western. Within the tradition of Chinese fiction, the writing of domestic fiction in the 1940s, with thematic emphasis on love, marriage, and family life, had antecedents in the talent-beauty, or *caizi jiaren*, novels and the mandarin-duck-and butterfly, or *yuanyang hudie*, novels popular, respectively, in the early Qing (seventeenth- and eighteenth-century) and late Qing, early Republican (late nineteenth, early twentieth-century) periods.[13] For Chang, in the 1940s and beyond, the most significant influences for her writing were the greatest of China's family novels, Cao Xueqin's *The Dream of the Red Chamber* (1791) and what may be termed a para-domestic novel of courtesan life, Han Bangqing's 1892–94 *Sing-Song Girls of Shanghai*, which Chang would begin translating in 1967 from the Wu dialect into both Mandarin Chinese and English, around the time that she published *The Rouge of the North* and *Yuannü*.[14] While using conventions from traditional Chinese fiction such as an episodic narrative structure, with loosely concatenated events—in contrast to the teleological directedness and temporal compression of the marriage plot—Chang nevertheless shows the influence of the nineteenth-century European domestic novel in her focalization of narrative through a single heroine, abstracted from the multiplicity of characters typical in Ming-Qing fiction. As an instance of such a singularized heroine, Yindi in *The Rouge of the North* exhibits ostensible parity with Fanny Price in *Mansfield Park*. These novels call upon their readers to scrutinize the predicaments of such singularized heroines in their respective household settings.

Austen and Chang may be said to approach the depiction of their heroines and households in the capacity of historians. That is to say, they depict in the realist mode the fictional worlds of their characters in ways that reflect particular historical actualities. While Austen cannot be said to bring an outright historicizing consciousness to her work on three or four families in a country village, the keenness of her observations of her contemporary world has made her novels appear to critics, increasingly in recent years, as repositories of historical insight into a changing English cultural milieu.[15] While she maintains the focus of her novels on gentry village life, she incorporates into this purview angles that open up onto issues of national and global significance: the Napoleonic Wars, English reaction to French revolutionary radicalism, abolition, colonialism, and imperialism. Since Edward Said's pathbreaking remarks in "Jane Austen and Empire" in 1993, *Mansfield Park* has figured with special importance in Austen's oeuvre as a text in which local goings-on at a Northamptonshire estate link to processes taking place at national and global levels.[16] While

Austen may function effectively, if not knowingly, as a historian of her contemporary moment, Chang in contrast brings a deliberately historicizing perspective to the period of transition from late imperial to Republican China. She would return again and again in her fictional work, as she herself moved farther and farther away in time and space, to this period as one of critical importance for Chinese modernity. In her essays of the 1940s, notably in the poetological "Writing of One's Own," she thematized this era as one in which "the old things are being swept away and the new things are still being born" and claimed that it is "this era that constitutes my artistic material."[17] In the same essay, she also explains that her writerly stance toward the era will not be from the perspective of the heroic, so often preferred in the rhetoric of nation-building reformism. "An emphasis on the uplifting and dynamic smacks more or less of the superman," she writes, "but the placid and static aspects have eternal significance: even if this sort of stability is often precarious and subject at regular intervals to destruction" (WO, 16). Throughout her oeuvre, Chang trains her gaze on the "placid and static" aspects of life, which, according to her, serve as the very "grounding" (*dizi*) for the "uplifting and dynamic," which may appear as just so much "froth" (*fumo*) in relation to the former (WO, 16). In *The Rouge of the North*, she thus maintains the focus of the narration on the domestic and familial, every now and then inserting, with the precision of a fine needle, allusions to dates and events of national importance. The sixtieth birthday party of a family patriarch becomes, for instance, the occasion for an offhand mention of civil unrest inland that has affected the Shanghai partygoers' sources of income. Like Austen, but with a more self-consciously historicizing bent, Chang makes large-scale processes of historical change legible with her foregrounding of the domestic and the quotidian.

Let us turn now to the two particular households in question in *Mansfield Park* and *The Rouge of the North*. These serve as the primary scenes of action and frameworks of significance for the heroines Fanny and Yindi. The narration of *Mansfield Park* begins with the affairs of the previous generation that had led to the child Fanny's arrival at Mansfield at age ten as the impoverished ward of her maternal aunt and uncle and swiftly moves by the end of Chapter 3 to Fanny at sixteen. The rest of the novel concentrates on the two or three years after Fanny reaches marriageable age and ends, of course, in keeping with the marriage plot, in her union with her cousin Edmund Bertram and ascendancy to the position of custodian, if not full mistress, of Mansfield Park. The narration of *The Rouge of the North* dilates over thirty-five years: it begins with Yindi becoming a bride at age eighteen and ends with her at fifty-three, now a widow, a grandmother, and a frustrated would-be matriarch. Like Fanny, Yindi marries "up" socially and economically. The orphaned daughter of sesame oil shopkeepers, she ascends the socioeconomic hierarchy by consenting to the marriage her brother and sister-in-law arrange for her to the blind and invalid second son of the Yao family, whose wealth and power were based on high-ranking service in the imperial bureaucracy. With her marriage, she moves physically from above the sesame oil shop to the multi-generational, multi-branched Yao family compound, then after the death of Old Mistress Yao, into a reduced "old, foreign-styled house" where she sets herself up as mistress with power over her son and a few retainers and, eventually, her son's wife, his concubine, and their children (99). While the action of *Mansfield Park* unfolds almost entirely in the eponymous country house, three consecutive domestic spaces serve as the scenes for the narration of episodes in Yindi's life. Nevertheless, among these spaces, it is the Yao household that serves as the epicenter of power and significance in Yindi's world, even in the 1940s, at the end of the novel, when its hierarchical operating logic and sociocultural organizing function seem out of sync with the changing times. *Mansfield Park* shows the conjoined movements of a household and a heroine toward positions of sociocultural exemplarity. In contrast, *The Rouge of the North* shows a heroine clinging on to a household logic that was becoming gradually superseded, with both heroine and household moving toward positions of sociocultural decadence and uncertainty.

What kind of a household is Mansfield Park? On the face of it, the estate seems comparable in status to other country houses named in the novel: Sotherton Court, the seat of the Rushworths nearby, and Ecclesford, the seat of a Lord Ravenshaw in Cornwall. Yet, we learn from one of the visitors to Mansfield, Mary Crawford, that Mansfield is not a hereditary estate but a "modern-built house."[18] Newly arrived from London to visit with her half-sister, Mrs. Grant, Mary surveys the estate with matrimonial prospects in mind, assessing the property thus: "a park, a real park five miles round, a spacious modern-built house, so well placed and well screened as to deserve to be in any collection of engravings of gentlemen's seats in the kingdom" (35). This particular gentleman's seat may take its place among estates that derive their wealth and power from a feudal-agricultural basis, but the substance of its wealth derives not from local land and labor but from elsewhere. Antigua figures in the novel as the distant and unseen site of Sir Thomas's business interests, most likely but not altogether unambiguously a sugar plantation. It is to Antigua that Sir Thomas goes away early in the novel, accompanied part of the time by his eldest son, Thomas, to attend to affairs that, according to the critical consensus, probably have to do with the recent abolition of the slave trade in 1807.[19] While the country house unit of Mansfield Park may manifest its power and exhibit its cultural significance locally in the county of Northampton—and nationally in relation to other like estates—it depends for this manifestation on wealth acquired far away across the Atlantic, through a newly evolving slave labor force. While maintaining the focus on Mansfield, Austen's narration casts peripheral glances to other sites—Antigua, London, Portsmouth, Liverpool—to suggest the commercial and colonial-imperialist foundations undergirding what appears at first glance to be an estate of the traditional landed aristocracy, complete with neighboring parsonage. What Austen's narration suggests without stating overtly is that the grounds sustaining the English country house as a political economic unit seem to be shifting from a feudal-agricultural to a commercial-colonialist basis. The latter assumes the trappings of the former while gradually rendering outmoded the substance of its power.

To this household built on colonial commerce and distant slave labor and secured with a baronetcy of probably recent acquisition, Fanny Price arrives as an unentitled and misplaced outsider. She is allotted first an attic room and then the room of the governess, a space that indicates her spatial and social marginality within the structure of the household. By the end of the novel, Fanny will achieve a sense of belonging at Mansfield Park. She will marry the second son of the family and move with him into the parsonage, which the syntactically complex last sentence of the novel informs us in its last part became "as dear to her heart, and as thoroughly perfect in her eyes, as every thing else, within the view and patronage of Mansfield Park had long been" (321). Fanny's probity of character and constancy of judgment are confirmed by her steady conduct and clear-eyed anticipation of the hectic turns of events in the dénouement—adultery, elopements, and mercenariness, on the part of other characters. Sir Thomas realizes, the narration concludes, in another of its strangely endogamous touches, that "Fanny was indeed the daughter that he wanted" (320). By the end, rightful occupancy, if not proprietorship, of Mansfield Park will come to be defined by criteria other than birth and rank. Fanny's "triumph" shows the estate as a hierarchical formal structure that admits access and mobility to those who recognize and affirm its formal justice. In terms of overall narrative action, *Mansfield Park* stages a change in the terms of entitlement to the commercial-colonial estate as a political economic unit of England as nation-state and imperial power, with Fanny as representative ordinary subject.

Like Fanny, Yindi is an outsider when she moves into the Yao household. She marries up in a mercenary arrangement, leaving the sesame oil shop to take her place in a "big family" household as wife to the second of the Yao sons. While she lives in the Yao family compound for only around twelve of the thirty-five years in the narration, or five out of the fifteen chapters of the novel, the ordering structure operative there continues to dictate Yindi's sense of social status and identity. Even after moving out after the death of her mother-in-law, she would continue talking in "stage whispers hissed across the room" in her new abode, for "anybody who has lived in a big family," the narration wryly notes, "could never get over the habit of whispering" (99). The boundaries and protocol of the family compound transfer themselves acoustically beyond the walls of the actual grand household itself.

The wealth and power of the Yao family derived from high-ranking service in the imperial-bureaucratic system of the Qing dynasty. It is clear that the deceased Old Master Yao had been a powerful and well-connected government official, although details of rank and duration of service—and the status of the Yaos in previous generations—remain ambiguous. All information pertaining to this question is filtered through the limited perspective of the poorly educated, at best semi-literate, Yindi. The narration repeatedly notes that the Yaos are from the north, perhaps Beijing—it is not clear—and only recent transplants to Shanghai, with its markedly different mercantile culture and the presence of foreign concessions. They are a traditional gentry-bureaucratic family, and the multi-generational, multi-branched household operates according to the principles of patriarchy and seniority, in conformity with the Confucian hierarchical ordering of relations. While she was alive, Old Mistress Yao exercised authority, both de facto and de jure, as the widowed matriarch in the domain. Yet she, too, as a woman, was confined to the household as a sequestered space or orbit, with only attenuated and indirect power over the affairs the men of the family could conduct beyond the jurisdiction and purview of the household. As a Yao daughter-in-law, Yindi is positioned within this structure, which is further complicated by the distinction between wives and concubines in a system of polygamy. Beyond the walls of the household, the gender economy gets complicated further by the extramarital category of singsong girls and, as Yindi is surprised to find, Peking opera female impersonators. Entering the Yao family household, Yindi acquires both the status and the limitations of being the wife of the Second Master of the family. That this Second Master is blind and sickly is accidental, rather than essential, to his position and to the position she derives from him by right.

Chang situates this household and its organizing logic at a cuspal moment of historical change. Subtending the timeline from Yindi's marriage at eighteen to the end of the narration when she is fifty-three is a timeline that dates from the last two or three years of the Qing dynasty, 1909–11 or so, to the early 1940s, when Shanghai was under Japanese wartime occupation. While the familial calendar and domestic events take precedence and occupy the foreground of the narration, glimpses are offered every now and then of events and developments of national significance. At the aforementioned sixtieth birthday party of a Yao patriarch, for instance, the general narratorial reticence about dates gives way to an exceptional explicitness. This dating is prompted by the question of whether a lavish celebration, including a Peking opera performance, would be socially in good form at the time.

> In their set such displays would seem out of place after the fall of the empire even if it was already twenty years after. They were people who had lost their country, so to speak, finding shelter in the foreign settlements. Their land in the interior was exposed to civil wars.... (133)

> 在姚家這圈子裏似乎不大得體。雖然大家不提這些，到底清朝亡了國了，說得上家仇國恨，托庇在外國租界上，二十年來內地老是不太平[20]

With the end of the Qing in 1911, this party would be taking place in the early 1930s, if "twenty years" is taken as an approximation, rather than a precise number of years. In the intervening time, the practice of footbinding had been abolished, the New Culture Movement of 1919 had transformed intellectual life, the Chinese Communist Party had formed in Shanghai in 1924, and brutal purges of political enemies by the Kuomintang government under Chiang Kai-Shek had taken place in 1927. And in 1931, an increasingly militaristic Japan would occupy Manchuria. Writing retrospectively to create the vignette of Yindi at a family celebration in 1931, Chang casts a deliberately historicizing gaze on this past moment. The character Yindi's attention is trained, however, on the immediate particulars before her, and her perspective on the goings-on is organized according to the framework of the traditional household. The unknowingness of this perspective as well as the fragility of this framework are brought into view by Chang's lightly but surely historicizing gesture, deftly transmitted in the somewhat catty, insiderish remarks of the narrator. Over a period of radical change involving republican politics and factional fighting as well as educational and cultural reform and the promotion of the education and sexual autonomy of women, the traditional household had become increasingly precarious as articulating framework for women's identity and agency.

As domestic novels, *Mansfield Park* and *The Rouge of the North* show households as sites of moral and political revision at moments of historical transition. The eponymous estate in *Mansfield Park* functions as a microcosm wherein the authority of England as a commercial society and colonialist power undergoes redefinition on the premises of a feudal-manorial model. Fanny serves in the novel as both the prime subject and observer of such processes of revision. In *The Rouge of the North*, the household figures as a site where traditional hierarchical articulations of authority gradually lose their efficacy. This crisis of the household is a function of a wider-scale reorganization of the relationship between the household and the state itself, as both move away from their earlier grounding in a Confucian system of familial and social ordering and political administration. Yindi functions in the novel as the subject caught in the confusion of such changes. Her confusion and indeed recalcitrance bespeak, curiously, Chang's double critique of both traditional patriarchy and positive, even triumphalist definitions of modernity that would seek simply to substitute for the old certitudes.

In the next sections, I examine how Austen and Chang incorporate theater and theatricality in *Mansfield Park* and *The Rouge of the North* as domestic novels. How might the household itself be considered a stage? What might the emergence of the household as stage in these novels show readers about the task of being modern?

Mansfield Park and the Drama of Ordination

In Volume 1, Chapters 13–17 of *Mansfield Park*, Austen inserts into the novel preparations for the staging of a play. John Yates, a friend of the younger Thomas Bertram, arrives at Mansfield from another country house, Ecclesford, "with his head full of acting" (86). He soon spreads his enthusiasm to most of the young people gathered there. Sir Thomas has been away in Antigua, delayed by business there. In his absence, he puts not his wife, the indolent Lady Bertram, in charge but her officious sister, Mrs. Norris, who also catches the "infection" of acting.[21] The party decides to rehearse *Lovers' Vows*, the same 1798 play by Elizabeth Inchbald that the party at Ecclesford had been rehearsing. All but Fanny and Edmund embrace the project, although Edmund eventually gives in. Fanny alone maintains her refusal to act in the play, on the grounds that doing so would violate a sense of household decorum. Facing pressure, she agrees to serve instead as prompter, assuming a position that puts her on the threshold of the play, indeed, on the threshold of the play and the novel. In the middle of rehearsals, Sir Thomas returns suddenly to Mansfield. The performance never takes place, for Sir Thomas disapproves, for reasons never made entirely clear, of play-acting and converting the house into a theater.

This episode of private theatricals has been the subject of a great deal of critical attention.[22] In *Sincerity and Authenticity*, Lionel Trilling reads Fanny's resistance to play-acting as akin to Rousseau's critique of the theater and the danger of hypocrisy posed by theatricality in the *Letter to D'Alembert*, among other writings.[23] Fanny, like Rousseau, according to Trilling, defends a notion of selfhood and a vision of moral conduct impervious to impersonation and self-dramatization, in contrast to the Crawford siblings from London, whose metropolitan predilection for theatricality seems to indicate a purely commercialist disregard for the difference between seeming and being. Trilling finds, moreover, Fanny's constancy of judgment and conduct—what Tony Tanner calls her being "never, ever wrong"—an exceptional example of categorical judgment rather than the dialectical mode that characterizes the learning processes of Austen's other heroines.[24] This unwaveringness on the part of Fanny makes her appear priggish, and it makes her seem a flatter character than Elizabeth Bennet, Elinor Dashwood, or Emma Woodhouse.[25] Indeed, in her characterization as a placeholder heroine making her way as an outsider in unaccommodating environs, Fanny resembles K. in Kafka's *The Castle* rather more than Elizabeth Bennet visiting Pemberley. Organizing the empiricist thickness of Austen's narration is a rigorous, abstract formalism that lays bare the structural logic of the household as primary scene of novelistic action. Contrary to Trilling's argument that Fanny occupies a position resistant to or outside of social life as a quasi-theatrical realm of appearances and imitations, I argue that the novel shows, rather, beginning with Fanny's refusal to act in *Lovers' Vows*, her exemplification of a different logic of inhabiting and acting in the household construed figuratively as stage of the modern.[26]

When beginning to work on *Mansfield Park*, Austen had written cryptically to her sister Cassandra, "Now I will try to write of something else;—and it shall be a complete change of subject—ordination."[27] The remark had long been taken by readers, including Tanner and Trilling (in an essay separate from *Sincerity and Authenticity*), to pertain to Edmund, who as the second of the Bertram sons is expected, in keeping with the patterns of primogeniture, to take orders in the Church of England and who eventually does so after being tested by his initial love interest, Mary Crawford.[28] In recent years, readers such as Michael Karounos and Daniel Stout have argued instead that Fanny is the novel's principal subject of ordination, with "ordination" taken to denote "arrangement in orders and classes" in general, rather than the specific arrangement of taking clerical orders.[29] I incline toward this shift to Fanny as the focal subject of the social ordering system at Mansfield Park, although I acknowledge that the ambiguity in the term "ordination" continues to be sustained in the novel in the union between Fanny and Edmund.

Mansfield Park stages its drama of sociopolitical ordination by incorporating within its narration two plays: *Lovers' Vows* and, less conspicuously, *Henry VIII* in Volume 3. The novel's drama of ordination, I contend, establishes itself genealogically in relation to these two plays. I propose now to examine how Austen makes use of these plays to advance the drama of ordination that constitutes the principal action of the novel.

After the party at Mansfield decide to stage a play, they then settle upon Inchbald's *Lovers' Vows*. Its appeal, exclaimed by Tom Bertram and endorsed by the others, was that it had been attempted at the Ravenshaws. Austen thus presents Inchbald's 1798 play as a choice for Regency-era country house theatricals, letting the irony of the choice present itself rather than commenting on it in the narration outright. Inchbald's play, adapted from August von Kotzebue's 1791 sentimental melodrama *Das Kind der Liebe*, had its premiere at Covent Garden in 1798 and was then performed on various stages in Bristol, Bath, and Newcastle.[30] If the principal events of *Mansfield Park* can be ascertained to date around 1810–13, the play would have been known for around ten to fifteen years.[31] Like its German prototype, Inchbald's play takes place in a mythical feudal domain ruled by the Baron von Wildenhaim, whose past misdeeds have come back to haunt him in the present. Exercising *droit du seigneur*, he had impregnated and abandoned in his youth a young villagewoman, Agatha. Both Agatha, now a beggarwoman, and the son he had disowned, Frederick, have returned to the vicinity, recognizing each other after a long separation. The play ends with the Baron's reconciliation with his illegitimate son and with him granting the marriage of his legitimate daughter Amelia to her tutor, Anhalt, rather than the foppish Count von Cassel. *Lovers' Vows* thus stages a familial drama of class dehierarchization in which patriarchal power revises itself and generational revaluation takes place. As both Inchbald's and Kotzebue's plays were associated with Jacobin sentiments of the 1790s, the transposition of this sentimental melodrama to such country houses as

Ecclesford and Mansfield, where it receives casual endorsement as material for private theatricals, presents obvious dissonances.

The relationship between Inchbald's play and Austen's novel has often been construed in terms of a Jacobinist advocacy of rapid change versus Burkean incrementalism.[32] It is striking, however, not just how much the two works oppose each other but how much they double and resemble each other. From the distance of a long-durational and cross-cultural perspective, I suggest, such doubling can be thought outside of binary terms, such that the play and the novel appear not so much as opposites of one another as more narrowly different expressions of moral-political systemic revision. The actions of both the play and the novel unfold primarily on the site of an aristocratic or post-aristocratic estate; they are structured by a marriage plot, with the marriages at the end symbolizing renewed definitions of community; in both cases, the patriarchs acknowledge their lapses in judgment and are open to redefinitions and redistributions of power and authority. Although on the level of story the novel puts an end to the performance of the play, it can be said on the level of discourse to continue the work of the play by different means. It, too, ends with a scenario of social mobility. By marrying Edmund, Fanny rises above the station of impoverished ward to which she had seemed destined a generation ago by the financial imprudence of her mother's marriage.

The rehearsals of *Lovers' Vows* serve to catalyze processes of change wherein Fanny, the unentitled outsider, begins to emerge as the unlikely heroine of the novel. As the prompter for the other characters who assume parts in the play, she alone occupies a position on not just the threshold of the play-within-the-novel but on the threshold between the play *and* the novel. By occupying this liminal space, Fanny functions as the privileged spectator within the novel. She is not just the critic and judge of the actors playing their parts in *Lovers' Vows* but, akin to both narrator and reader, of the other characters within the novel, too. The rehearsals allow these characters, as actors of other roles, to discover and enact illicit or yet unacknowledged desires toward one another that may not otherwise have come to the fore. They set into motion and facilitate the development of triangular relationships that unfold and revolve in the next two volumes. By contending for the role of Agatha, the Bertram sisters Maria and Julia establish themselves as competitors for the attentions of Henry Crawford, who plays the part of Frederick. Maria's interest in Henry makes Henry a rival of her fiancé, Rushworth. Mary Crawford's rehearsal of the role of Amelia with Edmund as Anhalt awakens and confirms in Fanny feelings of jealousy that had already begun kindling earlier. Fanny's watchfulness and clear-sightedness vis-à-vis the other characters is not, however, new. Already, on the excursion to Sotherton Court, the Rushworths's estate, she had witnessed the flirtations between Henry and Maria Bertram, the jealousy of Julia Bertram, and the obliviousness of Rushworth, along with growing signs of warmth between Edmund and Mary. At Sotherton, seated in the planted wood near the ha-ha, or iron gate, marking the limit of the wood and the park, Fanny was already positioned on another threshold as the observer of the others, in a way that looked forward to her role as prompter. What is remarkable about her position here is that Fanny is not overhearing anything that is not meant for her ears. She gathers insights into the illicit or unacknowledged desires of others, rather, by hearing directly the speeches of others who do not bother to conceal them from her, so inconsequential is she to their level of interaction. Even when Rushworth comes by, after his fiancée, Maria, has trespassed beyond the gate with Henry Crawford, he speaks to Fanny only in order to get confirmation of his own previous opinions: "Pray, Miss Price, are you such a great admirer of this Mr. Crawford as some people are? For my part, I can see nothing in him" (73). She obliges by echoing conformably, "I do not think him at all handsome" (73).

In the prevailing household hierarchy of *Mansfield Park*, the child and adolescent Fanny's position had been somewhere between the servants and the Bertrams. Without peers in this stratification, the child Fanny was isolated. The narration illustrates and analyzes her situation by playing conspicuously on the ambiguity of the word "kind" as part of both a moral vocabulary and a taxonomic term. It repeatedly stresses in the early chapters the absence of "kindness" the household shows the child Fanny upon her arrival—an absence for which Edmund constituted the sole exception and thus became identified by Fanny as like—indeed, of a "kind" with—her brother William.[33] Mary Crawford would, notably, also show Fanny a "kindness" at odds with the hierarchical ordering of kinds in the household that has excluded Fanny, by and large, from being treated as an equal.[34] There is no kindness at Mansfield except between those established as of a kind already. Instead of displaying a categorical judgment based on innate and unchanging criteria, Fanny's judgment may be said to have developed dialectically from her experience as a child interloper at Mansfield.

Fanny's de facto position in the household comes to the fore in the pivotal scene when she refuses to act a part in *Lovers' Vows*. Responding to Tom's demand that she play the role of the Cottager's Wife, she declares emphatically, "I could not act any thing if you were to give me the world. No, indeed, I cannot act" (102). Finding herself in an unaccustomed position of being "at that moment the only speaker in the room," she nonetheless repeats, "But I really cannot act" (103). Her first refusal is met with Tom's demurral that "it is a nothing of a part, a mere nothing" (102). Her second refusal is met with a chorus of objections that culminate in Mrs. Norris pronouncing "in a whisper at once angry and audible: 'What a piece of work here is about nothing—I am quite ashamed of you, Fanny, to make such a difficulty of obliging your cousins in a trifle of this sort,—So kind as they are to you!'" (103) Unrestrainable, Mrs. Norris continues, "I shall think her a very obstinate, ungrateful girl, if she does not do what her aunt and cousins wish her—very ungrateful indeed, considering who and what she is" (103). The repetition of the word "nothing" in Tom and Mrs. Norris's objections answers, paradoxically, the question of "who and what" Fanny *is* in the prevailing hierarchy of *Mansfield Park*, a system of which Mrs. Norris is the self-appointed prime enforcer. Fanny's declaration that she cannot play-act only exposes how she has never enjoyed, within the terms governing this household, any capacity for action or agency, to begin with.[35]

A dual transformation follows this refusal: the emergence of Fanny as the privileged spectator and moral judge in the narration and the transformation of what it means for the estate of Mansfield Park as a representative political economic unit in the state to serve as a stage for not just play-acting but action itself. Up to this point, the narration had already shown Fanny's watchfulness in its description, through both indirect and free indirect discourse, of her observations of others as well as the prospects and vistas of the Northamptonshire landscape. It has shown also how Fanny, by virtue of her marginal position in the household, has been privy to indiscretions that would have been hidden before more consequential eyes and ears. What the rehearsals of *Lovers' Vows* offer is the figuration in explicitly theatrical terms of Fanny's watchfulness within the world of Mansfield Park. Fanny's consciousness becomes increasingly aligned with that of the narrator in observing and reflecting on this world. À propos Julia, who has lost the role of Agatha to her sister Maria, the narration uses indirect discourse to report Fanny's observations:

> Fanny saw and pitied much of this in Julia; but there was no outward fellowship between them. Julia made no communication, and Fanny took no liberties. They were two solitary sufferers, or connected only by Fanny's consciousness.
>
> The inattention of the two brothers and the aunt, to Julia's discomposure, and their blindness to its true cause, must be imputed to the fulness of their own minds. They were totally preoccupied. (114)

If the first sentence of the narration clearly begins in indirect discourse, it slides after the semicolon into the indeterminate territory of free indirect discourse, where it is unclear whether the connections are being made by the narrator or by Fanny thinking of her own consciousness in the third person. The content of the beginning of the next paragraph could likewise be attributed equally to the narrator and to Fanny. The difference between the narrator's and Fanny's perspectives very nearly collapses in the passage: what maintains the difference is the pathos of Fanny's specific empathy with Julia, whose disturbance of desire reflects Fanny's own feelings upon watching Mary and Edmund. Fanny's role as prompter gives her insight into the derangements occasioned by play-acting:

> —So far from being all satisfied and all enjoying, she found every body requiring something they had not, and giving occasion of discontent to the others.—Every body had a part either too long or too short;—nobody would attend as they ought, nobody would remember on which side they were to come in—nobody but the complainer would observe any directions. (115)

Along with the narrator, she alone sees both the dissatisfaction and desires of the actors as well as the characters apart from their play-acting roles. Rather than being completely impervious to the dissatisfactions she perceives in others, however, Fanny too is far from "all satisfied and all enjoying." On the threshold of the play alone, unperceived by the characters, she may be outside of the play-acting "every body" who requires something they had not. On the threshold between the play *and* the novel, however, it is apparent to the reader with access to her interiority that she figures among the restless "every body" that Sir Thomas's interruption of the play would attempt to restore to their "proper," predesignated place. It is in the threshold between the play and the novel that the transformation of not just Fanny's status would begin, but the very terms according to which Mansfield Park may serve as a veritable stage for "every body."

If Fanny's refusal to play-act reveals how, according to the operating logic of Mansfield Park, she was unable also to act as an agent exerting her will and power, the end of the novel shows her finding "thoroughly perfect"—though not without the memory of "painful sensation"—everything "within the view and patronage of Mansfield Park" (321). What the novel shows in the process of Fanny's ordination as an entitled member of the estate is the transformation of Mansfield Park itself as a site where action is the right or entitlement of only the few, for which others provide infrastructural support. The rehearsals of *Lovers' Vows* had highlighted that division within the household, a division that corresponds to the classic

Aristotelian division between the *oikos* or household itself as site of private and ordinary life and the *polis* as public space of appearances and elevated domain for the pursuit of the good life. Austen's domestic novel focuses on the "modern-built" commercial-colonialist household, erected in differential resemblance to the feudal, aristocratic manor, as site for a reorganization of the relationship between ordinary life as infrastructural realm of necessity and public, political life as realm of freedom. By staging the drama of Fanny's ordination, *Mansfield Park* puts into question the traditional, hierarchical relationship between the *oikos* and the *polis*, along with the very conception of action itself that attends such hierarchy. Instead of freeing action entirely from the domain of labor and work, the novel advances in Fanny's ordination a conception of freedom and action that recognizes the infrastructural constraints without which freedom and action have no stage and cannot appear. That the space in which action takes place is not given, but made, and is an infrastructural artifice subject to remaking, is an insight that Austen's novel illuminates through Fanny's custodial consciousness. The subject of freedom and action that Fanny comes to exemplify is one split between being a singular performer of extraordinary deeds and the custodian as a participant in the collective work of ordinary life, which includes the very remaking and rearticulation of what would constitute a stage for action. Fanny as modern agent acknowledges the necessity of being a means to herself and others as ends.

The refusal to play-act in *Lovers' Vows* is not Fanny's only act of refusal in the novel. She refuses also Henry Crawford's offer of marriage, having become the object of his attention in her coming out and after the departure of the newly married Maria along with Julia. Fanny's refusal runs counter to the plans of Sir Thomas and constitutes, however mildly, another challenge to the prevailing authority governing Mansfield Park. For her defiance, she is banished to the home of her parents at Portsmouth. It is there that she comes consciously to realize that "Portsmouth was Portsmouth; Mansfield was home" (292). This realization is precipitated by the news that Tom Bertram has suddenly taken ill, and her desire to return to Mansfield is reinforced by the subsequent news of Maria's adultery with Henry Crawford and Julia's elopement with Yates. Her affirmation of Mansfield as home gains strength from her comparison of the decorum of life at Mansfield with the disorderliness of her childhood home.[36] And her affirmation of her own role and position at Mansfield is expressed specifically in terms of the related criteria of service and utility. "Could she have been at home," she thinks to herself, "she might have been of *service* to every creature in the house. She felt that she must have been of *use* to all" (293, emphasis mine). With a haste that critics have not failed to notice, Austen's narration accelerates at the end toward a dénouement in which Fanny comes to exemplify and articulate the principle of the general good at Mansfield—and to define for herself a role in the process—in revision of Sir Thomas's prior administration of the household order.

Utility figures as a key criterion in the redefinition of the general good at Mansfield and the affirmation of this criterion as a condition of belonging to the estate. "She was returned to Mansfield Park, she was useful, she was beloved," the narration summarizes at the beginning of the last chapter (312). "Fanny was indeed the daughter that he wanted," reports the narration toward the end of Sir Thomas's state of mind after he approves of the match between Edmund and Fanny (320). The outsider Fanny is ordained at the end of the novel as useful, beloved, and rightful subject of everything "within the view and patronage of Mansfield Park" (321). Utility displaces birth, rank, and money as the principal criterion of membership at Mansfield Park as an exemplary political economic unit. The disgraced Maria and Julia have been banished, with Mrs. Norris assigned to live with Maria, with Tom's health remaining uncertain at the end of the novel. Fanny's younger sister Susan has now moved into Mansfield, for Fanny has arranged for Susan to leave Portsmouth and to take her own place as Lady Bertram's companion. The narration presents this development in terms of a lesson learned by Sir Thomas: in seeing the merits of Fanny, Susan, and their brother, William, "all assisting to advance each other, and doing credit to his countenance and aid, Sir Thomas saw repeated, and for ever repeated reason to rejoice in what he had done for them all, and acknowledge the advantages of early hardship and discipline, and the consciousness of being born to struggle and endure" (321). The ending of the novel sees Mansfield Park redefined as an estate that serves to advance the mutual interests of those who consent to making themselves useful to each other rather than one that conserves the rights and privileges of those simply born to the household. Fanny is positioned as the counselor and custodian of this infrastructure-turned-stage, the artifice that serves as the condition of her and others' freedom and agency.

By maintaining the decorum and structure of the household, Fanny shows a peculiar resemblance to Mrs. Norris, whom Sir Thomas had entrusted with administrative duties. Right after hearing of Tom's illness and wishing to be back at Mansfield to be "of service to every creature in the house," she imagines the functions she would fulfill:

> She felt that she must have been of use to all. To all, she must have saved some trouble of head or hand; and were it only in supporting the spirits of her aunt Bertram, keeping her from the evil of solitude, or the still greater evil of a restless, officious companion, too apt to be heightening danger in order to enhance her own importance, her being there would have been a general good. (293)

The unnamed Mrs. Norris is imagined here as a rival or a double, with the pronominal confusion in the last two clauses of the second sentence enhancing the uncanniness of the resemblance. One a niece and the other a sister, both serve as companions to the lady of the house, claiming to maintain order and the general good. The officiousness of Mrs. Norris expresses itself, however, as an enforcement of the class hierarchy—an "evil" to be exorcised. In contrast, Fanny's concern with decorum would show a meliorism that affirms the structure of the household while redefining the criteria of membership and thus opening it up to greater enfranchisement.

As mentioned, the novel that is *Mansfield Park* does not so much expel *Lovers' Vows* as pursue the dehierarchizing impulse of the play by other means. It stages a prosaic drama of ordination in which the lowly, conformable, yet not uncritical Fanny Price comes to represent a revision of the household order and to embody a new logic of agency altogether. In staging this drama of ordination, the novel may be said curiously to repeat the second play Austen incorporates later in the narration, *Henry VIII*, the 1613 history play attributed in Austen's time to Shakespeare but today to Shakespeare and John Fletcher. Just as *Henry VIII* reflects on the significance of theater and theatricality in the redefinition of political authority at a time of historical transition, ending with prospects of a future heralded by the birth of a daughter as heir, so too does *Mansfield Park* showcase a redefinition of the very stage of political action on the plane of the ordinary, ending with a renewal of the state/estate under the stewardship of a daughter *cum* daughter-in-law.

A reading of excerpts from *Henry VIII* takes place in Volume 3, Chapter 3. The recently rejected but irrepressible Henry Crawford comes to call on Fanny and the Bertrams, accompanied by Edmund, who hopes to help Henry advance his suit. They arrive in the drawing room, where Fanny feigns deep absorption in her needlework. Crawford picks up and begins reading from the volume of Shakespeare from which Fanny had just been reading to Lady Bertram.[37] Crawford's reading was not only good, it was excellent. Fanny could not deny it:

> The King, the Queen, Buckingham, Wolsey, Cromwell, all were given in turn; for with the happiest knack, the happiest power of jumping and guessing, he could always light, at will, on the best scene, or the best speeches of each; and whether it were dignity or pride, or tenderness or remorse, or whatever were to be expressed, he could do it with equal beauty.—It was truly dramatic. (228)

After this reading, Edmund and Crawford discourse about Shakespeare. The newly ordained Edmund ponders next the relevance of eloquent reading to preaching. While the previous generation of those ordained had assumed that "reading was reading, and preaching was preaching," a recent "spirit of improvement" had led to the question of how "distinctness and energy may have weight in recommending the most solid truths" (230). Crawford toys with becoming a preacher too but stipulates that he would need to have an educated London audience and only preach every now and then—"not for a constancy; it would not do for a constancy" (232). Upon this last remark, Fanny, "who could not but listen, involuntarily shook her head" (232).

In this scene, Fanny functions as the principal audience member, critic, and judge of Henry Crawford's performance, occupying again a position akin to that she had held as prompter for *Lovers' Vows*. Significantly, moreover, Austen's novel may be seen to historicize itself as well as reflect on its own aesthetic and political status in relation to *Henry VIII*. The play dramatizes the political and religious break with Rome and the Catholic Church that Henry VIII effects through the occasion of his divorce of Katherine of Aragon and marriage with Anne Boleyn ("Anne Bullen" in the play). It stages the very founding of the Church of England—in which Edmund had just taken orders—as a watershed event that initiates a new era of English monarchical and national power. Clearly, *Mansfield Park* shows the complex continuity of the history of its own early nineteenth-century moment with this period of radical transition constitutive of early modernity in England. Remarkably, the play stages this history by calling attention to the very role of theater and theatricality itself in politics and political contestation.[38] The rivalry between Wolsey and Henry VIII is depicted in terms of theatrical manipulation. Wolsey, as master of ritual pageantry, is outmaneuvered by Henry, who begins showing his understanding of the power of political theater by staging a pastoral masque in Wolsey's own palace and courting Anne Bullen in the guise of a shepherd. Henry's staging of the public pageants of his wedding with Anne Bullen and, finally, the christening of Elizabeth shows what he has learned from

Wolsey's political dramaturgy; his trial of Wolsey resembles the trial of Buckingham that Wolsey had earlier engineered. *Mansfield Park* inherits not only the English political and religious history recounted in *Henry VIII* but the play's reflection on how such history is mediated by theater and theatricality.

In their discourse about Shakespeare, Crawford had said platitudinously to Edmund, "Shakespeare one gets acquainted with without knowing how. It is a part of an Englishman's constitution" (229). In reply, Edmund echoes in polite and equally platitudinous confirmation, "His celebrated passages are quoted by every body; they are in half the books we open, and we all talk Shakespeare" (229). As a production associated with the authorial proper name "Shakespeare," *Henry VIII* shows how an "Englishman's constitution," in political terms, is mediated and resettled by theatrical means. The likes of Henry Crawford, Edmund, and Fanny are not only fictions of historical subjects who participate in a tradition reconstituted by England's founding Protestant monarch. They are also fictions in the fictional medium of the domestic novel that reconstitutes, for a prosaic age, Shakespeare's national theater and relocates the stage of political action into the domain of the representative bourgeois household, where "woman" names the figure of the modern subject as an ordinary subject-in-the-making.

The Rouge of the North and the Afterlife of Ritual

At the very beginning of *The Rouge of the North*, a man is walking at dusk on a Shanghai side street in the days when "electric lights were as yet uncommon in the Old City" (1). He is tipsy, the text intimates. Between the end of the day and the beginning of night, between sobriety and drunkenness, he finds himself in the mood for opera. Alone on the "pebble-paved side street . . . with all the little shops boarded up for the night," the man turns the empty street into his theater: "He weaved happily from one side of the street to the other, humming Peking opera with an occasional 'Ti guh lung di dung' to simulate the musical accompaniment" (1). He is startled by something moving across his back.

> It was only his pigtail that had come loose.
> "Lay its mother!" he swore half laughing. To cover up his confusion in front of invisible spectators he flapped his fan loudly against his buttocks and swung into the slow measured "square step," walking with feet wide apart, toes pointing outwards in the manner of mandarins in Peking opera, and sang,
> "I, the king, drunk in the Peach Blossom Palace,

With Han Su-ngo of beauty matchless."
That reminded him. Turning around he looked about him and retraced his steps peering at all the familiar shopfronts until he came to the right one. He pounded loudly on the boards and shouted, "Miss! Miss!" (1–2)

他終於明白過來,是辮子滑落下來。

「操那!」

用芭蕉扇拍打著屁股,踱著方步唱了起來,掩飾他的窘態。

「孤王酒醉桃花宮,韓素梅生來好貌容。」

一句話提醒了自己,他轉身來四面看了看,往回走過幾家門面,揀中一家,蓬蓬蓬拍門。

「大姑娘!大姑娘!」(4)

The narration will soon indicate that the man is a carpenter, but it will never give this everyman a name. He disappears from the narration after the first few pages until the very end, when he returns in an involuntary memory of Yindi, when she recalls, thirty-five years later, his pounding on the door that evening and calling, "Miss! Miss!" (185)

What is the significance of the novel's opening with a scene of amateur, impromptu Peking opera? Although the unnamed carpenter will leave the story after the beginning, his performance prefigures how the heroine Yindi will also display a tendency to turn to Peking opera for analogies to her own situations at different moments in her life. What is the significance of this dimension of *The Rouge of the North* in both its Chinese and English versions? A 1943 essay by Chang, "Peking Opera through Foreign Eyes" (*Yangren kan jingxi*), sheds light on these questions.

Chang conducts in the essay the experiment indicated in the very title of the piece. She looks at China through Peking opera, and Peking opera, in turn, through foreign eyes. "To see China through the eyes with which foreigners watch Peking opera," the essay begins, "would be an exercise not entirely lacking in significance."[39] Ironically, the "foreign eyes" through which Peking opera and China are seen are Chang's own. In this experiment, she conducts an exercise of self-ethnography that is also an exercise of self-estrangement. Rather than saying that she sets out deliberately to conduct such self-estrangement, one may say, more accurately, that Chang responds to and reflects on a predicament of self-estrangement that has already affected both Peking opera and China. Such self-estrangement, the essay implies, has taken place in two interwoven contexts: in theatrical culture and in the very sociopolitical and moral ordering of life in China. In terms of theatrical culture and the history of theater, the self-estrangement of Peking opera had come in the form of a foreign import of Western provenance, modern spoken drama (*huaju* or *wenmin xi*, "civilized drama").[40] As Chang writes, "The realist new drama in China has defined itself in opposition to Peking opera from its very conception," before she goes on to observe, "but the very first spoken drama really to lodge itself in the hearts of the common people depends for its success on its heavy use of that same tradition. This is truly an astonishing fact" (PO, 107). After realist, spoken drama was introduced to China in the late nineteenth century, it began gaining momentum in the 1910s, especially after the May Fourth, or New Culture, Movement of 1919. This transformation in the history of Chinese theater is, of course, part and parcel of the general radical transformation of Chinese culture and society undertaken in the late nineteenth and early twentieth centuries in the name of reform and modernization.[41]

What Peking opera as a prominent form of late imperial Chinese theater and the traditional sociopolitical and moral order have in common is ritual. Peking opera is an art that depends for its expressive power on ritual gestures and cultural typologies. As Chang writes, "In Peking opera, it could be said that the repetition of the rules has reached its pinnacle. The highly conventionalized beauty of the movements of the actors across the stage is referred to by westerners as dance, when in reality it represents the essence of ritual protocol" (PO, 112). To a much greater degree than dance, the movements of Peking opera distill and stylize gestures associated with ritual practices and cultural types—for instance, the "slow measured 'square step'" of mandarins that the carpenter performs. The power of Peking opera to communicate with and move its audience depends on the latter's recognition of the artful manipulation of ritual gestures that evoke shared practices offstage. The skill of individual performers consists in the apt and subtle modulation of these gestures to generate a variety of aesthetic and emotional effects. In terms of character typology, Peking opera features major roles—*sheng* (male roles), *dan* (female roles), *jing* (painted face male roles), and *chou* (clowns)—which in turn divide into subcategories. The plays rehearse well-known stories: "Each of the scores of popular plays that make up the bulk of the operatic repertoires," Chang observes, "provide us with standardized and thus eternal narrative molds" (PO, 107). Dialogues and arias are rich with quotations and stock phrases. Like ritual, Peking opera is a practice that depends on the principle of repetition. If Peking opera quotes and distills recognizable ritual gestures, it participates in turn in a culture of iteration by enriching a cultural repertoire that can be drawn upon for various applications.

Toward the end of her essay, Chang zooms in on the evanescence of ritual practices in Republican-era China. "The custom of kowtowing in greeting has long since been eliminated. Apparently to kowtow with style required a great deal of skill," she quips (PO, 112). While many forms of traditional etiquette had been disembedded from their functions within a traditional political order, the old conventions still carry meaning in unofficial social interactions and thus continue to generate aesthetic and affective effects onstage, most evidently in Peking opera, but even in modern spoken drama. After claiming that the "realist new drama" defined itself "in opposition to Peking opera," she observes that operatic elements appear to account for the great popular success of a new spoken drama, the 1943 *Autumn Quince* (*Qiu haitang*) (107). Even after the double self-estrangement suffered by Chinese theatrical culture and social, moral, and political culture, Peking opera has an afterlife beyond a simple break between premodern and modern eras construed in temporally linear terms. It remains a vital way of looking at China through foreign eyes—those of foreigners to China as well as those of the Chinese who have undergone the foreignizing experience of self-estrangement.

Let us return to the carpenter's scene of improvisation. He responds to his own fright with dexterity, choosing on the spot a specific role and aria to master his own embarrassment. The couplet in Chinese reveals that the role is based on a famous historical figure whose exploits crossed over the domain of historical writings to become the stuff of fictional and dramatic embellishment—Zhao Kuangyin, a military commander who became the first emperor of the Song dynasty in 960 C.E.[42] And the aria in question is from an opera, *Zhan Huangpao* [Cutting the Imperial Robe], which dramatizes episodes at the beginning of the new emperor's reign. To master his embarrassment at being spooked by his pigtail, the carpenter sings the lines of a legendary heroic figure drunkenly bemoaning his solitary state and thinking of a lovely maiden. The words of the couplet trigger an association with a nearby lovely maiden, Yindi, the "sesame oil beauty," whose shopfront he then seeks out. In his improvisation, the carpenter finds a correlation between his own drunken solitude and that of the Song emperor, then unfolds from this basic analogy an erotic element, with Yindi as the counterpart to the emperor's object of interest.

This everyman shows himself to be a lay connoisseur of Peking opera. His connoisseurship manifests itself in the precision and aptness of his selection, whereby he finds a self-ironic analogy for his own mood and situation. In her 1943 essay, Chang remarks:

> The Chinese have always been alive to the pleasure of the apt quotation or set phrase. Lovely bons mots, words of wisdom and cautionary phrases, two-thousand-year-old jokes—all circulate freely in everyday speech. These invisible tissues constitute a living past. The body of tradition is continually strengthened by its application to new people, new things, and new situations . . .
>
>   Only in China does history perform itself so persistently in everyday life. (PO, 107)

中國人向來喜歡引經據典。美麗的，精警的斷句，兩千年前的老笑話，混在日常談吐裏自由使用著。這些看不見的纖維，組成了我們活生生的過去。傳統的本身增強了力量，因爲它不停地被引用到的人，新的事物與局面上 . . .

只有在中國，歷史仍於日常生活中維持活躍的演出。[43]

The body of tradition gains strength anew in the minor, everyday scene of a tipsy everyman applying a set piece from a cultural repertoire to interpret, master, and mock his own situation. History performs itself in such an ordinary scene.

  The carpenter demonstrates here, indeed, what it means to be a subject of history in a culturally specific way. He acts in a way that positions himself in relation to an analogous precedent, then moves horizontally to Yindi as the counterpart for another analogy; he finds correspondence in the conditions of solitude and drunkenness; and he thereby restores the equilibrium he had just lost. He manifests and activates the potentiality of the ritual positioning system that Peking opera abstracts from actual life and supplements as theatrical medium. The subject manifests his capacity to act in the calibration of elements in a discrete episode, unrepeatable in the combination of particular elements but dependent nevertheless on the principle of repetition. In the calibration of elements, he reads the occasion by means of the resources of a tradition, honoring the uniqueness of the moment and activating the tradition anew. While the particular analogy he draws on makes him equivalent to the emperor in the embarrassment of their drunkenness, the discernment motivating the analogy makes him the equal of the emperor in another sense—in the structural understanding of how carpenter and emperor are both subject to and subjects of mutual articulation in relation to one another, and to others, in the flexible warp and weft of a cultural operating system. While he may be play-acting, his play-acting reveals the conditions of action itself within a specific cultural framework. Moreover, it is an act of freedom, wherein freedom is not absolute and unconditional, outside of culture, but conditioned within the historically shifting frameworks of particular cultures. This act of freedom transcends and comments on the very framework of articulation that serves as its condition of possibility, while it still participates, playfully, within this framework. Chang begins *The Rouge of the North* with a minor, easily misrecognized scene of freedom, enacted on the stage of an ordinary side street, inviting readers, Chinese and foreign, to see China through Peking opera, and Peking opera through foreign eyes.

After this prologue, the focus of the narration shifts to Yindi, where it remains for the rest of the novel. She, too, will refer to Peking opera for analogies with situations in her own life. However, while the carpenter is precise and self-ironic, Yindi will be vague and conventional, at first earnestly and later cynically, in the way she turns to the operatic imaginary for reflections of her own status and identity. To begin with, her knowledge of Peking opera is limited, for as "a native of Shanghai she had trouble understanding the lyric and jokes" (156).[44] Rather than renewing the vitality of "the body of tradition" through the limber application of quotations and precedents, she displays, rather, what Chang calls in another essay the "unhealthy" transformation of life into drama, wherein "the line between life and its dramatization becomes difficult to draw."[45] Not unlike Emma Bovary, Yindi shows a penchant for self-dramatization based on secondhand sources, although her sources are not romance novels but a combination of stock Peking opera types and cognate cultural associations.

What, then, can be learned from looking through a perspective as limited as Yindi's? In telling the story of Yindi's life over thirty-five years, the narration foregrounds the household as principal site of action and activity and the framework of significance wherein Yindi derives her status and identity. As the site where ordinary life takes place, the household is a scene of unremarkable routines, where the activities and processes necessary to sustain biological life takes place, and where the commemoration of familial deaths marks that without which the continuity of life itself has no significance. These activities—food preparations, daily chores, birthdays, marriages, births, and deaths—are repeated in such temporal increments as the day, the season, the year, and the generation. They occupy the foreground of the narration, which invites readers to scrutinize them at eye level through the perspective of Yindi. At the same time, through subtle, peripheral glances, the narration opens up, beyond Yindi's perspective, to events and developments of national significance. In so doing, it shows how the traditional household as framework of significance rests on shifting foundations in early twentieth-century China. Remarkably, it interweaves in its allusions to changes in the political, social, and moral ordering of China also allusions to changes in the history of its theatrical practice and culture. It thus shows through Yindi's perspective the disjunctions occasioned by these shifts. "Woman" emerges as the focal subject of the cultural disjunctions and contradictions of Chinese modernity. Significantly, while analyzing the limits and limitations of Yindi's perspective, the narration continues to affirm the scene of the ordinary, scaffolded by a ritual positioning system, as the abiding scene of Chinese history and, thus, the very promise of Chinese modernity.

In the rest of this section, I will take a closer look at three moments, interspersed over twenty years or so, in which Yindi refers to Peking opera for analogy to her own situation. They coincide with moments of ritual passage or ritual commemoration in her life in the Yao household: namely, right after she has consented to become a bride of the family; upon the sixtieth birthday of her deceased father-in-law, the late Old Master Yao; and, climactically, upon the sixtieth birthday of Old Master Gunglin, a patriarch of the extended family, when a Peking opera performance is actually staged at the celebration. Let us turn to the first of these moments.

Right after agreeing to marry into the Yao family, Yindi sits alone in her room above the shop, anticipating her future: "So the man she married would never see what she looked like. Part of her died at this" (21). Her horror gives way to other imaginings:

> But amidst the sense of danger and treachery she already saw him as the young Peking opera actor in a night scene sitting with an elbow on the table, eyes closed on the handsome face painted pink and white. It was as if she was to live out the rest of her life on a lighted stage with music accompanying her every movement. Or on a lighted lantern like the painted figures on it, their red sleeves turned a pale orange against the light. (21)

> 但是她一方面警誡自己，已經看見了他，像個戲台上的小生，肘彎支在桌上閉著眼睛睡覺，漂亮的臉搽得紅紅白白。她以後一生一世都在台上過，腳底下都是電燈，一舉一動都有音樂伴奏。又像燈籠上畫的美人，紅袖映著燈光成爲淡橙色。(23–24)

In this first instance when Yindi refers to Peking opera to imagine her own situation, she draws on the image of a stock type—the *xiaosheng*, or "young gentleman" role—to imagine her future husband, the blind Second Master Yao, in terms more physically flattering than she will soon find that he lives up to. The narration does not have her dwell on imagining herself in the counterpart role of *dan*, or "young lady," but shows her moving fleetingly to another stock image, painted beauties on a lantern. The rapidity and disconnectedness of her associations, which continue until she falls into a fitful sleep, belie an anxiety before the unknown, as she will soon leave the familiar environment of the sesame oil shop and the side street for the grand space of the Yao family compound.

Poised on this transition from one space to another, and passage from one phase of her life to another, she imagines the grander space of the Yao household in theatrical terms. This space, in which her role as yet remains vague to her, will be one in which she intuits being exposed to heightened visibility and a visibility regulated by a more elaborate set of rules than she has been subject to as the orphaned daughter of the Chai family and the "sesame oil beauty" of the shops. As a grand household, the Yao compound comprises within its walls multiple branches: the Yao sons, with their wives, concubines, and children, all presided over by the widowed matriarch and attended to by servants. She is to join the second branch of this family with the task of bearing a son to ensure its continuity. Given the imperial-bureaucratic status of the family, the operations of the household approximate those of the court, taking Yindi away from the relative informality of the shop. Chang figures Yindi's intuition of her new surroundings in explicitly theatrical terms. In her inhabitation of the framework of the traditional household, Yindi will show herself guided and misguided in her understanding of her new role by a Peking opera imaginary.

With her marriage, Yindi's very identity as "woman" is determined by the positioning system of the traditional patriarchal hierarchy. She is defined as the second daughter-in-law of the Yao family. It is as such that she understands herself to behave and to be viewed within the confines of the household as well as in public. A few years after her marriage, upon the occasion of the posthumous celebration of the sixtieth birthday of the late patriarch, Yindi takes her place among the Yao women in a "string of open carriages" as they process through Shanghai to a temple (72). Weaving between indirect and free indirect discourse, the narration comments:

> The cavalcade and the baby marked her high respectability and the rouge placed her as a northerner. There was no danger of her being mistaken for one of those singsong girls that drove to Chang Park for tea. Still it was a theatrical look; she felt that they were a troupe of players incongruously out

under the sun sailing along the traffic. She was acting and enjoyed it, posing as the loved and admired one. (72)

她們這浩浩蕩蕩的行列與她車上的嬰兒表出她的身分,那胭脂又一望而知是北方人,不會拿她誤認爲坐馬車上張園吃茶的倌人。但是搽這些胭脂還像是唱戲,她覺得他們是一個戲班子,珠翠滿頭,暴露在日光下,有一種突兀之感;扮著抬閣抬出來,在車馬的洪流上航行。她也在演戲,演得很高興,扮做一個爲人尊敬愛護的人。(82)

The indeterminacy between the narrator's external perspective and Yindi's own reflections—might Yindi be referring to herself in the third person?—suggests the degree to which her own perspective is marked by culturally coded indices of feminine status and identity. This imagination begins with the insignia of rank (the size of the entourage, the presence of the infant son) and provenance (the northern custom of applying rouge), then darts aside to her anxiety of being mistaken for a singsong girl, and ends with the analogy to a troupe of players. The ceremonial elaborateness of the occasion heightens the degree to which the display of ritual order approximates theatrical performance. The aside to singsong girls, a running motif in the novel, betrays the anxious rivalry that the legitimacy and respectability of her position still do not protect her from.

The foundations underlying the legitimacy and respectability of this position have been shifting, however, as Chang's narration indicates through a peripheral mention of current affairs: "They had more relatives than ever this year, so many were fleeing the revolution seeking shelter in the foreign settlements" (73). The year is likely 1912 or 1913, a year or so after the end of the Qing dynasty. The hearsay does not just include changes to the structure of political authority but reports, concurrently, changes undertaken by reformers, "wild youngsters mostly," to theatrical practice itself:

Here in Shanghai under the protection of the foreign settlements they attracted more attention than elsewhere with their own newspapers and their speechifying plays, called "civilized plays" because they were imported, at a time when the reformers deemed most native things barbaric. Those shows with just talk and no singing were very much the vogue just now but she had yet to see one. (74)

一向在上海因爲有租界保護,鬧得更兇些,自己辦報紙,組織戲團唱文明戲,言論老生動不動來篇演說,大罵政府,掌聲不絕。現在非常出風頭,銀娣是始終沒看見過。(84)

Significantly, the event of revolution first appears in the novel in conjunction with revolution in the institution of the theater. These disturbances merely occupy the periphery of Yindi's field of perception. Tellingly, what interests her most about these changes are rumors about the offstage behavior of the actors: "The civilized actors, as they were called, including female impersonators who still took all the women's parts, were notorious for the number of their affairs with singsong girls and concubines" (74). In Chinese, Chang's text is more succinct:

唱文明戲的都是吊膀子出名的,名聲太壞。(84)

The actors of "civilized plays" were all known for their liaisons. They were notorious. (my translation)

In the English text, she inserts a gloss of the period slang *diao banzi* (literally, "dangling arms," which I render as "liaisons") and spells out what remains more understated in Chinese. With such deviations throughout, where the English provides not-so-stealthy glosses (also in the previous passage explaining the term "civilized plays"), Yindi inhabits a much less reticent world in English than in Chinese. With different degrees of tact and intimacy, both English and Chinese versions of the passage nevertheless show in common that the political and cultural-symbolic grounds of Yindi's status and identity have shifted. They show, at the same time, how little she is aware of the consequences of the shift. The main disturbance she experiences to her framework of significance comes from the potential sexual threats posed by actors, including female impersonators, and singsong girls, who, along with concubines, constitute the proliferating enemies of wives in the gender economy of traditional patriarchy.

Almost twenty years after the excursion to the temple, the extended Yao family gathers again for another sixtieth birthday, this time for Old Master Gunglin. After the death of Old Mistress Yao a few years ago, the grand household had separated into smaller branches. A widow with a grown son, Yindi is now in the position of a matriarch rather than a daughter-in-law. Upon this occasion, excerpts from various plays are staged in a private performance of Peking opera. It is the early 1930s. From chatter on the balcony and through Yindi's consciousness, we learn how times have changed: hemlines have gotten longer and sleeves shorter, Big Master has started working for the nationalist government, sons are being sent overseas to study, and even "girls went to school in the last couple years" (146). And, besides four well-known female impersonators, actresses—the recent development of women playing female roles in Peking opera—will appear onstage. Yet, the performances onstage are not what matter to Yindi. Second Mistress Sun calls her attention to the spectacle of an actress offstage. From the balcony, the two women look together upon this apparition, who goes by the stage name "Pink Cloud":

> The actress was walking past the front row followed by her train of admirers, turning to nod at friends in the audience. She wore a man's gown and an English checked cap at a rakish angle. A pigtail hung down her back. The footlights alongside shone brightly on the vermilion mouth and round silver face. (136)
>
> 那女戲子正在樓下前排走過，後面跟著一群捧場的。她回過頭來向觀眾裏的熟人點頭，台前一排電燈泡正照著她一張銀色的圓臉，硃紅的嘴唇。下了裝，穿著件男人的袍子，歪戴著一頂呢鴨舌帽，後面拖著根大辮子。(154)

For both women looking upon her, the actress functions as an ambiguous figure of femininity and modernity who disturbs what Yindi and Second Mistress understand to be a woman. As a modern professional woman, she possesses a certain degree of independence from a patriarchal economy, yet she plays roles that correspond to a traditional typology of femininity. In the figure of the Peking opera actress, moreover, the naturalistic biases of spoken realist drama meet the ritual expressivism of Peking opera, where the actual gender of the performer does not matter to the mastery of stylized gestural and vocal conventions.[46] Pink Cloud thus poses a double enigma to the onlooking Yindi. Her visibility showcases how the category of "woman" has been untethered from its traditional moorings. And her very existence as an actress betokens an estrangement of Peking opera from itself as medium through which to view oneself, others, and China.

Upon the puzzling phenomenon of Pink Cloud Yindi projects fantasies of matriarchal power. Sometime after the party, she talks with her son Yensheng at home on the opium couch and teases him with the idea of making Pink Cloud his concubine, at a time when both opium and polygamy were on the decline. The narration enters her thoughts through indirect discourse. In Pink Cloud and other actresses, she sees traces of her younger self:

> The women on the stage had rouged eyelids continuous with the deep pink cheeks just like she herself when she was young. Their spangled head-dress full at the back and cut into a pointed arch over the forehead reminded her of the pearl cap she used to wear. The comediennes wore the jacket and trousers fashionable about ten years ago, like hers, just flashier and

embroidered all over, which looked right over the footlights. The resemblance was so haunting she was easily moved by the story. (156–57)

但是剛巧唱花旦的那身打扮也就是她自己從前穿的襖袴，頭上的亮片子在額前分披下來作人字式，就像她年輕的時侯戴的頭面。臉上胭脂通紅的，直搽到眼皮上，簡直就是她自己在夢境中出現，看了很多感觸。(178)

Her musings move next offstage and into the future:

> If it was possible to take such a one into the house, then that glittering world that once she could only eavesdrop on from the veranda in the dark, she could go in at last even if it was only in the role of the dowager empress. Like the old lady in *A Dream in the Red Chamber* who likes to be surrounded by beauties and served only by them. Even their own Old Mistress here had had her court made up of her sons' wives and concubines, all chosen for their charms and then relegated to a manless life. It would be different with her son and his famous beauty, they would attend on her like the Golden Boy and White Jade Maid of the Goddess Kwannon, with a mysterious smile between the three of them that came of her knowledge of that love she had brought about and shut away for life. (157)

> 真要是娶這麼一個到家裏來，那她從前在黑暗的陽台上偷聽樓下划拳唱戲，那亮晶晶的世界從來不容她插足的，現在到底讓她進去了，即使只能演太后的角色。向來老太太們喜歡漂亮的女孩子，是有這傳統的。像《紅樓夢》裏的老太太，跟前只要美人侍奉。就連他們自己家的老太太不也是這樣？娶媳婦一定要揀漂亮的，後來又只喜歡兒子的姨奶奶們，都是被男人擱在一邊的女人，組成一個小朝廷，在老太太跟前爭寵。她要是給兒子納妾，那當然又兩樣，娶個名美人來，小兩口子是觀音身邊的金童玉女，三個人之間有一種神秘的微笑，因為她知道他們關上房門以後的事，是她作成他們 . . . (178)

Not only does she discern a phantom resemblance between the costumes and roles of the actresses onstage and her younger self offstage, she imagines how such an actress may figure into an offstage dramaturgy of the household in which she herself would play the role of matriarch. For the casting of such a matriarch, she draws upon four icons of female authority: the dowager empress; closer to home, her own late mother-in-law; from the literary domain, the old lady in *The Dream of the Red Chamber*; and from religion, the Buddhist Goddess of Mercy, Kwannon. Like the dowager empress, she could govern indirectly. Like the old lady in *The Dream of the Red Chamber* and her mother-in-law, she could preside over a grand household with a select entourage. The final vision, based on a popular configuration of the Goddess of Mercy, shows an entourage of only two, a reduction compensated for by the private satisfaction betokened by the shared mysterious smile. Her own satisfaction would derive vicariously from her being the dramaturge of the smile of erotic satisfaction she imagines she would have the power to bring about between the younger couple. Insofar as she sees in the figure of the Peking opera actress reflections of her younger self and the erotic power of this younger self, her fantasy of satisfaction carries also the extra perversity of an incestuous twist.

The passage sketches an imaginary autobiography through Peking opera. This autobiography begins not with her birth or childhood, but with her youth and entry into the grand Yao household as what Chang's Chinese text terms—in a sentence absent from the English version—*xiaojia biyu*, literally the "jade ornament of the small household," an idiomatic expression for a young woman of modest background. In the sharp-tongued and saucy *huadan* roles, Yindi sees reflected images of her own class origins before she draws on other cultural types to imagine her ascent of the hierarchy as matriarch and finally as goddess. This imaginary autobiography is articulated through the evocation of cultural types embedded in a traditional patriarchal framework that is, in turn, mediated by the typology of Peking opera. The fantasy of matriarchal power here has no operativity, however. The passage ends with Yindi's own admission that "it was all make-believe, enough for some women when they were old enough" (157). The dramaturgical scheme would lead nowhere beyond the mother and son's opium-hazed conversation.

Chang stages in this passage two entwined crises: that of the articulation of feminine identity and that of the framework of Peking opera as medium for such articulation. Undergirding these crises is the radical shift in the entire sociopolitical system in which the category of "woman" is defined. Through Yindi's perspective, the novel shows how "woman" functions as the focal subject of a systemic crisis. "Woman" here does not simply designate Yindi as "traditional woman" and the actress as a modern alternative. Rather, "woman" designates the split between Yindi as the one who sees and the actress as the one seen, a split that Yindi tries to overcome by assimilating the latter to an outmoded framework of social organization.[47] The narration shows here how the fractures to this framework that Yindi had experienced as tremors on the scale of the everyday have widened, over the course of years, to a chasm.

Throughout the novel, Chang's episodic narrative structure depicts Yindi in a concatenation of scenes over thirty-five years repeatedly bound by and straining against the rules that define her position in the traditional patriarchal order. Her will to transgress and be defined otherwise ends only in the increasingly reactionary embrace of static precedents. The novel ends with the return of a memory triggered by a typical act of petty sadism on Yindi's part. Retiring in the evening for the night, she burns the wrist of her slave girl with a small lamp to keep her from nodding off. The sight "reminded her of the time she had burned a man's hand," that of the carpenter pounding on her door thirty-five years ago. "Everything she drew comfort from was gone, had never happened," the narration reports, moving ambiguously between indirect and free indirect discourse. "Nothing much had happened to her yet" (185). [她引以自慰的一切都沒有了，根本沒有這些事，她這輩子還沒經過什麼事。(207).] In this domestic moment on an unremarkable evening, the novel shows another act of routine violence on the part of an embittered woman as well as the crisis of a framework of significance, according to which, from her own perspective as well as that of the narration, "nothing much had happened to her yet."[48]

The term that best describes the mood or mode of this scene is "desolation," *cangliang*, which Chang famously uses to describe her own poetics. In the 1944 essay "Writing of One's Own," she states plainly, "I do not like heroics. I like tragedy and, even better, desolation" (WO, 16–17). The effect of desolation is produced by the technique of creating equivocal, rather than stark, contrasts. Chang explains this technique through an analogy with color: "Tragedy" (*beizhuang*), she writes, "resembles the matching of bright red with deep green: an intense and unequivocal contrast. And yet it is more exciting than truly revelatory" (WO, 17). Desolation, in contrast, has the power to reveal through the juxtaposition of moderate hues, for instance, "the conjunction of scallion green with peach red" (WO, 17). Desolation thus has a greater capacity for what Chang terms *qishi* or *qifa*, which Andrew Jones renders approximately in his translation as "revelation." The poetics of desolation taps into a palette of inexhaustible gradations that can enter into a likewise inexhaustible multiplicity of combinations to temper the field of perception and extend the space of reflection. "Tragedy is a kind of closure," Chang explains, "while desolation is a form of revelation" (WO, 17). In terms of characterization, she prefers also to work with "equivocal characters" (*bu chedi de renwu*): while they "are not heroes, . . . they are of the majority who actually bear the weight of the times" (WO, 17).

Yindi is such an equivocal character. She has functioned throughout the narrative as the focal subject on which the weight of the times can be measurably discerned. The principal site for her activity as a woman is the household. As the relationship between the household and the state changes in the transition from Confucian administrative principles toward republicanism, so does the category of woman undergo rearticulation. Chang does not offer through Yindi or other characters any unequivocal, positive iterations of modern femininity. As David Der-wei Wang writes, "Compared with contemporary women writers such as Ding Ling (1907–86) and Xiao Hong (1911–42), Chang shows little intent either to record or to imagine revolutionary alternatives for Chinese women" (xviii). She makes "woman," rather, the site of contradiction and disjunction, the focal subject who experiences the discontinuities of her time. In so doing, Chang offers a conception of Chinese modernity itself as an ongoing and still inchoate process, rather than one moving according to a developmental agenda toward a preconceived image of the future. While she critiques the repressiveness of traditional patriarchy, she puts into question also the impatient knowingness of positivist reformers eager to raze and replace the habits and practices that make up the very habitat of the ordinary and the everyday.

Thus, while she exposes the limitations of Yindi and the confusions of her perspective, she shows the inscription or embeddedness of this vantage point within a preexisting framework of inhabitation that always already conditions communication and mutuality. Peking opera serves as the figure for this mediating social apparatus in a changing lifeworld in China. It is an apparatus that, like other forms of history, can be used or abused for life—by the likes of Yindi or the everyman carpenter. But it remains the apparatus in which a lifeworld abides, day after day. In her writing of the domestic novel, Chang affirms the scene of the ordinary as the scene in which the experience of history takes place and where the promise of modernity opens up in the immanent context of an inherited and changing lifeworld. In this shift, *The Rouge of the North* positions itself qua domestic novel in a critical-aesthetic genealogy in relation to Peking opera as a theatrical medium with which to see China through foreign eyes.

Austen's Wit, Chang's Desolation: Irony and Companionability in the Accommodation of the Ordinary

In the preceding sections of this chapter, I have examined how Austen and Chang train their lenses on the predicaments of female protagonists in households at changing historical moments. Their domestic novels show how "woman" functions as focal subject in respective moments of entry into modernity. They show how, in both the contexts of early nineteenth-century England and early twentieth-century China, the entry into modernity involves a revaluation of the household as, traditionally, the site of ordinary life—that is, the site where the activities of production and reproduction take place that sustain the continuity of life itself in its biological and material senses. The household was traditionally the domain of women and slaves, those who took care of the necessities of life considered infrastructural to the pursuit of the "good life," wherein human beings may manifest virtues of nobility and heroism and distinguish themselves as unique and memorable. The traditional configuration of the relationship between the household and the polis or the state is hierarchical, with the realm of the good life figured in an elevated and visible position. The traditional configuration is likewise patriarchal, as women and slaves attend to the needs of men who can interact with each other as peers outside of the space of the household. In the traditional configuration, freedom and equality were reserved for the few, and the male few, rather than the many. Insofar as modernity involves the activation of freedom and equality as universal principles, attributable to all human beings as subjects capable of exercising reason to give laws to one another, modernity involves the reconfiguration of the relationship between the household as the site where the many engage in the activities of ordinary life and the polis or state as the site of higher activities enjoyed by the few.

Both *Mansfield Park* and *The Rouge of the North* explore the repositioning or relocation of the pursuit of the good life, the question of a life worth living, in the domain of ordinary life. As subject of the household, woman functions proleptically and exemplarily as figure of the modern subject who may coexist with others in freedom, equality, and mutuality. In *Mansfield Park*, Fanny Price emerges from a position of marginality and inferiority, where she is of merely infrastructural importance, to embody a new custodial consciousness that revises the very relationship between infrastructure and structure itself. The stage of the private theatricals serves in the novel as microcosm of the stage of higher, more meaningful action that the household as infrastructure of the polis is supposed to support. Austen's novel puts into question such a hierarchical conception of the stage and shows through the critical consciousness of Fanny an alternative conception of the stage of meaningful action. In this alternative conception, the infrastructure of ordinary life is acknowledged as that which makes and remakes, forms and transforms, the stage or scene in which significant action can take place and be perceptible. Fanny exemplifies the modern subject as one who participates in the stewardship of the infrastructure that conditions the stage on which she and others can pursue free and meaningful action. In so doing, she consents to serving as means to both herself and others as ends. The subject of freedom and equality is not a wholly independent or autonomous entity but one whose equal claim to freedom is implicated in the care for ordinary life and predicated on the grounds of mutuality. The hidden, infrastructural nature of ordinary life as grounds of mutuality comes to the fore in the domestic novel as a form of modernity.

In *The Rouge of the North*, Chang manifests a similar concern with ordinary life as the grounds of mutuality. In "Writing of One's Own," she remarks, with reference to many of her Chinese contemporaries, "I have discovered that people who like to write literature usually concentrate on the uplifting and dynamic aspects of life and neglect those that are placid and static, though the latter is the ground of the former" (WO, 16). A couple of paragraphs later, she adds, "Without this grounding, uplift is like so much froth. Many works are forceful enough to provide excitement but unable to offer any real revelation, and this failure results from not having grasped this notion of grounding" (WO, 16). The routines, habits, and interactions of everyday life, concentrated in the arena of the household and organized by ritual practices, already instantiate principles and practices of mutuality that undergird and constitute the very substance of freedom and equality. In her reorientation of the discourse about Chinese modernity toward the "placid and static," away from the "uplifting and dynamic," Chang offers a counter-vision to both Chinese and foreign contemporaries who espouse a simplistic and standardizing conception of modernity based on the rationalist equation of knowledge and power. For such contemporaries, the modern subject is the subject of knowledge, presumed to be autonomous and independent. Chang grounds this subject and the possibility of her claim to freedom in the mutuality of ordinary life, where the unknownness of aspects of *doing*, praxis, precedes the consciousness and tempers the willfulness of *knowing*. In her affirmation of the ordinary and the everyday as grounds of modernity, Chang also opens up the inherited grounds of tradition for complex inspection. Her approach makes possible finer distinctions between practices that produce and reproduce a patriarchal, authoritarian harmony and practices that enact a supple and creative mutuality that would undergird new articulations of freedom and equality.

In Yindi's predicament, Chang shows failure and confusion, rather than the working custodial consciousness of Fanny as modern subject. She shows Yindi's equivocation between transgressive assertions of desire and reactionary applications of patriarchal norms. The growing inefficacy of these norms at a time of sociopolitical reorganization produces the effect of desolation. Insofar as she continues to be oriented in her status as matriarch by patriarchal norms, Yindi cannot be the custodian of a free and equal mutuality. With dim hope, but with hope nonetheless, Chang affirms the scene of Yindi's ordinary life as the grounds for the very possibility of cultural renewal. She positions the reader in this situation of a desolation that offers, paradoxically, strength and dim hope.

Where do such strength and hope come from? They come from the process of mourning at work in the scrutiny of the inherited grounds of tradition that constitute the imperfect habitat of the ordinary. If Yindi is incapable of performing such work of mourning but is caught in a melancholic space detached from efficacious reality, the novel solicits and orients the reader precisely in this work of reviewing objects of lost love and meaningfulness as well as their articulation within a symbolic order that gives expression to such investments and attachments. It is in such work that loves and losses are identified and the displacement of attachments and substitution of lost objects can take place, and it is in such work that lost causes of love and attachment can be found and reclaimed for life. Chang's poetics of desolation solicits the reader as a witness and companion in the work of mournful affirmation, which the willfulness of heroic dynamism and the knowingness of tragic closure would forgo in their distanced perspectives on ordinary life.

Austen and Chang are both critical writers whose unsentimental approaches to the domestic novel lay bare the social structures in which their heroines operate. Their incorporation of elements of theater and theatricality further exposes how their own novelistic practices operate within the frameworks of particular theatrical cultures and succeed and displace theatrical traditions that mediate sociality. In comparison with Austen, Chang's writing displays yet another critical dimension: that of seeing China and Chinese culture through foreign eyes. The self-estrangement inherent in this practice acknowledges the difference between lifeworlds, foreignizing China while calling into question the narcissistic fantasy of coherence and the claims to universalism of foreign eyes. Such self-estrangement effects a mutual provincialization of the claims to coherence of both China and foreign eyes.

Both writers lay bare the changing social frameworks in which their heroines seek to inhabit ordinary life. Both thus provide in their novels a legend to read the changing sociological structures and signifying codes that shape the lifeworlds of their heroines. Besides providing such a legend to read what, after Roland Barthes in *Camera Lucida*, may be called the *studium* of these separate lifeworlds, Austen and Chang offer further the less stable and predictable guide of irony for the task of accommodating the ordinary.[49] In Austen, this irony expresses itself in the form of wit; in Chang, as the experience of desolation.

If Fanny comes to embody a custodial consciousness that valorizes the criterion of utility, irony, in the form of wit, is what keeps this consciousness from conforming completely with a functionary utilitarianism and keeps open the delicate space of difference. At the beginning of the last chapter of the novel, Volume 3, Chapter 17, the narrator makes a sudden conspicuous appearance, calling her protagonist "my Fanny" and summing up, as if in conclusion, "She was returned to Mansfield Park, she was useful, she was beloved" (312). Syntactically and semantically, this formulation echoes a sentence toward the end of Volume 3, Chapter 3, after Henry Crawford's reading aloud from *Henry VIII*: "She was at liberty, she was busy, she was protected" (234). Focalized through Fanny's consciousness, the earlier sentence uses indirect discourse to express the relief Fanny feels upon the entry of the servant Baddely with the afternoon tea service, a routine that interrupts and protects Fanny from Crawford's unstoppable courtship. Anne-Lise François detects, in the "comic and welcome relief" this sentence conveys, the sense "that such protection—such business—is enough for now (and for as long as need be) to guarantee her liberty" and notes the incongruity between the "usually opposed terms—liberty, work, and protection"—in the three short clauses.[50] The routine of taking tea serves, oddly enough, as the occasion of liberty. With the arrival of the tea service, "Mr. Crawford was obliged to move" (234). In the mutual, polite deference to a routine, in which all present are obliged to participate, a space of liberty opens up in which Fanny thinks and does as she pleases. The condition for this slight exercise of liberty is the imperative of household decorum. And the not unpleasant discovery of this liberty affirms not only the propriety of household decorum, but the impropriety it allows for. At the end of the novel, at a distance from Fanny, the narrator pronounces synoptically, "She was returned to Mansfield Park, she was useful, she was beloved." The resonance produced by the echo of the earlier passage suggests that rightful inhabitation as useful and beloved member of Mansfield Park involves comic appreciation of how liberty is not unconstrained but conditioned by a structure of mutuality. The comedy happens with the recognition that constrained liberty is liberty nonetheless, despite one's expectations to the contrary. It is a liberty that one cannot think in advance but that emerges immanently from the everyday arrangements of ordinary life—and that survives the disillusion of a purer, untrammeled conception of freedom.

Strangely enough, Chang's poetics of desolation serves as the occasion also of an unexpected freedom. While *The Rouge of the North* and other fictions present equivocal characters caught and constrained by changing norms in changing circumstances, Chang refrains from imposing positive models of modern subjectivity. Her fictions stage, rather, scenes of ordinary life wherein structures of mutuality are undergoing revaluation. Her writing positions both her characters and readers in relation to phenomena and sensibilia that serve as props of significance that allow mournful revaluation to take place on the scale of the everyday. Her writing thus enlists readers as witnesses and companions to changes in the everyday, orienting them in relation to signifiers undergoing resignification within the operating structure of a particular lifeworld, but leaving the readers free to perceive and reassign significance to these signifiers. In "Writing of One's Own," she explains this orientation of the reader by quoting and commenting on a stanza from an ancient poem, *"Jigu,"* or "Beating the Drums," from the *Shijing,* or *Classic of Poetry,* the foundational collection of the Chinese literary tradition:

> "Life and death are so far apart / I make my vow to you / and take your hand to grow old together." This is a mournful poem, but how very affirmative is its posture toward human life. (16)
>
> 「死生契闊，與子成說；執子之手，與子偕老」是一首悲哀的詩，然而它的人生態度又是何等肯定。(115)

The very gesture of quotation is an act of reiteration that affirms the means of operativity of Chinese literary culture and that interpellates the reader accordingly. The content of the quotation is the wife's marriage vow, itself remembered and reiterated in the longer context of the entire poem by the soldier-husband at a time of war.[51] In repeating these words, likewise at a time of war in 1943, Chang allegorizes anew the terms of a companionship that puts the reader in contact with the workings of a tradition but leaves this reader also the precarious freedom to interpret what is to come.

Both Austen and Chang posit freedom within the immanent framework of an ordinary lifeworld, as an effect to which all have equal claim within changing structures of mutuality. In this freedom, one distinguishes oneself as singular from one's identity as type or function in a system of operativity in which one nevertheless plays a part. In this freedom, the habitat of ordinary life emerges as comprehensible but also strange and thus subject to remaking as stage for action and happiness. The domestic novels of

Austen and Chang solicit their readers as companions in the estrangements upon which such remaking is predicated.

As mentioned, while both Austen and Chang are critical writers who prompt reflection on the conditions of their own representations, Chang's writing features the further critical dimension of cultural self-estrangement. In such cultural self-estrangement, the different conditions of operativity of different lifeworlds are acknowledged, while the claims to totality of these conditions and the claims to centrality and coherence of culturally situated perspectives are called into question. Such cultural self-estrangement effects a mutual provincialization whereby, I argue, a genuine cosmopolitanism may begin.

What is this "genuine cosmopolitanism?" It is not a cosmopolitanism that assumes the uniformity of a world in which commerce and the equivalence of markets motivate the drive toward commensurability. It is, rather, a cosmopolitanism that supplements, complicates, and tilts the instrumentalist and flat uniformity of such a global order with the multi-dimensionality of worlds inhabited in languages that bear the heterogeneous histories of operativity and affectivity. Such a cosmopolitanism puts into question the limits of the European Enlightenment episteme that has functioned as the governing episteme of the uniform global order. It puts into question likewise critical approaches to the inequities of the global economic order that remain within the confines of an aculturalist or monoculturalist model. Such a cosmopolitanism does not presume the uniformity of a global order but attends, rather, to how the world opens up differently to human beings that inhabit different languages and cultures with complex histories and potentialities.

From the perspective of a uniform world guided by assumptions of individualist autonomy and empowered subjecthood of modern Western derivation, writers such as Chang might appear quaint and queer, niche curiosities. According to the logic of a "world stage" made visible by the totalizing satellitic propensity of scientific modernity, a writer such as Chang cannot but appear as a deviation rather than squarely as a "woman writer of world importance." What the comparative reading of Austen and Chang shows, I hope, is that the world that appears in the mutual provincialization of their reading is not one simply available to uniform illumination. The world that appears in their juxtaposition consists, rather, of the coexistence of locally and linguistically inhabited perspectives in complex and oblique communication with one another.

Resonance describes the mode of this oblique communication. The comparative reader is one who hears the resonance that implies the possibility of a connection and communication across cultural contexts but also, paradoxically, the impossibility of this communication taking place directly, on the instrumentalist plane of language presumed to be a transparent medium or tool. The comparative reader hears both the strangeness between languages and the strangeness of languages to themselves. Such hearing involves hearing not just what is being said but an attunement to the figures, devices, and conventions that condition and inflect how something is said. It thus involves an attentiveness to the caesurae within language itself, the caesurae that arise from the difference between literal and figurative, constative and performative, dimensions of language. Such caesurae produce a silence or hollowness within language that gets redoubled, in turn, between languages, generating the very effect of resonance. The comparative reader is one who hears and learns to listen to this resonance in and from literature, which, more than any other discourse, proceeds with ironic insight into how language says more and less than what it means.

In Volume 1, Chapter 16 of *Mansfield Park*, we learn that one of the books Fanny has been reading in her attic East Room is a volume about Lord George Macartney's 1793 embassy to China.[52] How would this reader, as one of Austen's figures of the reading subject, have made sense of the famous encounter between East and West on the stage of the Qing court with both parties futilely asserting their claims to sovereign, imperial power? Might this reader anticipate the possibility of a mutual reading and shared world in which the companionability of cultures begins not on the stage of sovereign power but with the acknowledgment of ordinary lives embedded in histories and structures of mutuality? To such readers this book looks forward.

Coda

In Samuel Taylor Coleridge's 1798 poem "Frost at Midnight," the ruminating speaker writing late at night finds his attention drawn to a piece of film fluttering over his fireplace grate. "In all parts of the kingdom these films are called *strangers*," Coleridge explains in a footnote appended to early editions of the poem, and "are supposed to portend the arrival of some absent friend."[1] Contemplating the fluttering film, the "sole unquiet thing" in the frozen stillness of the winter night, the lyric speaker muses:

> Its motion in this hush of nature
> Gives it dim sympathies with me who live,
> Making it a companionable form,
> Whose puny flaps and freaks the idling Spirit
> By its own moods interprets, every where
> Echo or mirror seeking of itself,
> And makes a toy of Thought. (17–23)[2]

The image of this "companionable form" recalls for him school-day memories of watching similar films over other grates and yearning for the arrival of some absent friend. Seeing the film takes him on an imaginative journey back in time and then forward as he envisages a future happier than his own for the infant son sleeping in a cradle next to him. The "companionable form" echoes or mirrors his spirit's own seeking, serving as the delicate vehicle wherein the desire for companionability, however ephemerally and spectrally, nevertheless attains expressive form.

By examining forms of modernity in Romantic England and Romantic China on the horizon of world literature, this book has brought together in each chapter, in effect, strangers as companionable forms. The companionability of such forms—the literary manifesto, the tale collection, the familiar essay, and the domestic novel—is predicated on a shared definition of literature as imaginative writing and on the condition of world literature as a discursive framework wherein local writing practices and textual traditions come into encounter and undergo reclassification and revaluation in dialectical relation to one another. These forms appear similar at first glance, and they serve as vehicles and sites for the pursuit of shared questions: what does it mean to attain a voice? What is a common reader? How does one dwell in the ordinary? And what is a woman? But close examination of the texts has shown how the uses of these forms tap into heterogeneous textual and philosophical traditions and operate according to different sociocultural logics of address. The efforts to write literary modernity in different lifeworlds activate elements of different literary historiographical constellations.

On the Horizon of World Literature has approached such efforts to write literary modernity as efforts to enact political modernity according to shared principles of liberty, equality, and mutuality. While such principles have universal valence in what may be called world modernity, their actualization has taken place and continues to take place locally in plural and uneven ways within languages and cultures as inherited mediums of imagination and inhabitation. The universality of shared political criteria makes literary modernities comparable and companionable to one another, but the plural instantiation of such criteria puts into question false and often unwittingly provincial universalisms that attempt to determine and stabilize the content of what it means to exist in conditions of liberty, equality, and mutuality. In its comparison of select forms across languages and cultures, this book has aimed to shed light on not just the terms of comparability of literary forms but on the terms of companionability of different cultures, treating literary forms as fictive institutions that serve as the testing grounds for modern sociopolitical forms of life.

Besides investigating the companionability of literary forms across cultures, this book has studied how literary forms serve *within* cultures as experiments in new forms of companionability, as reimaginations and reinventions of ways of being-with. The sequence of chapters traces an arc that moves toward ordinary life and daily existence as the grounds on which modernity and reinventions of being-with take place in resilient and sustainable ways. The chapters move from the high, proclamatory register of the literary manifesto, in which speakers claim a certain elevation above those whom they address, to the lower, middling registers of the tale collection, the familiar essay, and the domestic novel, in which the claim to speak and the act of address issue from an eye- and ear-level relationship to others. At stake in these registers are different critical relationships to language itself as medium of communication that is always in danger of ossification and thus always in need of renewal. In moving from a higher, heroic register to registers of the middling, the chapters move also from texts that operate with a high level of conceptual abstraction to texts that engage with the sensuous particulars of lifeworlds that would not be immediately available and recognizable to one another. The sequence shows how the critical process of putting language itself into question necessarily involves abstraction but, rather than establishing a meta-language for higher thought, returns to the originative potential and critical intimacies of ordinary life and everyday language. The process of putting language into question does not harden, thus, into critical positions that can be used to preside over aesthetic-ideological programs of cultural consolidation. It remains attuned, rather, to the ongoingness of language and languages as locally lived, to their potentialities for reimagining and reinventing ways of being-with in companionable yet stranger scenes of the everyday.

In its practice of a deprovincialized close reading, this book has sought to compare not just texts but textual and historical processes that condition acts of iteration. It has shown how texts operate as fields of interlocking developments, wherein processes in one culture and locale connect to processes in another within a common epistemic framework but depend for their meaningfulness on heterogeneous traditions and cultural contexts of address. In so doing, it aims to offer a model for comparative reading attuned to the potentialities of a plurally shared and intimately lived world modernity and open to the promise of companionabilities to come portended by the forms of fluttering strangers.

Acknowledgments

For a book that shuttles between East and West, it seems oddly fitting that I began this book at one institution, National Tsing Hua University in Hsinchu, Taiwan, and finished it at another, Barnard College in New York. I have benefited in the process from the encouragement, expertise, advice, and insight of many friends and colleagues in both places and beyond.

I would like to thank my editors at Fordham University Press for making this book a reality. Years ago, before any part of the manuscript had come into being, Sara Guyer was one of the first people to encourage me to pursue the particular research direction I was considering. Brian McGrath's importance as an interlocutor in the early stages of the project only grew in the later stages, to the point of utter indispensability. His questions have been invaluable to the improvement of the manuscript. I am indebted to Tom Lay for his thoughtful and careful stewardship of the manuscript and for advice that has helped me give the book a more expansive reach. I thank Aldene Fredenburg and Eric Newman for their meticulous copy editing of the manuscript and Sophia Basaldua and C. J. Sheu for their work indexing the book.

I am indebted to the two readers of the manuscript for their careful readings and illuminating comments and suggestions. It was a privilege to benefit from their erudition and critical acumen and a pleasure to engage with their feedback. I was honored to discover that one of the readers was Wai-yee Li, whose scholarly and professional example I have long admired and learned from deeply. Her insights have helped this book immensely.

Among former colleagues at Tsing Hua, I am indebted to Y. C. Tsai for giving me the chance to develop my interest in literary relations between China and the West on both individual as well as institutional levels. The elegance of his own work has been an inspiration to me. I learned a great deal from working with colleagues and students in the Department of Foreign Languages and Literatures and from interacting with colleagues in various other departments and institutes in the College of Humanities and Social Sciences in workshops and events hosted by the Center for Comparative Literature. I am especially grateful to Juliette Yueh-tsen Chung for being a sheer force of nature and a close interlocutor and friend. And I thank Kean-Fu Guan not only for his intellectual fellowship while I was at Tsing Hua but also for bringing me back to Hsinchu from New York as a presenter at two conferences he organized.

At Barnard, I am indebted to Peter Connor for his generous and gracious support and to him and Peter Platt for their thoughtful readings of the manuscript. Anupama Rao made me feel welcome at Barnard in more ways than I can count. Rachel McDermott helped me make a decision about the structure of the book and, along with Max Moerman and Jack Hawley, shed light on questions beyond my own range of expertise. Rachel Eisendrath not only responded helpfully to a draft of my book proposal but also suggested, with graceful ease, the deft switch that resulted in the book's final title. Sondra Phifer and the crew of colleagues on the third floor of Milbank provided a sustaining flow of support and camaraderie.

I am grateful to Yu-yu Cheng for the invitation to speak about my book project at National Taiwan University and to Earl Jackson for an occasion to present an early version of Chapter 1 in a lecture at National Chiao Tung University. Thanks go also to audiences at conferences of the North American Society for the Study of Romanticism, the International Conference on Romanticism, the American Comparative Literature Association, and the World Congress in Translation Studies for feedback on my work in progress.

Part of Chapter 1 appeared under the title "Shelley's Voice: Poetry, Internationalism, and Solidarity" in the *European Romantic Review* 30.3 (2019): 239–247. A version of Chapter 2, "Shakespearean Retellings and the Question of the Common Reader: Charles and Mary Lamb's *Tales from Shakespeare* and Lin Shu's *Yinbian Yanyu*," appeared in the *Journal of the History of Ideas in East Asia* 13 (December 2017): 89–130. I thank the readers and editors at these journals for their helpful comments.

Various friends and colleagues read and responded to parts of the manuscript at multiple stages. I am particularly indebted to Jared Stark and Ulrich Baer for reading versions of the Introduction and individual chapters and offering me crucial formulations. I thank Eyal Peretz for holding me fast to my overall theoretical conception of the book. For valuable feedback and timely encouragement at various stages of my work, I thank Jennifer Ballengee, Elisabeth Bronfen, Shun-liang Chao, Alex Des Forges, Eric Eisner, Michael Fei, Ludovico Geymonat, Harrison Huang, Michael Keevak, Peter Manning, Barry McCrea, David Wang, Alex Woloch, and Yang Tse. Along with advice and encouragement, Lydia Liu provided warm hospitality to me in Morningside Heights in her capacity as director of the Institute for Comparative Literature and Society at Columbia.

Thanks go to Cathy Caruth, Shoshana Felman, Paul Fry, Connie Harsh, and Lynn Staley for their early and steadfast encouragement of my writing of this book, and to Michael Levine, Pericles Lewis, Jonathan Mulrooney, Sarah Raff, and Emily Rohrbach for timely interactions and conversations that helped me stay on course.

My mother, Alice Yu; my brother, Edward Sun; my sister-in-law, Felicia Lu, and now little Riley Sun make sure that Taipei is always a home for me. My father, Raymond Sun, has been a source of consistently warm and gentle supportiveness.

Finally, I thank Clay Ruede and Maggie Gordon-Ruede for making our home life so much fun and so loving. Maggie and this book have grown up together. I dedicate this book to Clay and to the memory of my grandmother Alice Tsai Yu, who died in 2018 before this book could be completed. From both of them I feel fortunate indeed to have received richly the gift of extraordinarily fine listening.

Notes

Introduction: Reading Literary Modernities on the Horizon of World Literature

1. Johann Wolfgang von Goethe and Johann Peter Eckermann, "Conversations on World Literature," in *The Princeton Sourcebook in Comparative Literature: From the European Enlightenment to the Global Present*, ed. David Damrosch, Natalie Melas, and Mbongiseni Buthelezi (Princeton, N.J.: Princeton University Press, 2009), 22. The editors of this volume reprint with some alterations John Oxenford's translation of *Conversations with Eckermann* (Washington, D.C., and London: M. Walter Dunne, 1901).

2. Ibid.; Oxenford translation modified.

3. See the entry on "Literature," in Raymond William's *Keywords: A Vocabulary of Culture and Society* (Oxford: Oxford University Press, 2015), 134–38.

4. See James Turner, *Philology: The Forgotten Origins of the Modern Humanities* (Princeton, N.J.: Princeton University Press, 2014), particularly Chapter 4, "'Deep Erudition Ingeniously Applied': Revolutions of the Later Eighteenth Century," and Chapter 5, "'Genuinely National Poetry and Prose': Literary Philology and Literary Studies, 1800–1860."

5. See Liang Qichao, *Xiaweiyi youji* [Travels to Hawaii], in *Yinbinshi heji: Zhuanji* [Collected Writings from the Ice-Drinker's Studio: Collected Works] (Shanghai: China Books, 1936), 22:190–91. The fiction writer Zeng Pu refers in a letter to Hu Shih in 1928 a conversation he had with Chen Jitong at the turn of the century in which Chen advocates leaving national literature behind and getting involved in world literature. Secondary citation from Hu Shih, *Hu Shi jingpinji* [Selections from Hu Shih], ed. Hu Ming et al. (Beijing: Guangming Daily Press, 1998), 6:349. See Jing Tsu, "Chen Jitong's 'World Literature,'" in *Sound and Script in Chinese Diaspora* (Cambridge, Mass.: Harvard University Press, 2011), 112–43.

6. See Zhou Zuoren's 1922 essay "*Gujing zhongwai pai*" [On the Ancient/Modern, Chinese/Foreign School], in *Zhou Zuoren daibiaozuo* [Representative Works of Zhou Zuoren], ed. Zhang Juxiang (Zhengzhou: Huanghe wenyi, 1987), 58.

7. Franco Moretti, "Conjectures on World Literature," in *Distant Reading* (London: Verso, 2013), 45.

8. David Damrosch, *What Is World Literature?* (Princeton, N.J.: Princeton University Press, 2003), 281.

9. Emily Apter, *Against World Literature: On the Politics of Untranslatability* (London: Verso, 2013), 2.

10. My use of "provincialize" here is indebted to Dipesh Chakrabarty's formulation in *Provincializing Europe: Postcolonial Thought and Historical Difference* (Princeton, N.J.: Princeton University Press, 2008).
11. Moretti, "Conjectures on World Literature," 45.
12. Damrosch, *What Is World Literature?*, 4.
13. Apter, *Against World Literature*, 3.
14. Immanuel Kant, *Critique of Judgment*, trans. Werner Pluhar (Indianapolis: Hackett, 1987), 103–17.
15. See Hannah Arendt, "The Discovery of the Archimedean Point," in *The Human Condition* (Chicago: University of Chicago Press, 1998), 257–68.
16. I have learned much from the comparative work on traditions of textual interpretation undertaken by Sheldon Pollock and other collaborators in *World Philology*, ed. Sheldon Pollock, Benjamin Elman, and Ku-Ming Kevin Chang (Cambridge, Mass.: Harvard University Press, 2015).
17. I am indebted to Gayatri Spivak's formulation "intimate reading" as an interpretation of "close reading" that acknowledges the ineradicable workings of desire in the practice of reading; see Spivak, "The Politics of Translation," in *Outside in the Teaching Machine* (New York: Routledge, 2008), 200–225.
18. Pheng Cheah, Introduction, "Missed Encounters: Cosmopolitanism, World Literature, and Postcoloniality," and Chapter 1, "The New World Literature: Literary Studies Discovers Globalization," in *What Is a World? On Postcolonial Literature as World Literature* (Durham, N.C.: Duke University Press, 2016), 1–45.
19. Williams, *Keywords*, 134–38.
20. Ibid., 136.
21. David Der-Wei Wang, Introduction, "Worlding Literary China," in *A New Literary History of Modern China*, ed. David Der-Wei Wang (Cambridge, Mass.: Harvard University Press, 2017), 6.
22. On the writing of literary histories in China, see Chen Guoqiu (also known as Leonard Kwok-kou Chan), *Wenxueshi shuxie xingtai yu wenhua zhengzhi* [The Forms and Cultural Politics of Literary History] (Beijing: Peking University Press, 2004).
23. Paul de Man, "Literary History and Literary Modernity," in *Blindness and Insight: Essays in the Rhetoric of Contemporary Criticism* (Minneapolis: University of Minnesota Press, 1983), 142–65.
24. Ibid., 162–63.
25. Goethe and Eckermann, "Conversations on World Literature," 22. I have modified the translation that Damrosch, Melas, and Buthelezi reprint with some alterations from John Oxenford's translation of *Conversations with Eckermann*. The German text can be found in Goethe, *Sämtliche Werke: Briefe, Tagebücher und Gespräche*, ed. Friedmar Apel et al. (Frankfurt am Main: Deutscher Klassiker Verlag, 1986–99), Part 2, 12:224f.
26. Goethe and Eckermann, "Conversations," translation modified.
27. Ning Ma, *The Age of Silver: The Rise of the Novel East and West* (Oxford: Oxford University Press, 2017), 169. For reference to Goethe's reading of *Haoqiu zhuan*, *Yujiao li*, and other translated Chinese texts, see Patricia Sieber, *Theaters of Desire: Authors, Readers, and the Reproduction of Early Chinese Song-Drama, 1300–2000*

(New York: Palgrave Macmillan, 2003), 14. Reinhart Meyer-Kalkus surmises that, instead of *Haoqiu zhuan*, it was another seventeenth-century Chinese novel, *Yujiao li*, that Goethe was reading that day in Jean-Pierre Abel Rémusat's French translation, *Iu-kiao-li, ou, Les deux cousines* (Paris: Moutardier, 1826). See Meyer-Kalkus, "World Literature beyond Goethe," in *Cultural Mobility: A Manifesto*, ed. Stephen Greenblatt et al. (Cambridge: Cambridge University Press, 2010), 96–122.

28. Thomas Percy, Preface, *Hau Kiou Choaan, or The Pleasing History* (London: R. and J. Dodsley, 1761), vii. Percy rehearses in the Preface the history of the transmission of Wilkinson's manuscript. See James St. André, "Modern Translation Theory and Past Translation Practice: European Translations of the *Haoqiu zhuan*," in *One into Many: Translation and the Dissemination of Classical Chinese Literature*, ed. Leo Tak-hung Chan (Amsterdam: Rodopi, 2003), 39–66; and Chen Shouyi, "Thomas Percy and His Chinese Studies," in *The Vision of China in the English Literature of the Seventeenth and Eighteenth Centuries*, ed. Adrian Hsia (Hong Kong: Chinese University Press, 1998), 301–24.

29. Eun Kyung Min, *China and the Writing of English Literary Modernity, 1690–1770* (Cambridge: Cambridge University Press, 2018); see Chapter 5, "Thomas Percy's Chinese Miscellanies and the Reliques of Ancient English Poetry." See also Peter Kitson, "Thomas Percy and the Forging of Romantic China," in *Forging Romantic China: Sino-British Cultural Exchange, 1760–1840* (Cambridge: Cambridge University Press, 2013), 26–44; and David Porter, "Thomas Percy's Sinology and the Origins of English Romanticism," in *The Chinese Taste in Eighteenth-Century England* (Cambridge: Cambridge University Press, 2010), 154–83.

30. Chris Murray's book *China from the Ruins of Athens and Rome: Classics, Sinology, and Romanticism, 1793–1938* (Oxford: Oxford University Press, 2020), analyzes how Anglophone writers coming into contact with Qing China turned to ancient Greek and Roman classics to interpret Chinese concepts, effectively establishing a dialogue between cultural pasts.

31. Ning Ma's *Age of Silver* is one example of ambitious, exciting recent work on this topic.

32. Jorge Luis Borges famously refers to an unknown or perhaps apocryphal contributor to an imperial Chinese encyclopedia in his 1942 essay "John Wilkins's Analytical Language," in *Selected Nonfictions*, ed. Eliot Weinberger, trans. Esther Allen, Suzanne Jill Levine, and Eliot Weinberger (New York: Penguin, 2000), 229–32. Michel Foucault memorably cites this reference at the beginning of *The Order of Things* (New York: Pantheon, 1970).

33. Jacques Derrida, *Acts of Literature*, ed. Derek Attridge (London: Routledge, 1992), 36.

34. Writers like Guo Muoro and Xu Zhimo tended to equate Romantic writing simply with such expressivism. See Leo Ou-fan Lee, *The Romantic Generation of Modern Chinese Writers* (Cambridge, Mass.: Harvard University Press, 1973).

35. See Suh-Reen Han's Introduction to "English Romanticism in East Asia," the collection of essays she edited for the December 2016 issue of the online journal *Romantic Circles Praxis Series* (https://romantic-circles.org/praxis/eastasia). In Section 10 of her Introduction, she writes eloquently of Romanticism "as one form of

Enlightenment's self-criticism" that brings into "critical discourse a Kantian insistence on universal hospitality and cosmopolitan right against the aggravation of global wars and colonial violence. . . . Far from erasing historical differences and local particularities, rethinking East and West and their relationship through the prism of Romanticism will allow us to contemplate the shared *and* divergent forms, experiences, and questions of modernity."

36. Walter Benjamin, *Selected Writings*, vol. 4, *1938–1940*, ed. Howard Eiland and Michael W. Jennings (Cambridge, Mass.: Harvard University Press, 2003), 397.

37. Jacques Khalip and Forest Pyle offer an explanation of the untimely criticality of Benjamin's notion of the constellation in their Introduction "The Present Darkness of Romanticism," to their edited collection *Constellations of a Contemporary Romanticism* (New York: Fordham University Press, 2016).

38. Martin Puchner, *Poetry of the Revolution: Marx, Manifestos, and the Avant-Gardes* (Princeton, N.J.: Princeton University Press, 2006).

39. Among the numerous titles that have addressed this topic are *The Arabian Nights in Historical Context: Between East and West*, ed. Saree Makdisi and Felicity Nussbaum (Oxford: Oxford University Press, 2008), Srinivas Aravamudan's *Enlightenment Orientalism: Resisting the Rise of the Novel* (Chicago: University of Chicago Press, 2011), and Ros Ballaster's *Fabulous Orients: Fictions of the East in England 1662–1785* (Oxford: Oxford University Press, 2005).

40. See Yan Jianfu [also known as Kean Fu Guan], *Wanqing xiaoshuo de xin gainian ditu* [A Conceptual Remapping of Late-Qing Fiction] (Taipei: National Taiwan University Press, 2014).

41. See Douglas Howland, *Translating the West: Language and Political Reason in Nineteenth-Century Japan* (Honolulu: University of Hawaii Press, 2001), and *Personal Liberty and Public Good: The Introduction of John Stuart Mill to Japan and China* (Toronto: University of Toronto Press, 2005). As the editors of *Keywords in Chinese Culture* write in their Introduction to the volume, "*Ziyou* 自由 has the dual sense of 'self-willed' and 'carefree' in pre-modern texts, but comes to be understood [in the late Qing] as the equivalent of 'freedom' or 'liberty,' the individual's defense against encroachment on his or her rights"; *Keywords in Chinese Thought*, ed. Wai-yee Li and Yuri Pines (Hong Kong: Chinese University of Hong Kong Press, 2019), 22.

42. Charles Taylor, *Modern Social Imaginaries* (Durham, N.C.: Duke University Press, 2004).

43. Stanley Cavell, *In Quest of the Ordinary: Lines of Skepticism and Romanticism* (Chicago: University of Chicago Press, 1988).

1. Literary Modernity and the Emancipation of Voice: Defenses of Poetry by Percy Bysshe Shelley and Lu Xun

1. The essay appeared in 1908 in the February and March issues of *Henan* monthly, signed under the pen name "Ling Fei." The young Zhou Shuren would not adopt the pen name of "Lu Xun" for another ten years. For contextual purposes, I note that, between 1903 and 1908, the number of Chinese students in Japan reached upward of 8,000—one historian estimates 13,000—before dwindling after the 1911

Revolution. See Robert A. Scalapino, "Prelude to Marxism: The Chinese Student Movement in Japan, 1900–1910," in *Approaches to Modern Chinese History*, ed. Albert Feuerwerker, Rhoads Murphey, and Mary C. Wright (Berkeley: University of California Press, 1967), 192.

    2. As "Lu Xun" is a pen name rather than a compound consisting of a patronym and a given name, I cite the name in full throughout instead of using "Lu" as shorthand.

    3. Southey uses the phrase in the Preface to *A Vision of Judgement*.

    4. Thanks go to Max Moerman for bringing this connotation to my attention.

    5. Lu Xun tells the famous story of this decision in the Preface to his 1922 collection of stories *Nahan*, or *Outcry*.

    6. Beginning in the 1970s, Kitaoka published a series of articles on the probable sources Lu Xun used in writing the essay. These articles are collected in *Rojin Bungaku no engen wo saguru: "Mara Shi Ryoku Setsu" Zaigen Ko* [An Inquiry into the Origins of Lu Xun's Literature: A Study of the Sources for "On the Power of Mara Poetry"] (Tokyo: Kyuko Shoin, 2015).

    7. John Addington Symonds, *Shelley* (London: Macmillan, 1878). On the influence of Symonds's biography in Shelley's reception in Victorian England, see Eric Eisner's chapter "Shelley's Glamour," in *Nineteenth-Century Poetry and Literary Celebrity* (New York: Palgrave Macmillan, 2009), 91–114.

    8. See the classic articulation of this idea in Immanuel Kant's *Grounding for the Metaphysics of Morals*, trans. James W. Ellington (Indianapolis: Hackett, 1993).

    9. All quotes from Shelley in this chapter are from *Shelley's Poetry and Prose*, ed. Donald Reiman and Neil Fraistat (New York: Norton, 2002). Quotations of poetry are cited by line number and quotations of prose by page number within the body of the chapter.

    10. Commentators have long discerned a universalist aspiration in lines 4–5 of "Ode to the West Wind," as Shelley compares the leaves being driven to cyclical destruction and renewal by the West Wind to "yellow, and black, and pale, and hectic red, / Pestilence-stricken multitudes." Shelley's language in these lines repeats in the color of the leaves post-Linnaean taxonomic markers of racial difference that informed nineteenth-century Western discourse. Such color-coding entered Chinese discourse itself toward the end of the nineteenth century. What is important to register is the critical complexity that accompanied the local assimilation of such rhetoric. In his 1908 essays, Lu Xun targets his countrymen for the internalization and domestication of a hierarchical classification of races, criticizing among his fellow Chinese tendencies for slavish imitation of Europeans, adulation of "strong" peoples and nations, and contempt for "weaker" nations. In so doing, he situates his critical stance in relation to crude eugenicist and social Darwinist thinking among reformist groups of late Qing and, proleptically, Republican China. On the assimilation of racial color-coding in East Asian discourse, see Michael Keevak's *Becoming Yellow: A Short History of Racial Thinking* (Princeton, N.J.: Princeton University Press, 2011).

    11. On Shelley and Chartism, see Anne Janowitz, *Lyric and Labour in the Romantic Tradition* (Cambridge: Cambridge University Press, 1998), and Stephanie Kuduk

Weiner, *Republican Politics and English Poetry, 1789–1874* (New York: Palgrave Macmillan, 2005).

12. In Lu Xun's account of Shelley's 1811 pamphlet *The Necessity of Atheism*, it is Shelley himself who plays the figure of Byronic defiance, resisting first the clergy and then his father while getting expelled from Oxford. See note 20.

13. See Casie Legette, "From Citation to Recitation: Shelley's 'Men of England,'" in *Remaking Romanticism: The Radical Politics of the Excerpt* (Cham, Switzerland: Palgrave, 2017), 167–213.

14. For an analysis of the political implications of the poem's "hyper-reflexivity," see Marc Redfield's "Masks of Anarchy: Shelley's Political Poetics," in *The Politics of Aesthetics: Nationalism, Gender, Romanticism* (Stanford, Calif.: Stanford University Press, 2003), 148–71.

15. For a recent collection of essays revisiting the tension between the terms *shijie* and *tianxia* (literally "all under heaven"), see *Chinese Visions of World Order*, ed. Ban Wang (Durham, N.C.: Duke University Press, 2017).

16. On the influence of Zhang Taiyan on Lu Xun, see Viren Murthy's *The Political Philosophy of Zhang Taiyan: The Resistance of Consciousness* (Leiden: Brill, 2011).

17. For the introduction of the term *ziyou* as translation of "freedom" and "liberty," see Douglas Howland, *Personal Liberty and Public Good: The Introduction of John Stuart Mill to Japan and China* (Toronto: University of Toronto Press, 2005).

18. See Jon von Kowallis, "On the Critical Reception of Lu Xun's Early Classical-Style Essays from the Japan Period," *Journal of Chinese Literature and Culture* 3, no. 2 (November 2016): 357–98.

19. Lu Xun, excerpt from "On the Power of Mara Poetry," trans. Shu-ying Tsau and Donald Holoch, in *Modern Chinese Literary Thought: Writings on Literature, 1893–1945*, ed. Kirk Denton (Stanford, Calif.: Stanford University Press, 1996), 99. Citations of this translation will be henceforth integrated by page number into the body of the chapter.

20. Lu Xun, "Moluo shi lishuo," in *Lu xun zuopin ji* [Collected Works of Lu Xun] (Taipei: Fengyun shidai chuban gongsi, 1989), 6:66. Citations of this text will be henceforth integrated by page number into the body of the chapter.

21. According to Stephen Owen, "It is uncertain exactly when the 'Great Preface' reached its present form, but we can be reasonably sure that it was no later than the first century A.D."; Owen, *Readings in Chinese Literary Thought* (Cambridge, Mass.: Harvard University Press, 1992), 37.

22. The passage that Lu Xun reformulates in the "Great Preface" is as follows, in Stephen Owen's translation: "The affections (*ch'ing*) emerge in sounds [or "voices" for *sheng*]; when those sounds [*sheng*] have patterning (*wen*), they are called "tones." The tones of a well-managed age are at rest and happy; its government is balanced. The tones of an age of turmoil are bitter and full of anger; its government is perverse. The tones of a ruined state are filled with lament and brooding; its people are in difficulty" (ibid., 43). For readings of how Lu Xun reformulates key concepts in the "Great Preface," see John Crespi, *Voices in Revolution: Poetry and the Auditory Imagination in Modern China* (Honolulu: University of Hawaii Press, 2009), 25–27, and Ban Wang, *The Sublime Figure of History: Aesthetics and Politics in Twentieth-Century China* (Stanford, Calif.: Stanford University Press, 1997), 65.

23. Martin Puchner, *Poetry of the Revolution: Marx, Manifestos, and the Avant-Gardes* (Princeton, N.J.: Princeton University Press, 2005).

24. For a Peacockian reading of how the language of the new human sciences inhabits already Shelley's poetry, see Maureen McLane's *Romanticism and the Human Sciences: Poetry, Population, and the Discourse of the Species* (Cambridge: Cambridge University Press, 2000).

25. Lu Xun, "Toward a Refutation of Malevolent Voices," trans. Jon von Kowallis, *Boundary 2* 38, no. 2 (2011): 39–62. References to this translation will be henceforth incorporated into the body of the chapter.

26. Yang Xiong, *Exemplary Figures / Fayan*, trans. Michael Nylan (Seattle: University of Washington Press, 2013), 76–77. The passage is found in *Wenshen*, "Asking about Divine Insight," 5, no. 13 (2013). I have taken the liberty of modifying Nylan's translation from "speech is the heart's sounds" to "speech is the voice of the heart" in accordance with Lu Xun's tendency to use the word *sheng* as "voice."

27. Lu Xun, "Po esheng lun," in *Wang hui du lu xun* [Wang Hui Reads Lu Xun] (Hong Kong: Chinese University of Hong Kong Press, 2013), 166.

28. Von Kowallis renders the term "becoming master of one's own soul."

29. Wang Hui, "The Voices of Good and Evil: What Is Enlightenment? Rereading Lu Xun's 'Toward a Refutation of Malevolent Voices,'" trans. Ted Huters and Yangyang Zong, *Boundary 2* 38, no. 2 (2011): 92.

30. See the annotations von Kowallis provides along with his translation of Lu Xun's "Toward a Refutation of Malevolent Voices."

31. Kant, *Perpetual Peace and Other Essays*, trans. Ted Humphrey (Indianapolis: Hackett, 1983), 41.

32. Friedrich Nietzsche, *Kritische Studienausgabe in 15 Bänden*, ed. Giorgio Colli and Mazzino Montinari (Berlin: Deutsche Taschenbuch Verlag / de Gruyter, 1999), 4:265.

33. Lu Xun, "Po esheng lun," 165.

2. Shakespearean Retellings and the Question of the Common Reader: Charles and Mary Lamb's *Tales from Shakespeare* and Lin Shu's *Yinbian Yanyu*

1. Stanley Wells, "Tales from Shakespeare," *Proceedings of the British Academy* 73 (1987): 125–52.

2. According to Wells in his 1987 essay, there were almost "200 editions in English, and . . . at least forty translations extending beyond the major European languages to Burmese, Swahili, Japanese, Macedonian, Chinese . . . , Hungarian, and the African dialects of Ga and Ewe . . . 1879 was a bumper year, with seven editions, three of them in Calcutta" (ibid., 131).

3. Alexander Huang mentions *Xiewai Qitan* as an earlier translation that appeared in 1903 but did not make nearly the impact on readers as *Yinbian Yanyu*. See Chapter 3, "Rescripting Moral Criticism: Charles and Mary Lamb, Lin Shu, and Lao She," in Huang's *Chinese Shakespeares: Two Centuries of Cultural Exchange* (New York: Columbia University Press, 2009), 71.

4. Lin would translate, over the course of his career, an estimated 180–200 Western literary works. See a list of titles of "Lin Shu's Classic Translations," in *Renditions* (Autumn 1975): 22–24.

5. For a critical account of the Godwins's project, see Chapter 6, "A Juvenile Library; or, Works of a New Species," in Julie Carlson's *England's First Family of Writers: Mary Wollstonecraft, William Godwin, Mary Shelley* (Baltimore: Johns Hopkins University Press, 2007).

6. Marina Warner rehearses this well-known, bizarre episode in English literary and cultural history in her Introduction to Charles and Mary Lamb's *Tales from Shakespeare* (London: Penguin, 2007), xxiv. All subsequent references to this edition of the Lambs's *Tales* will be incorporated by page number within the body of the essay.

7. Lydia Liu provides an important and useful analysis of this process in *Translingual Practice: Literature, National Culture, and Translated Modernity, 1900–1937* (Stanford, Calif.: Stanford University Press, 1995).

8. On the fate of Lin's advocacy of *guwen* in the 1920s, see Chapter 2, "Transplanting the Lady of the Camellias," in Hu Ying's *Tales of Translation: Composing the New Woman in China, 1899–1918* (Stanford, Calif.: Stanford University Press, 2000), and Michael Gibbs Hill, *Lin Shu, Inc.: Translation and the Making of Modern Chinese Culture* (Oxford: Oxford University Press, 2013).

9. Robert Altick, *The English Common Reader: A Social History of the Mass Reading Public 1800–1900* (Chicago: University of Chicago Press, 1957), 6–7.

10. G. K. Chesterton, *Robert Browning* (Urbana, Ill.: Project Gutenburg, 2004), retrieved March 31, 2017, from https://www.gutenberg.org/files/13342/13342-h/13342-h.htm.

11. Ibid.

12. I use here the translation by George Kao of Qian Zhongshu's "The Translations of Lin Shu," in *Twentieth-Century Chinese Translation Theory*, ed. Leo Tak-hung Chan (Amsterdam and Philadelphia: John Benjamins, 2004), 106. I indicate in brackets my clarification of the terms Qian uses for "world" and my reinsertion of a segment of Qian's text that Kao chooses to skip in translation. Qian's text in Chinese can be found in *Qianzhongshu Yangjiang Sanwen*, ed. Wen Xiang and Li Hong (Beijing: China Broadcasting Service Press, 1997), 172–212.

13. See Lorraine Daston, *Classical Probability in the Enlightenment* (Princeton, N.J.: Princeton University Press, 1995), and Ian Hacking, *The Emergence of Probability* (Cambridge: Cambridge University Press, 1975) and *The Taming of Chance* (Cambridge: Cambridge University Press, 1990).

14. See the chapter "Authors and Readers," in Perry Link's *Mandarin Ducks and Butterflies: Popular Fiction in Early Twentieth-Century Chinese Cities* (Berkeley: University of California Press, 1981), 156–95, and Leo Ou Fan Lee and Andrew J. Nathan's "The Beginnings of Mass Culture: Journalism and Fiction in the Late Ch'ing and Beyond," in *Popular Culture in Late Imperial China*, ed. David Johnson, Andrew J. Nathan, and Evelyn S. Rawski (Berkeley: University of California Press, 1985), 360–95.

15. Jon Klancher, *The Making of English Reading Audiences, 1790–1832* (Madison: University of Wisconsin Press, 1987), 14.

16. On the popularity of translations of the *Arabian Nights* and other foreign tale collections in eighteenth- and nineteenth-century England, see Warner,

Introduction, in Lamb, *Tales from Shakespeare*. Ros Ballaster treats an earlier period in her lively and path-breaking *Fabulous Orients: Fictions of the East in England 1662–1785* (Oxford: Oxford University Press, 2005).

17. Huang focuses in the chapter "Rescripting Moral Criticism," in *Chinese Shakespeares*, on moral didacticism in the *Tales* and *Yinbian Yanyu*. While benefiting and learning from Huang's work, I am interested in how the texts go beyond message-driven moralism to open up perspectives beyond simple reproduction of dogmatic orthodoxies.

18. Nancy Armstrong, *Desire and Domestic Fiction: A Political History of the Novel* (Oxford: Oxford University Press, 1987), 3.

19. Paul Fleming, *Exemplarity and Mediocrity: The Art of the Average from Bourgeois Tragedy to Realism* (Stanford, Calif.: Stanford University Press, 2009), 51.

20. Ibid., 59. Fleming cites and translates Gotthold Ephraim Lessing from *Werke und Briefe in zwölf Bänden*, ed. Wilfried Barner and Klaus Bohnen (Frankfurt am Main: Deutscher Klassiker Verlag, 1985), 4:175.

21. See Xiaohuan Zhao, *Classical Chinese Supernatural Fiction: A Morphological History* (Lewiston, N.Y.: Edwin Mellen, 2005). For *chuanqi* as a form of Ming-Qing drama, see Wilt Idema on "Traditional Dramatic Literature," in the *Columbia History of Chinese Literature*, ed. Victor Mair (New York: Columbia University Press, 2001), 785–847.

22. Hill, Chapter 3, "The Name Is Changed, but the Tale Is Told of You," in *Lin Shu, Inc.*

23. I use here the translations by Alexander Huang in *Chinese Shakespeares*, 80.

24. Lin Shu and Wei Yi, *Yinbian Yanyu* (Shanghai: Shangwu yinshuguan, 1904). The pages of the Preface are not numbered. All further references to this text will be incorporated by page number, where relevant, in the body of the essay.

25. Jonathan Hay, "Double Modernity, Para-Modernity," in *Antinomies of Art and Culture: Modernity, Postmodernity, Contemporaneity*, ed. Terry Smith, Okwui Enwezor, and Nancy Condee (Durham, N.C.: Duke University Press, 2008), 113–32.

26. Charles Lamb, *The Complete Works and Letters* (New York: Modern Library, 1935), 727.

27. Ibid.

28. After citing Huang's translations of other titles, I note here that my translation of "Ju Yin" as "Storm Ruse" differs from Huang's preference of "A Tempestuous Cause."

29. Patrick Hanan, *The Chinese Vernacular Story* (Cambridge, Mass.: Harvard University Press, 1981), 26. See also Yang Lien-Sheng, "The Concept of *Pao* as a Basis for Social Relations in China." in *Excursions in Sinology* (Cambridge, Mass.: Harvard University Press, 1969).

30. See Hill, "The Name Is Changed, but the Tale Is Told of You."

31. Letter of January 29, 1807; Lamb, *Complete Works and Letters*, 763.

32. See Michel Foucault's argument on the market as the site of veridiction of governmental practices in the modern age of political economy in *The Birth of Biopolitics: Lectures at the Collège de France, 1978–1979* (New York: Picador, 2010), 27–50.

33. Raymond Williams, *Marxism and Literature* (Oxford: Oxford University Press, 1977), 126.

34. Ibid., 123–24.

3. Estrangements of the World in the Familiar Essay: Charles Lamb and Zhou Zuoren's Approaches to the Ordinary

1. See Denise Gigante's Introduction to *The Great Age of the English Essay: An Anthology* (New Haven, Conn.: Yale University Press, 2008), xiii–xxxiii.

2. William Hazlitt, *Lectures on the English Comic Writers* (London: Taylor and Hessey, 1819), 186.

3. Zhou Zuoren, "Belles Lettres" [*Meiwen*], in *Zhou Zuoren Daibiao Zuo* [Representative Writings of Zhou Zuoren], ed. Zhang Juxiang (Zhengzhou: Huanghe wenyi chuban she, 1987), 13–14. All quotations from Zhou's essays will be from this edition and will be henceforth cited by page number and integrated into the body of the chapter.

4. Modified from a translation by Susan Daruvala, in *Zhou Zuoren and an Alternative Chinese Response to Modernity* (Cambridge, Mass.: Harvard University Press, 2000), 171.

5. On the Republican-era Chinese essay and its sources, see Charles Laughlin, *The Literature of Leisure and Chinese Modernity* (Honolulu: University of Hawaii Press, 2008), and Tam King-Fai's Introduction to *A Garden of One's Own: A Collection of Modern Chinese Essays, 1919–1949*, ed., trans. Tam King-Fai (Hong Kong: Chinese University of Hong Kong Press, 2012).

6. See Theodore Huters, *Bringing the World Home: Appropriating the West in Late Qing and Early Republican China* (Honolulu: University of Hawaii Press, 2005).

7. Jonathan Hay, "Double Modernity, Para-Modernity," in *Antinomies of Art and Culture: Modernity, Postmodernity, Contemporaneity*, ed. Terry Smith, Okwui Enwezor, and Nancy Condee (Durham, N.C.: Duke University Press, 2009), 113–32.

8. *Zhou Zuoren: Selected Essays*, ed., trans., with an Introduction by David Pollard (Hong Kong: Chinese University of Hong Kong Press, 2006).

9. See Jane Aaron's *A Double Singleness: Gender and the Writings of Charles and Mary Lamb* (Oxford: Clarendon, 1991).

10. Marilyn Butler, *Romantics, Rebels, Reactionaries* (New York and Oxford: Oxford University Press, 1981), 177.

11. See David Pollard's Introduction to his edition of *Zhou Zuoren: Selected Essays*.

12. Butler, *Romantics, Rebels, Reactionaries*, 176.

13. Charles Taylor, *Sources of the Self: The Making of the Modern Identity* (Cambridge, Mass.: Harvard University Press, 1989), 211. Quotations from this text will henceforth be integrated according to page number within the body of the chapter.

14. *Politics* 1252b, in *The Basic Works of Aristotle*, ed. Richard McKeon (New York: Random House, 1941), 1129.

15. Charles Taylor, *Modern Social Imaginaries* (Durham, N.C.: Duke University Press, 2004).

16. Zhou Zuoren, *Zhongguo xin wenxue de yuanliu* [Sources of the New Chinese Literature] (Nanjing: Jiangsu Literature and Art Publishing House, 2007).

17. See Daruvala, Chapter 3, "The Aesthetics of Place and Self," in *Zhou Zuoren and an Alternative Chinese Response to Modernity*.

18. See Chapter 3, "A Syncretist's Critique of Ch'eng-Chu Orthodoxy," in Edward T. Chien's *Chiao Hung and the Restructuring of Neo-Confucianism in the Late Ming* (New York: Columbia University Press, 1986), 67–113.

19. Charles Lamb, "Old China," in *The Complete Works and Letters of Charles Lamb* (New York: Modern Library, 1935), 218. Quotations from the essay in this edition will henceforth be integrated by page number into the body of the chapter.

20. Elizabeth Chang, *Britain's Chinese Eye: Literature, Empire, and Aesthetics in Nineteenth-Century Britain* (Stanford, Calif.: Stanford University Press, 2010), 78–83.

21. See Chapter 1, "China for Sale: Porcelain Economy in Lamb's *Essays of Elia*," in Karen Fang's *Romantic Writing and the Empire of Signs: Periodical Culture and Post-Napoleonic Authorship* (Charlottesville: University of Virginia Press, 2010).

22. See Simon P. Hull, *Charles Lamb, Elia and the London Magazine: Metropolitan Muse* (London: Pickering and Chatto, 2010), 82–83.

23. See William Morris, "The Lesser Arts," in *News from Nowhere and Other Writings*, ed. Clive Wilmer (London: Penguin, 2004), 231–54.

24. I am indebted to Mark McGurl's insights into narration, scale, and global history in his essay "Gigantic Realism: The Rise of the Novel and the Comedy of Scale," *Critical Inquiry* 43 (Winter 2017): 403–30.

25. Erwin Panofsky, *Perspective as Symbolic Form* (Cambridge, Mass.: Zone, 1997), 30–31.

26. Laughlin translates the title as "Herbs of My Hometown" in his reading of the essay in *The Literature of Leisure and Chinese Modernity*, 49–52.

27. The technique of *jiejing* originated in the aesthetics of Chinese garden architecture and landscaping and was mentioned in the 1631 Ming dynasty treatise *Yuanye*, or *The Craft of Gardens*. On the relationship between garden aesthetics and literary writing, see Waiyee Li, "Gardens and Illusions from Late Ming to Early Qing," *Harvard Journal of Asiatic Studies* 72, no. 2 (December 2012): 295–336.

28. The quote is from the section "*Li Lou 2*," in James Legge, *The Works of Mencius* (New York: Dover, 1970), 322.

29. Theodore de Bary and Irene Bloom, eds., *Sources of Chinese Tradition*, 2nd ed. (New York: Columbia University Press, 2000), 1:867–68.

30. *Almost Island* is the name of an online journal (almostisland.com) and publishing company based in Mumbai, India. Since 2008, it has been hosting every December an annual gathering of international writers in New Delhi and has sponsored also, as a separate event, China-India Dialogues.

31. The memory of Goswami's metaphor returned to me a year and a half later, when I came across this passage in William Jones's "On the Poetry of Eastern Nations," the reading for a workshop at the 2019 meeting of the International Conference on Romanticism: "But it is not sufficient that a nation have a genius for poetry, unless they have the advantage of a rich and beautiful language, that their expressions may be worthy of their sentiments; the Arabians have this advantage also

in a high degree: their language is expressive, strong, sonorous, and the most copious, perhaps, in the world; for, as almost every tribe had many words appropriated to itself, the poets, for the convenience of their measure, or sometimes for their singular beauty, made use of them all, and, as the poems became popular, these words were by degrees incorporated with the whole language, like a number of little streams, which meet together in one channel, and, forming a most plentiful river, flow rapidly into the sea." The passage is in William Jones, *Poems, Consisting Chiefly of Translations from the Asiatick Languages: To Which Are Added Two Essays. I. On the Poetry of the Eastern Nations; II. On the Arts, Commonly Called Imitative* (London: Printed by W. Bowyer and J. Nichols for N. Conant, 1777), 172. Struck by how much Goswami's metaphor resonates with the ending of this quote, I inquired if Jones and Goswami may both be citing or alluding to a popular turn of phrase or a locus classicus in South Asian poetics. My colleague Rachel McDermott confirmed the frequency of riverine imagery in Bengali poetry and referred also to famous stream-to-river-to-ocean images in the *Upanishads*, where "the conjoining of streams is used as an analogy for what happens to souls after death: they all join the one Brahman, or Absolute Spirit" (cited from e-mail exchange). I am grateful to Rachel for shedding light on these poetic sources, which both speak through and were spoken by Goswami and Jones, and I thank Sharmistha Mohanty and Jack Hawley for further clarifying confirmations.

4. Between the Theater and the Novel: Woman, Modernity, and the Restaging of the Ordinary in *Mansfield Park* and *The Rouge of the North*

1. Louisa Chiang and Perry Link, "Before the Revolution," *New York Review of Books*, June 7, 2018.

2. Kam Louie, Introduction, in *Eileen Chang: Romancing Languages, Cultures and Genres*, ed. Kam Louie (Hong Kong: Hong Kong University Press, 2012),16.

3. Book Review, "Eileen Chang's Vivid Recreation of Life in China in the 1930s," *South China Morning Post*, March 30, 2016.

4. Letter to Anna Austen, September 9–18, 1814, in *Jane Austen's Letters*, ed. Deirdre Le Faye (Oxford: Oxford University Press, 1995), 276.

5. Te-hsing Shan, "Eileen Chang as a Chinese Translator of American Literature," *Modern China and the West: Translation and Cultural Mediation*, ed. Hsiao-yen Peng and Isabelle Rabut (Leiden: Brill, 2014), 106–25.

6. See David Der-wei Wang's Foreword to *The Rouge of the North* (Berkeley: University of California Press, 1998), xxix, note 2; and Xiaojue Wang, "Eileen Chang, *The Dream of the Red* Chamber, and the Cold War," in *Eileen Chang*, 126. Quotations from Chang's *The Rouge of the North* will be from the 1998 University of California edition and henceforth will be incorporated by page number into the body of the chapter.

7. For a detailed account of Chang's multiple rewritings of the same story, see Jessica Tsui Yan Li's "Self-Translation/Rewriting: The Female Body in Eileen Chang's 'Jinsuo ji,' *The Rouge of the North*, *Yuannü*, and 'The Golden Cangue,'" *Neohelicon* 37 (2010):391–403.

8. Leo Bersani, *A Future for Astyanax* (New York: Columbia University Press, 1984), 77. See also Kingsley Amis, "What Became of Jane Austen?," *Spectator*, October 4, 1957, 339–40; Nina Auerbach, *Romantic Imprisonment: Women and Other Glorified Outcasts* (New York: Columbia University Press, 1985); Tony Tanner, Introduction to Penguin Classics edition of *Mansfield Park*, reprinted in Jane Austen, *Mansfield Park*, ed. Kathryn Sutherland (London: Penguin, 1996), 440–64.

9. Lionel Trilling, *Sincerity and Authenticity* (Cambridge, Mass.: Harvard University Press, 1972), 1.

10. See Trilling, Chapter 3, "The Sentiment of Being and the Sentiments of Art," in *Sincerity and Authenticity*, 53–80.

11. See Nancy Armstrong, *Desire and Domestic Fiction: A Political History of the Novel* (Oxford: Oxford University Press, 1987).

12. Nicole Huang, *Women, War, Domesticity: Shanghai Literature and Popular Culture of the 1940s* (Leiden: Brill, 2005), 35.

13. For the importance of such genres for the writing of love and sentiment in early Republican China, see Haiyan Lee, Part I, "The Confucian Structure of Feeling," in *Revolution of the Heart: A Genealogy of Love in China, 1900–1950* (Stanford, Calif.: Stanford University Press, 2007).

14. On Chang's critical writing on *The Dream of the Red Chamber*, see the aforementioned essay by Xiaojue Wang, "Eileen Chang, *The Dream of the Red Chamber*, and the Cold War," and, also by Xiaojue Wang, "Creation and Transmission: Eileen Chang and 'Sing-song Girls of Shanghai,'" *Chinese Literature: Essays, Articles, Reviews (CLEAR)* 36 (December 2014): 125–48.

15. See William Galperin, *The Historical Austen* (Philadelphia: University of Pennsylvania Press, 2006), and Mary Favret, Chapter 4, "Everyday War," in *War at a Distance: Romanticism and the Making of Modern Wartime* (Princeton, N.J.: Princeton University Press, 2010).

16. Edward Said, *Culture and Imperialism* (New York: Knopf, 1993), 93–97.

17. Chang, "Writing of One's Own," in *Written on Water*, trans. Andrew Jones, coedited, with an Introduction by Nicole Huang (New York: Columbia University Press, 2005), 17. Further references to this essay will be incorporated in the body of the chapter with the abbreviation "WO," followed by page number.

18. Austen, *Mansfield Park*, ed. Claudia Johnson (New York: Norton, 1998), 35. Further references to this edition of the novel will be incorporated by page number into the body of the chapter.

19. Claudia Johnson annotates in her edition for Norton of *Mansfield Park* that Sir Thomas Bertram's sugar plantation in Antigua may have been losing money because of "decreased crop production stemming from exhausted soil; increased competition from other sugar-producing islands; and/or increased production costs resulting from the abolition of the slave trade" (19, note 2).

20. Zhang Ailing, *Yuannü* (Taipei: Crown, 2016), 150. Further references to this text will be incorporated by page number into the body of the chapter.

21. On the metaphor of acting as an infection, see Joseph Litvak, "The Infection of Acting: Theatricals and Theatricality in *Mansfield Park*," in *Caught in the Act: Theatricality in the Nineteenth-Century English Novel* (Berkeley: University of California

Press, 1992), 1–26. On the metaphorics of purity and hygiene in the novel, see Ruth Yeazell, "The Boundaries of Mansfield Park," *Representations* 7 (Summer 1984): 133–52.

22. Besides the aforementioned texts by Litvak, Yeazell, and Trilling, see also David Marshall's "True Acting and the Language of Real Feeling: *Mansfield Park*," in *The Frame of Art: Fictions of Aesthetic Experience, 1750–1815* (Baltimore: Johns Hopkins University Press, 2005), 72–90.

23. Trilling, *Sincerity and Authenticity*, 58–73.

24. Tanner, Introduction to Penguin Classics edition of *Mansfield Park*, 441.

25. Trilling, *Sincerity and Authenticity*, 77.

26. Litvak and Marshall have also argued that Fanny is not exempt from the theatricality she sees others enacting. The comparative juxtaposition of *Mansfield Park* with *The Rouge of the North* highlights even more how there is no metaphysical "outside" to theatricality but, rather, interruptions, displacements, and revisions of the historical and cultural terms and conditions of seeing and being seen by others.

27. Letter to Cassandra Austen, January 29, 1813, in *Jane Austen's Letters*, 202.

28. See Tanner's Introduction to the Penguin Classics edition of *Mansfield Park*. Trilling's essay on *Mansfield Park* is included in Trilling, *The Moral Obligation to be Intelligent: Selected Essays*, ed. Leon Wieseltier (Evanston, Ill.: Northwestern University Press, 2000), 292–310.

29. Michael Karounos, "Ordination and Revolution in *Mansfield Park*," *Studies in English Literature, 1500–1900* 44, no. 4 (Autumn 2004): 715–36; Daniel Stout, Chapter 2, "The One and the Manor: On Being, Doing, and Deserving in *Mansfield Park*," *Corporate Romanticism: Liberalism, Justice, and the Novel* (New York: Fordham University Press, 2017), 53–95.

30. On Elizabeth Inchbald's adaptation of Kotzebue, see Christoph Bode, "Unfit for an English Stage? Inchbald's *Lovers' Vows* and Kotzebue's *Das Kind der Liebe*," *European Romantic Review* 16, no. 3 (2005): 297–309.

31. On the dating of the actions and events in *Mansfield Park*, see Brian Southam, "The Silence of the Bertrams," *Times Literary Supplement*, Feb. 17, 1995.

32. See Alistair Duckworth, "*Mansfield Park*: Jane Austen's Grounds of Being," in *The Improvement of the Estate: A Study of Jane Austen's Novels* (Baltimore: Johns Hopkins University Press, 1994), 35–80.

33. In just Vol. 1, Chapter 2, the narration of Austen's *Mansfield Park* uses numerous variations on the word "kind": "Nobody meant to be unkind, but nobody put themselves out of their way to secure her comfort" (12); "He had never knowingly given her pain, but he now felt that she required more positive kindness" (14); "Their brother Edmund urged her claims to their kindness" (15); "Edmund was uniformly kind himself" (15).

34. In Austen, Mansfield Park, Vol. 1, Chapter 15, the narration enters Fanny's mind via indirect discourse: "Fanny did not love Miss Crawford; but she felt very much obliged to her for her present kindness" (104).

35. Fanny's public refusal to act, and the resonance throughout the scene of the word "nothing," resembles Cordelia's famous refusal to speak her love in Act I,

Scene I of Shakespeare's *King Lear*. See my analysis of that latter scene in Emily Sun, *Succeeding King Lear: Literature, Exposure, and the Possibility of Politics* (New York: Fordham University Press, 2010), 17–24.

36. See Ruth Yeazell's fine reading in "The Boundaries of *Mansfield Park*" of how a passage of description in Vol. 3, Chapter 15 registers Fanny's subtle yet unmistakable sense of revulsion toward the dirt and disorder at Portsmouth.

37. It is quite possible that the volume of Shakespeare from which Fanny was reading aloud to Lady Bertram was Samuel and Henrietta Bowdler's 1807 four-volume edition of *The Family Shakespeare*, which included *Henry VIII* in Volume 3.

38. See Isobel Armstrong's analysis of the significance of *Henry VIII* in the novel in Armstrong, *Jane Austen: Mansfield Park* (London: Penguin, 1988), 79–87.

39. Chang, "Peking Opera through Foreign Eyes," in *Written on Water*, 105. Further references to this essay will be incorporated in the body of the chapter with the abbreviation "PO," followed by page number.

40. See Xiaomei Chen, "Twentieth-Century Spoken Drama," in *The Columbia History of Chinese Literature*, ed. Victor Mair (New York: Columbia University Press, 2001), 848–77.

41. See Haiyan Lee on the moral and aesthetic consequences of the realist turn in Chinese theater in "Chinese Feelings: Notes on a Ritual Theory of Emotion," *Wenshan Review of Literature and Culture* 92 (June 2016): 1–37.

42. Zhao's exploits were retold and popularized in the late Ming dynasty or sixteenth-century historical military romance *History of the Southern and Northern Song Dynasties* (*Nanbei liangsong zhizhuan*).

43. Ailing, "*Yangren kan jingxi ji qita*," *Huali yuan* (Taipei: Crown, 2018), 14.

44. The Chinese text adds, "In fact, she didn't know much more about Peking opera than he [her son Yensheng] did, but she had always listened intently to what others said" (my translation); Ailing, *Yuannü*, 177.

45. Chang, "From the Mouths of Babes," in *Written on Water*, 8.

46. See Lee, "Chinese Feelings."

47. In Chapter 3 of *Woman and Chinese Modernity*, Rey Chow locates Chang's resistance to a dominant twentieth-century narrative of modernity-as-revolution in her writerly attentiveness to details deemed frivolous and irrelevant to the monumental historiography of Chinese nation-building. My reading follows Chow's by tracing how Chang, in addition to resisting the dominant narrative of Chinese modernity, makes the unstable status of "woman" the site of subtle—and detailed—feminist self-critique; Chow, "Modernity and Narration—in Feminine Detail," *Woman and Chinese Modernity: The Politics of Reading between West and East* (Minneapolis: University of Minnesota Press, 1991), 84–120.

48. I reread the significance of this moment in an essay, "Reverberations: Traumatic Histories, Cultural Difference, and the Drama of Listening in Eileen Chang's *Yuannü* and *The Rouge of the North*," for a collection, edited by Jennifer Ballengee and David Kelman, titled *Reading Catastrophe: Trauma and Literature in an Age of Globalization* (London: Routledge, forthcoming).

49. Roland Barthes, *Camera Lucida*, trans. Richard Howard (New York: Hill and Wang, 1982), 25–27.

50. Anne-Lise François, Chapter 4, "Fanny's 'Labour of Privacy' and the Accommodation of Virtue in Austen's *Mansfield Park*," in *Open Secrets: The Literature of Uncounted Experience* (Stanford, Calif.: Stanford University Press, 2008), 249.

51. The poem "*Jigu*" is among the "Airs of Bei." The same verses are famously cited by the male protagonist Fan Liuyuan in Chang's *Love in a Fallen City*.

52. The volume among Fanny's books in the East Room was, according to Claudia Johnson's annotation, probably John Barrow's 1807 *Some Account of the Public Life, and a Selection from the Unpublished Writings of the Earl of Macartney* (Norton Critical Edition of *Mansfield Park* (New York: Norton, 1998),109, note 4). The Macartney Embassy or Mission, led by George Macartney in 1793, was the first British diplomatic mission to China. The members of the mission met with the Emperor Qianlong on September 14. The mission failed to accomplish the official objectives of opening new ports for British trade in China, establishing a permanent embassy in Beijing, and securing an island off the southern coast for British use. These objectives, along with the goal of selling opium from India to China and tea from China to India, would be forcibly achieved a half century later in the Opium Wars. The Macartney Mission famously included the episode of the British refusing to perform the ritual of kowtowing, choosing rather to genuflect, in keeping with British court protocol.

Coda

1. Samuel Taylor Coleridge, *The Major Works*, ed. H. J. Jackson (Oxford: Oxford University Press, 2000), note to "Frost at Midnight," 701–2.

2. Ibid., 87.

Index

Addison, Joseph, 18, 73, 75
Against World Literature (Apter), 3–4, 145n9
À la recherche du temps perdu (Proust), 85
ambiguity, 8, 25–26, 30, 32, 48
Analects, 43
Antigua (British colony), 99–100, 103, 157n19
The Arabian Nights, 16, 55
Arabic (language), 89–90
Aristotle, 21
Athenäum (Schlegel), 37
Austen, Cassandra, 104–5, 158n27
Austen, Jane, 19, 92–98, 104–5, 133–34, 156n4, 157n15
Autumn Quince (*Qiu haitang*) (Qin Shou'ou), 117

Barbauld, Anna Letitia, 63–64
Bath (city in England), 105
Beijing (city in China), 18, 73, 77, 80, 85–86, 89, 101
Bengali (language), 89–90
Biographia Literaria (Coleridge), 37
Bristol (city in England), 105
Borges, Jorge Luis, 11–12, 147n32
Brandes, Georg, 25
British East India Company, 10, 18, 51, 76, 81
Browning, Robert, 52
Buddhism, 5, 41, 45, 125: Zen Buddhism, 22
Burney, Frances, 96
Burke, Edmund, 106
Byron, Lord, 15, 23–25, 33–34, 76: Byronism, 15, 24–25, 29

Camera Lucida (Barthes), 131, 159n49
Canton. *See* Guangzhou (city in China)

Carlyle, Thomas, 52
The Castle (Kafka), 104
Chang Ping-lin. *See* Zhang Taiyan
Chang, Eileen, 19, 92–98, 119, 133–34, 156nn5–7, 159n45
Chang, Elizabeth, 81, 155n20
Chao K'uang-yin. *See* Zhao Kuangyin
Chapman, George, 53
Chen Jitong, 1, 145n5
Chesterton, G. K., 18, 52–53, 73, 75, 152n10
Chiang Kai-Shek, 102
Chiang, Louisa, 92, 156n1
Ch'ien Chung-shu. *See* Qian Zhongshu
China, 11–13, 22–23, 27, 51, 54, 71, 73–74, 77, 81, 83–85, 93–94, 96, 115–17, 124, 128, 131, 137; early twentieth-century, 2, 4, 6–7, 12–13, 16, 21, 23, 33, 50, 53–54, 77, 93, 96–97, 116, 119–20, 128, 152n14; Han dynasty, 33, 36, 43–45; Ming dynasty, 18, 58–59, 74–76, 79, 86, 89, 97; People's Republic of, 19, 23, 76; Qin dynasty, 44–45; Qing dynasty, 1, 8, 15–17, 23, 38, 51, 58–60, 76, 86, 97–98, 101–2, 122, 135; Republican, 8, 12, 15–16, 18–20, 23, 27, 38, 51, 53, 60, 73–74, 79–80, 93, 96–98, 117, 123; Song dynasty, 33–34, 117; Tang dynasty, 58
China and the Writing of English Literary Modernity, 1690–1770 (Min), 11, 147n29
Chinese (language), 8, 17, 20–21, 23–24, 26, 28, 34, 50–51, 53, 58–59, 73–74, 85, 87–90, 93–94, 97, 115, 123, 126, 150n18; classical, 16–17, 21, 33–34, 37, 44–45, 47, 51, 53, 58–59, 73, 88, 152n8; dialects of, 21, 97
Ching Ming Festival. *See* Qingming (Tomb-Sweeping) Festival

Index

Chou Tso-jen. *See* Zhou Zuoren
chuanqi, 17, 58–59, 61–62, 153n21
classical Chinese poetics, 16, 35–37, 155n27; Gongan School, 79; Jingling School, 79. *See also Shijing*
classical Chinese thought. *See* Confucianism
close reading, 5–6, 14–15, 18, 20, 25, 139
Cold War, 93
Coleridge, Samuel Taylor, 63, 75–76, 160n1
common reader, 12, 17–19, 50–58, 61–62, 69, 138. *See also* the ordinary (life)
The Communist Manifesto (Marx and Engels), 37
comparative literature, 2, 3, 5–6, 9, 11, 34
comparative reading, 3, 9, 20, 26, 48, 134–35, 139, 147n30; of Jane Austen and Eileen Chang, 92–99, 101, 103, 128–34, 156n3, 158n26; of Charles Lamb and Zhou Zuoren, 74–75, 77–78, 80–81, 84–85, 89–91; of the Lambs and Lin Shu, 51, 54–55, 59–62, 66–69, 71; of Lu Xun and Percy Shelley, 25–26, 28, 33, 37–39, 42, 45–49, 150n12
Confucianism, 5, 17, 20–21, 23, 26, 38, 41, 43, 45, 68, 79, 89–90, 101, 103, 127–28; as subject of civil service examination, 6, 33–34, 38, 51, 76
"Conjectures on World Literature" (Moretti), 3, 4, 145n7
Conversations (Goethe), 1, 9–11, 145n1
cosmopolitanism, 4, 6, 12, 25, 52, 80, 96, 134. *See also* internationalism
Critique of Judgment (Kant), 4–5, 146n14
Croesus (king of Lydia), 82

Daoism, 5, 22, 41, 45, 66
Das Kind der Liebe (Kotzebue), 105, 158n30
Daston, Lorraine, 53, 152n13
deconstruction, 48
A Defence of Poetry (Shelley), 15–16, 22, 26, 37–42, 45–46, 48–49
democracy, 13, 20, 21, 53, 58, 75, 77. *See also* equality (egalitarianism); freedom (liberty); modernity; mutuality (fraternity)

Derrida, Jacques, 12, 147n33
Desire and Domestic Fiction (Armstrong), 57, 153n18
desolation, 127, 130–31
Deux ans de vacances (Verne), 52
Dickens, Charles, 52
Ding Ling, 128
"The Discovery of the Archimedean Point" (Arendt), 146n15
"Discourse on the Childlike Mind-Heart" (Li), 89, 155n29
disembeddings (Karl Polanyi), 21, 78, 117
The Dream of the Red Chamber (Cao), 97, 125, 157n14
Du Fu, 55, 60–61. *See also* literature: national
Dutch (language), 10
Dzien Tsoong-su. *See* Qian Zhongshu

Eckermann, Johann Peter. See *Conversations* (Goethe)
Egypt, 33
empire, 28, 92; British, 17, 50, 97, 100–1, 103; Chinese, 21, 51; technologico-scientific, 42
England (Britain), 22, 27, 29–32, 38, 50, 52, 54–55, 61, 71, 82–83, 95–96, 100–1, 103, 113; eighteenth-century, 10–11, 13, 17, 95–96; Elizabethan, 12, 55; Jacobean, 53; Regency, 16, 50, 54, 57, 74, 105; Restoration, 11–12; Romantic, 2, 10–13, 20, 137; Victorian, 12, 16, 25, 28–29, 50–51, 54, 75
English (language), 3, 6, 8, 10, 15, 20, 24–25, 28, 39, 50, 52–53, 73–74, 77, 87, 89–90, 93–94, 97, 115, 123, 126
The English Common Reader (Altick), 51–53, 152n9
Enlightenment (European), 13, 22, 25, 37, 46, 49, 74, 134, 149n8
equality (egalitarianism), 13, 20–21, 25, 28, 33, 39, 45–46, 48–49, 58, 71, 78, 129–30, 138. *See also* freedom (liberty); modernity; mutuality (fraternity)
Essays, Letters from Abroad, Translations and Fragments (Shelley), 37

Exemplarity and Mediocrity (Fleming), 57–58, 62, 153nn19–20

familiar essay, 12, 18, 73–75, 80–89, 137–38, 154nn1,5
Family Shakespeare (Bowdlers), 50, 159n37
femininity, 19, 22, 51, 57, 83, 88, 96, 124, 126, 128
Fletcher, John. *See Henry VIII* (Shakespeare and Fletcher)
"The Four Ages of Poetry" (Peacock), 41–42, 151n24
Foucault, Michel, 71–72, 153n32
Fraistat, Neil, 28, 149n9
France, 38
French (language), 10
French Revolution, 20, 49, 52, 75–76, 97, 105–6
freedom (liberty), 13, 20–21, 25, 30–33, 36, 39, 45–46, 48–49, 67–68, 72, 110–11, 119, 129–30, 132–33, 138, 148n41. *See also* equality (egalitarianism); modernity; mutuality (fraternity)
"Frost at Midnight" (Coleridge), 137

Galsworthy, John, 73
Gan Bao, 60
German (language), 10, 15, 24, 47
Germany, 55
Gissing, George, 73
Goswami, Joy, 89–90, 155–56n31
Greek (ancient language), 39, 77
Grotius, Hugo, 78
Guangzhou (city in China), 10
Guanyin. *See* Kwannon
Guillén, Claudio, 4
guwen. See Chinese (language): classical

Hacking, Ian, 53, 152n13
Haggard, Rider, 16, 52–53, 60
Hanan, Patrick, 68, 153n29
Han Pang-ch'ing. *See Sing-Song Girls of Shanghai* (Han)
Haoqiu zhuan (*The Pleasing History*), 10–11, 146–47n27
Hawthorne, Nathaniel, 73

Hay, Jonathan, 62, 74, 153n25
Hazlitt, William, 76
Henry VIII (Shakespeare and Fletcher), 19, 95, 105, 112–13, 113–14, 114, 132, 159nn37–38
Hermann und Dorothea (Goethe), 10–11
Hesiod, 42
History of Chinese Literature (Sasagawa), 8
The History of Napoleon Bonaparte (Lockhart), 71
Hodgkins, Thomas. *See* Juvenile Library (Godwins)
Holoch, Donald, 35, 43
Homer, 53
Hong Kong (city), 92–93
Hsiao Hung. *See* Xiao Hong
Hungarian (language), 15, 24
Hu Suh. *See* "Some Modest Proposals for the Reform of Literature" (Hu)

India, 33
In Quest of the Ordinary (Cavell), 21, 148n43
internationalism, 23, 25, 27–28, 30–33, 149–50n11. *See also* cosmopolitanism
irony, 8, 18–19, 48, 105, 115, 117–19, 131–32, 135
Irving, Washington, 52, 73
Italy, 29

"Jane Austen and Empire" (Said), 97, 157n16
Japan, 23–25, 77, 86, 102
Japanese Haiku Dictionary (*sajiki*), 86, 89
Japanese (language), 15, 20, 23–25, 59, 149n4
Jesuit, 10–11
"*Jigu*" ("Beating the Drums"), 133, 160n51
Jones, Andrew, 127
Journey to the West (Wu Cheng'en), 52–53
Juvenile Library (Godwins), 16, 50, 76, 152n5

Kan Bao. *See* Gan Bao
Kant, Immanuel, 46, 151n31
Karounos, Michael, 105, 158n29

Keats, John, 52–53, 76
Keywords (Williams), 1, 7, 145n1
Kinder- und Hausmärchen (Grimms), 55
Kitaoka Masako, 25, 149n6
knowledge, 7–8, 11, 32, 34, 39, 63–65, 74, 89, 130; as insufficient, 3, 8, 22, 41, 46, 130–31; (re)organization of, 1, 7–8, 12, 15, 37–38, 51, 74–75, 89, 154n6; of self, 32
Kowallis, Jon von, 43–44
Kwannon, 125–26

La Dame aux camélias (Dumas), 50
Lamb, Charles, 18, 51, 73–78, 80, 89–91, 153n26
Lamb, Mary, 51, 76, 152n6
Latin (language), 83
Lermontov, Mikhail, 15, 24
Les Siècles de littérature française (1772), 7
Lessing, Gotthold Ephraim, 57–58
Letter to D'Alembert on Spectacles (Rousseau), 104
Liang Qichao, 1, 38, 52; collected works, 145n5
Lin Chuanjia, 7–8
Link, Perry, 92, 156n1
Lin Shu, 50–54, 58, 68, 71, 151n4, 153n22
Lin Shu, Inc. (Hill), 58–59
"Literary History and Literary Modernity" (de Man), 8–9, 146n23
literary manifesto, 12, 15–17, 22, 26, 33, 37–38, 48–49, 137–38
literature: definition of, 1, 2, 4, 7–8, 37–38, 49, 137–38; national, 1, 7–8, 10–12, 15–16, 28–29, 38, 55, 60–61, 74–75, 79, 114, 146n22; revolution of, 1, 37, 41, 96, 116, 123; traditions of, 4–9, 11–12, 14–15, 18, 20–22, 25–26, 28, 33, 35, 38, 40–42, 45, 47–49, 53–54, 59, 60–61, 69, 73–75, 77, 79, 86, 93, 97, 118, 133, 137–38
Liverpool (city in England), 100
Locke, John, 78
London (city in England), 10, 18, 53, 63, 75, 80, 82, 84, 99, 100, 104, 113, 155n22
Los Angeles (city in the United States), 92

Louie, Kam, 92, 156n2
"The Lovely Lasses on the Boats to the Tombs" (Chinese folk rhyme), 87–88
Lovers' Vows (Inchbald), 19, 95, 103–10, 112–13
Lu Xun, 15–16, 18, 22–28, 47–48, 75–77, 149n2
Lyrical Ballads (Wordsworth and Coleridge), 10–11, 37

Macartney, George, 135, 160n52
Madame Bovary (Flaubert), 119
The Making of English Reading Audiences, 1790–1832 (Klancher), 54, 152n15
Manchuria (colony of Japan), 102
Manifesto of Futurism (Marinetti), 38
Mansfield Park (Austen), 19, 94–101, 103–14, 129–33, 135, 157nn8, 18, 157–58n21, 158nn22, 31–34, 158–59n35, 159nn36–38, 160n50
Marxism and Literature (Williams), 72, 154n33
"The Mask of Anarchy" (Shelley), 27–32, 150nn13–14
May Fourth Movement, 18, 50, 77, 102, 116
Mencius, 89, 155n28
Mendelssohn, Moses, 58
Mickiewicz, Adam, 15, 24
Modern Social Imaginaries (Taylor), 21, 78, 148n42
modernism, 12, 37–38
modernity, 8, 12–14, 16–22, 26, 28, 33, 38–39, 41–43, 45–46, 51, 53–54, 60, 78, 103, 124, 128–30, 137–38; Chinese, 13, 38, 74, 77, 79, 98, 120, 128, 130; English, 48, 113; heterogenous, 75, 78; history of, 78; linear and nonlinear, 79; literary, 2, 5, 7–13, 15, 20, 22, 25–26, 28, 34, 37–39, 46, 48–49, 51, 138; non-Western, 78; otherly, 62, 74; poetic, 38–39, 46, 48; political, 138; revolutionary, 41; scientific, 46, 51, 83, 134; secular, 41, 51, 96; shared, 26, 76, 95; Western, 62, 78, 96; world, 22, 26, 48–49, 51, 72, 138–39

Mohanty, Sharmistha, 90
Montaigne, Michel de, 73
Morris, William, 83, 155n23
mutuality (fraternity), 13, 20–21, 28, 47, 49, 128–33, 135, 138. *See also* freedom (liberty); equality (egalitarianism); modernity

Nanjing (city in China), 85
Naples (city in Italy), 60
nationalism, 28, 31, 38, 43, 45, 51, 60, 98. *See also* internationalism; provincialization
Newcastle (city in England), 105
New Culture Movement. *See* May Fourth Movement
New Delhi (city in India), 89–90, 155n30
Nicolai, Friedrich, 58
Nietzsche, Friedrich, 25, 47–48, 151n32. *See also* comparative reading: of Lu Xun and Percy Shelley
Northamptonshire (county of England), 94, 97, 100, 108
novel, 17, 95–96, 119; Chinese, 10, 53, 58, 93, 97, 157n13; domestic, 12, 19, 20, 94, 96–97, 103, 110, 114, 128, 130–31, 137–38; English, 10; as a global form, 11, 147n31

"Old China" (Lamb), 18–19, 80–84, 89, 155n21
"On the Concept of History" (Benjamin), 14, 148nn36–37
"On the Periodical Essayists" (Hazlitt), 73–74, 154n2
"On the Power of Mara Poetry" (Lu Xun), 15, 23–29, 32–39, 42, 46–49, 148–49n1, 150nn19–20
On the Sources of the New Chinese Literature (Zhou), 79–80, 155n16
the ordinary (life), 12, 18–22, 49, 61, 75–81, 84, 87, 89–93, 95–96, 98, 100–1, 110, 112, 114, 118–20, 128–35, 138–39. *See also* modernity
Ovid, 42, 61

patriarchy, 96, 98, 101–2, 103, 105, 106, 120, 121, 123–24, 126–28, 129, 130–31
Peking. *See* Beijing (city in China)
Peking opera, 19, 95, 101–2, 114–26, 128
"Peking Opera through Foreign Eyes" (Chang), 115–18, 159nn39,43
Peking University, 74, 77; as the Imperial University of Peking, 8
The Peony Pavilion (Tang), 59, 60
Percy, Thomas, 10, 147n28
Persia, 33
Perspective as Symbolic Form (Panofsky), 84, 155nn24–25
Petőfi, Sándor, 15, 24
Phillips, Adam, 75
philology, 1, 5, 8, 16, 26, 33, 45, 47–48, 145n4, 146n16
Poetry of the Revolution (Puchner), 15, 37–38, 148n38
Polish (language), 15, 24
Politics (Aristotle), 78, 109–10, 154n14
Pollard, David, 75, 154n8
Portsmouth (city in England), 100, 110–11
Portuguese (language), 10
postcolonial, 6
Prometheus Bound (Aeschylus), 16, 41
Propp, Vladimir, 57
provincialization, 4, 5, 11, 14, 20, 131, 134, 138–39, 146n10
Pseudo-Ossian, 12
Pushkin, Alexander, 15, 24
P'u Sung-ling. *See Strange Stories from a Chinese Studio* (Pu)

Qian Zhongshu, 52–53, 152n12
Qingming (Tomb-Sweeping) Festival, 87, 87–88

rationalism, 13, 26, 39, 42, 45, 60, 130
Rawls, John, 22
realism, 18, 83–84, 90, 97, 116–17, 124, 159nn40–41. *See also* theater
reason, 13, 39, 41, 129
Record of Qing Festivals (*Qing Jia Lu*) (Gu Lu), 86–87, 89

Records of the Historian (Sima), 43
Reiman, Donald, 28, 149n9
religion: Abrahamic, 9; poetic language as secular (Percy Shelley), 41; popular (Chinese), 43, 45. *See also* "Toward a Refutation of Malevolent Voices" (Lu Xun)
Reliques of Ancient Poetry (Percy), 10–12, 147n29
resonance, 17, 24–26, 28, 30–32, 35, 37, 47–49, 77, 92, 94, 132, 134–35
Richardson, Samuel, 10, 11, 96
Romanticism, 12–13, 15, 21–24, 37, 46, 50, 147n34, 147–48n35; English, 13, 27, 51, 75, 77
Romantics, Rebels, and Reactionaries (Butler), 76–77, 154n10
Rome (city in Italy), 113
Rothschild, Nathan Mayer, 82
The Rouge of the North (Chang), 19, 93–99, 101–3, 114–15, 117–33, 159n48. *See also Yuannü* (Chang)
Ruskin, John, 52
Russia, 38
Russian (language), 15, 24

Sanskrit, 23–24, 34, 47
Scott, Walter, 52
Shakespeare, William, 16–17, 50–51, 55–63, 69, 71, 112–14, 158–59n35
Shanghai (city in China), 92–94, 96, 98, 101–2, 114, 119, 121–22
Shaoxing (city in Jiangsu Province, China), 76
Shelley, Percy Bysshe, 15–16, 23–29, 33, 37–38, 41–42, 46–48, 76, 149nn9–10
shijie (world), 33, 52, 150n15; *de wenxue* (world literature), 2
Shijing (*Classic of Poetry*): 36, 133, 150nn21–22
Shishuo Xinyu (*The New Account of the Tales of the World*) (Liu Yiqing), 74
Sincerity and Authenticity (Trilling), 95–96, 104, 157n9
Sing-Song Girls of Shanghai (Han), 97

Sino-Japanese War (Second), 18, 77
skepticism, 21–22, 26, 32, 77, 80, 90
Slowacki, Juliusz, 15, 24
"Some Modest Proposals for the Reform of Literature" (Hu), 38
Sources of the Self (Taylor), 78, 154n13
Southey, Robert, 76; Satanic School (poetry), 15, 23, 149n3
Spanish (language), 89–90
Ssŭ-ma Ch'ien. *See Records of the Historian* (Sima)
Storia della letteratura italiana (Girolamo Tiraboschi), 7
Stout, Daniel, 105, 158n29
Strange Stories from a Chinese Studio (Pu), 52–53, 60
Swift, Jonathan, 52
"Symbolist Manifesto" (Moréas), 38
Symonds, J. A., 25, 28–29, 149n7

Taizhou School, 79, 155n18
Taizu (Song dynasty emperor). *See* Zhao Kuangyin
tale collection, 12, 16–18, 55, 58, 60, 69, 137–38, 148n40, 152–53n16
Tales from Shakespeare (Lambs), 16–17, 50–51, 54–71, 76, 151nn1–2, 152n6, 153n17
Tanner, Tony, 104–5, 158n24
Taoism. *See* Daoism
Taylor, Charles, 79
Tcheng Ki-tong. *See* Chen Jitong
The Tempest (Shakespeare), 17, 55, 59–69, 72
textual tradition. *See* literature: traditions of
theater, 95, 103–4, 113, 115–16, 120–22, 128–29, 131, 139
"This Lime-Tree Bower my Prison" (Coleridge), 75
tianxia. See *shijie*
Ting Ling. *See* Ding Ling
Tokyo (city in Japan), 85
Tomb-Sweeping Festival. *See* Qingming (Tomb-Sweeping) Festival
"Toward a Refutation of Malevolent Voices" (Lu Xun), 15, 26–27, 38–39, 42–46, 48, 151n25, 151nn27–28, 30

translation, 3–4, 7, 10–11, 16, 20, 23–25, 28, 43–44, 47, 50–55, 58–59, 61, 66–68, 71, 75, 77, 85, 87–90, 93–94, 97, 123, 127, 146n17, 148nn39,41, 150n17, 152n7
Trilling, Lionel, 104–5, 158n28
Ts'ao Hsüeh-ch'in. See *The Dream of the Red Chamber* (Cao)
Tsau, Shu-Ying, 35, 43
Tu Fu. *See* Du Fu

Über die neuere deutsche Litteratur (Herder), 7
Uncle Tom's Cabin (Stowe), 50, 68

Verne, Jules, 16
voice, 12, 15–16, 23–40, 42–43, 45, 47–49, 138
voicelessness, 25, 33, 35, 42–46

Wang, David Der-wei, 8, 128, 146n21
Wang Hui, 44–45, 48, 151n29
Wang Yangming, 79
The Water Margin (Shi Nai'an), 52–53
Wei Yi, 50–51, 59, 71
Weltliteratur. See world literature
wenlun. See literary manifesto
West Lake Sites (*Xihu Youlanzhi*) (Tian Rucheng), 86–87, 89
What Is a World? (Cheah), 6, 146n18
What Is World Literature? (Damrosch), 3–4, 145n8
"Wild Vegetables of My Hometown" (Zhou), 18, 80–81, 84–89, 155n26
Wilkinson, James, 10, 147n28
woman, 12, 19–20, 87, 94–95, 101–3, 114, 120–24, 126–29, 138, 159n47; in *Tales from Shakespeare* (Lambs), 56–57, 60, 62–66, 70, 154n9

Women, War, Domesticity (Huang), 96, 157n12
Wordsworth, William, 37, 70, 76
world literature, 1–2, 4, 10–13, 137–38; definition of, 2–3, 9, 11; as plurality, 5, 6, 9, 11, 13, 22, 48
"Writing of One's Own" (Chang), 98, 127, 130, 133, 157n17
Wuxi (county in Jiangsu Province, China), 52–53

Xiao Hong, 128

Yang Xiong, 43, 151n26
Yinbian Yanyu (Lin), 17, 50, 54–55, 58–62, 66–69, 71–72, 151n3, 153nn23–24,28
Yuannü (Chang), 19, 93–95, 97, 102, 114–15, 117–27, 157n20, 159nn44,48. See also *The Rouge of the North* (Chang)

Zhan Huangpao (Cutting the Imperial Robe), 117
Zhang Ailing. *See* Chang, Eileen
Zhang Binglin. *See* Zhang Taiyan
Zhang Dai, 79
Zhang Taiyan, 33, 47, 150n16
Zhao Kuangyin, 117, 159n42
Zhejiang (province of China), 77, 80, 85–88
Zhou Guisheng, 52
Zhou Zuoren, 18, 73–78, 80, 89–91, 145n6, 154n3; as younger brother of Lu Xun, 18, 24–25, 75–77
Zhou Zuoren and an Alternative Chinese Response to Modernity (Daruvala), 79, 154n4
ziyou. See freedom (liberty)

Emily Sun is Visiting Associate Professor in Comparative Literature and Translation Studies at Barnard College. She is author of *Succeeding King Lear: Literature, Exposure, and the Possibility of Politics* (Fordham, 2010) and co-editor of *The Claims of Literature: A Shoshana Felman Reader* (Fordham, 2007).

Sara Guyer and Brian McGrath, series editors

Sara Guyer, *Reading with John Clare: Biopoetics, Sovereignty, Romanticism.*

Philippe Lacoue-Labarthe, *Ending and Unending Agony: On Maurice Blanchot.* Translated by Hannes Opelz.

Emily Rohrbach, *Modernity's Mist: British Romanticism and the Poetics of Anticipation.*

Marc Redfield, *Theory at Yale: The Strange Case of Deconstruction in America.*

Jacques Khalip and Forest Pyle (eds.), *Constellations of a Contemporary Romanticism.*

Geoffrey Bennington, *Kant on the Frontier: Philosophy, Politics, and the Ends of the Earth.*

Frédéric Neyrat, *Atopias: Manifesto for a Radical Existentialism.* Translated by Walt Hunter and Lindsay Turner, Foreword by Steven Shaviro.

Jacques Khalip, *Last Things: Disastrous Form from Kant to Hujar.*

Jacques Lezra, *On the Nature of Marx's Things: Translation as Necrophilology.* Foreword by Vittorio Morfino.

Jean-Luc Nancy, *Portrait.* Translated by Sarah Clift and Simon Sparks, Foreword by Jeffrey S. Librett.

Karen Swann, *Lives of the Dead Poets: Keats, Shelley, Coleridge.*

Erin Graff Zivin, *Anarchaelogies: Reading as Misreading.*

Ramsey McGlazer, *Old Schools: Modernism, Education, and the Critique of Progress.*

Zachary Sng, *Middling Romanticism: Reading in the Gaps, from Kant to Ashbery.*

Emily Sun, *On the Horizon of World Literature: Forms of Modernity in Romantic England and Republican China.*

Robert Mitchell, *Infectious Liberty: Biopolitics between Romanticism and Liberalism.*

CPSIA information can be obtained
at www.ICGtesting.com
Printed in the USA
LVHW090129110321
681197LV00010B/392

9 780823 294794